European Community Law

WILLIAM RAWLINSON

C.B.E., M.A.(Oxon), of the Inner Temple, Barrister

and

MALACHY P. CORNWELL-KELLY

LL.B. (London), A.K.C., Solicitor of the Supreme Court

Foreword by the Rt. Hon. Lord Justice Woolf

WATERLOW PUBLISHERS

First edition 1990
© W. Rawlinson and M. Cornwell-Kelly 1990

Waterlow Publishers
Paulton House
8 Shepherdess Walk
London N1 7LB
A division of Pergamon Professional & Financial Services PLC

ISBN 0 08 033103 3

British Library Cataloguing in Publication Data

Rawlinson, William
  European Community law (Waterlow practitioner's library)
  1. European Community. Law
  I. Title II. Cornwell-Kelly, Malachy
  341.094

Printed in Great Britain by
B.P.C.C. Wheatons Ltd, Exeter

Contents

Foreword

BY THE RT. HON. LORD JUSTICE WOOLF

We all are—or rather we all should be—European lawyers now. Alas we are not. This is not entirely our fault. Some, like myself, still seek to be excused because we completed our training long before the United Kingdom became a member of the European Community. Even those lawyers who cannot rely on this excuse can, with justification, complain that our system of academic and professional education allows us to describe ourselves as lawyers without ever having had to study Community law. Community law is still not a compulsory or core subject in order to become a barrister or solicitor. I only hope that the position will have changed by 31 December 1992, that being the date on which all member States are committed to complete the single market.

Already the areas of our domestic law on which Community law does not have an impact have shrunk dramatically. It is becoming increasingly difficult to operate in any field as a lawyer without having to take into account the effect of our membership of the Community. At home and abroad all those engaged in the law are going to be faced with greater competition. In addition to the Green and White Papers and the resulting legislation now making its way through parliament, there is the EEC Directive on the Recognition of Professional Qualifications (89/48/ EEC).

The publication of this book could not be better timed. It is ideally suited to meet the challenge with which we are faced. Whether you are a novice seeking a painless introduction to the subject or an expert requiring a clear and concise textbook to check the accuracy of your recollection, you will find that you are well served. The authors have managed to distill into a remarkably small package an immense amount of information with clarity and precision. A glance at the Contents will indicate the sensible and practical way in which the material has been marshalled. Having been provided with an advance copy of the text, I have already benefited.

I am not surprised by what the authors have achieved. When I was junior counsel to the Treasury (the Treasury Devil) one of the myriad areas in which I had to act for the Government was in relation to Community law. It was a subject in which I was more dependant than usual on receiving first class instructions. Fortunately I obtained the assistance which I needed from the Solicitor to the Customs and Excise and the members of his office, thanks to the industry of the present authors, and William (Bill) Rawlinson, in particular, who were both at that time heavily engaged in Community law on behalf of Her Majesty's Customs and Excise. They had a special insight into Community legislation in many spheres, because they had been engaged in the detailed negotiations which preceded its introduction. They were in an admirable position to know the background and the policy of the legislation which is so important to its proper interpretation.

I am delighted that now, having left the Government's legal service, they have made their intimate knowledge of Community law available to a wider audience. I am confident that this book will be of immense value to the practitioner and the student who are confronted with problems as to Community law. Certainly it is to this book's pages that I will return when I need to be instructed as to European law.

January 1990   *H.W.*

Preface

It is now approaching twenty years since the United Kingdom joined the European Communities, and over thirty years since they were established. Community law has, in the meantime, grown to such proportions that there are few areas of national law which are unaffected by it. The lawyer practising in a Member State will thus be unlikely to be able to avoid having regard to the impact which Community law has upon his work, while lawyers in non-Community countries, whose clients are involved in trade with the Community, or who have branches of their business there, are similarly in need of a knowledge of this subject.

But, as the scope of this book indicates, there is sense in which it is difficult to speak meaningfully of Community law as a subject at all. There is, of course, the central corpus of law concerning the institutions and the general principles and procedures which form the framework within which the specific sectoral provisions have their existence. But it is with some artificiality that we categorise customs law and the law on freedom of establishment, the law on competition and that on water pollution, as one single subject.

"English law", containing an even wider range of topics than this, is indeed spoken of in similar terms as a single body of law, but the peculiarity of Community law is that it does not exist in isolation. It is, on the contrary, always encountered in the context of the legal systems of the Member States. There, it pervades and overlays the domestic law of the states to the point at which no lawyer can be said to have an adequate view of any legal topic without a knowledge of the Community law relevant to the sector in question.

The aim of this book is therefore to chart the way for the legal adviser, and those who must have a working knowledge of the law, in identifying the main themes of Community law relevant to their area of interest. The volume of Community legislation enacted every year, and at any time extant, is immense and requires a book of greater size than this simply to list it. Our coverage is therefore intended to enable the practitioner either to answer a question involving Community law, or to indicate a path which could be followed where a problem has to be considered in greater depth. We have tried to avoid academic discussions of theories which may be of little help in finding solutions to specific problems, and our intention is that this book should make it possible for the reader to be at ease with a directory of Community legislation.

We have, in general, not included reference to future plans or proposals for Community legislation in view of the uncertainty which so often accompanies them. We have sought to state the law as at 1 September 1989 and it has been possible to include certain changes made up to 1 January 1990.

Our particular thanks are due to Heather Cornwell-Kelly, formerly of the Legal Department of the Ministry of Agriculture, Fisheries and Food, and to Geraldine Tickle of Wragge & Co, who contributed the chapters on agriculture and competition respectively. We also record our debt to the unfailing helpfulness of the executive staff at the Solicitor's Office of H.M. Customs and Excise, in particular to Mr Michael Kelly.

London   W. R.
January 1990   M. P. C-K.

Table of Cases

xi

Table of Treaties and Conventions

Table of UK Statutes

Table of Regulations, Directives and Decisions

Directives and Decisions
("16A" indicates that the Directive or Decision is listed in the Annex to Chapter 16)

Year	No.	Ref.		No.	Ref.		No.	Ref.
1960	Directive of 11 May			387-8	16A		329	16A
	12.23, 12.24-7, 12.29			451	10.06		346	16A
				457	6.61		408-9	16A
1962	2645	16A		458	6.60		483	16A
				522-3	10.05		553	11.24
1963	21	12.27		524	6.57		556-7	10.06
	340	10.14					561-2	10.06.1, 15.07
	474	12.28	**1971**	118	6.55			
				127	16A		577	6.55
1964	54	16A		161	6.60			
	220	10.05		307	16A	**1975**	33	16A
	221	8.08, 10.11		316-20	16A		34-5	10.11
	222-3	10.06		347-9	16A		106-7	16A
	225	12.02					117	9.03, 9.09
	432-3	6.55	**1972**	156	12.28, 12.29		130	15.16
				166	12.09		268	6.83
1965	65-6	16A		194	8.08		318-19	16A
	264	10.14		245	16A		324	16A
				276	16A		362-3	10.05
1966	400-4	6.60		306	16A		410	16A
				430	12.09		442	16.11
1967	227	11.04		461-2	6.55		443	16A
	548	16A		464	11.08		716	16.10
							726	16A
1968	68	16A	**1973**	23	16A			
	151	13.04		44	16A	**1976**	114-16	16A
	193	6.60		79	11.24		118	16A
	297	11.63, 15.23		117	16A		135	15.11
	360	8.07, 8.08		148	10.05		160	16.09
	363-4	10.06		173	16A		207	2.19, 2.41, 9.07, 9.08
	367-8	10.06		183	12.10			
				239	12.04, 12.07		211	16A
1969	75	4.36		240	12.06		308	4.53, 4.66, 11.65, 11.68
	169	11.17, 11.64		241	16A			
	208	6.60		360	16A		403	16.11
	335	11.24		363	16A		621	16A
	464-7	6.59		404	16A		756-62	16A
	493	16A		437	16A		764-9	16A
							889-91	16A
1970	156	16A	**1974**	60-1	16A		893	16A
	157	16.12, 16A		63	6.57		895	6.59
	220-2	16A		69	4.34		914	15.04
	311	16A		148	16A			
	357	16A		150-1	16A	**1977**	91	13.05
	373	6.56		297	16A		92	10.06

Year	No.	Ref.
1975 (cont)	2771	6.18
	2777	6.18
1976	101	7.02
	103	7.23
	110	7.24
	199	5.17
	754	4.44
	1209	8.11
	1418	6.18
	3164	15.03
	3237	3.26, 15.08
1977	93	6.59
	222	3.22
	355	6.83
	1055	6.38
	1079	6.40
	1722	6.38
	2830	15.10
	2831	15.05
	3024	15.03
1978	1117	6.18
	1360	6.83
	2112	15.08
	2183	15.10
	2210-11	5.12
	2213-16	5.13
	2212	5.12
	2217	5.14
	3062	15.03
	3180-1	6.69
1979	1430	4.61
	1697	4.30, 4.57
	2622	7.18
1980	565	6.29
	1224	4.24, 4.30, 11.43-4
	1440	5.22
	1475	6.29
	1496	4.31
	2083	6.83
	3508	5.11
1981	553	4.21
	562	5.10
	1390	8.11
	1468	4.52
	1577	4.32
	1785	6.18
	3020	3.26, 15.08
	3670	5.11
	3795	8.11
	3796	7.16, 7.19
	3825	5.10
1982	3515	15.03
	3599	4.16
1983	170	7.03
	918	4.11, 4.13
	1615	2.49
	1983-4	14.42
	2001	8.11
	2026	6.29
	2763	4.43
	2950	9.14
	3158	4.32
	3568	15.05
1984	542	6.84
	856	6.40
	1932	6.83
	2151	4.03
	2176	4.46, 5.02
	2349	14.42
	2626	6.69
	2641	5.02
	3440	7.10
	3565	5.14
	3621	15.03
	3636	15.20
1985	123	14.42
	417-18	14.42
	678-9	3.06, 3.25
	797	6.83
	870	6.81
	1055	4.24
	1620	4.16
	1677	6.73, 6.75
	1678	6.70
	1766	4.31
	1999	4.37-8
	2137	11.72, 13.12
	2220	6.33
	3066	6.69
	3152	6.70
	3153	6.73, 6.78
	3155	6.73
	3632	4.63
	3644	6.84
	3677	15.03
	3678	6.82
	3681	5.11
	3765	6.56
	3820-1	15.06
	3824	9.14
	3826	6.38
1986	125	5.19
	426	6.18
	548	6.79
	1866	7.10
	2473	4.42
	3094	7.10
	3677	4.39
	3913	6.33
	3973	5.13
	4028	7.14
	4055-8	5.13
1987	822	6.18
	1062	3.25
	1181	6.33
	1636	6.70
	1674	3.22
	1760	6.83
	1825	5.19
	1889	6.76
	2082	6.33
	2096	4.16
	2144	4.54
	2658	4.06-7
	2827	3.25
	3183	6.64
	3251	7.13
	3665	6.29
	3773	4.32
	3846	6.29
	3860	4.17
	3940	7.23
	3975-6	15.14-15
	3991	6.18
	3995-8	6.18
	4163	5.14
1988	562	6.84
	569	6.38
	571	6.84
	1031	4.54
	1094	6.83
	1096	6.83
	1272	6.83
	1734	16.11
	1841	15.04
	1956	7.13, 7.18
	1969	12.35
	1970	4.42
	1991	15.05
	2048	6.62, 6.65, 6.67
	2321	7.14
	2671-3	15.14
	2868	7.18
	3272	4.31
	3494	6.79
	3578	6.73, 6.75-6
	3719	6.30-3
	3772	4.32
	3993	6.29

Abbreviations

Article	refers (unless otherwise stated) to an Article of the Treaty
CAP	common agricultural policy
CCT	common customs tariff
CFP	common fisheries policy
CMLR	Common Market Law Reports
CN	Combined Nomenclature
Commission	Commission of the European Communities
Community	refers to the EEC unless the context otherwise requires
Council	Council of the European Communities
Court	Court of Justice of the European Communities (or, where appropriate, the Court of First Instance)
ECR	European Court Reports*
ECSC	European Coal and Steel Community
ECU	European currency unit
EEC	European Economic Community
EEIG	European economic interest grouping
Euratom	European Atomic Energy Community
FEOGA	European Agricultural Guidance and Guarantee Fund (common agricultural policy)
GATT	General Agreement on Tariffs and Trade
MCAs	monetary compensation amounts (common agricultural policy)
NAFO	Northwest Atlantic Fisheries Organisation
OJ	Official Journal of the European Communities:
	C: series containing communications and information
	L: series containing legislation
	S. Edn: English special edition of OJ containing Acts passed before the UK's accession
STC	Simon's Tax Cases
TAC	total allowable catch (common fisheries policy)
Treaty	European Economic Community Treaty (Treaty of Rome)

---

*C preceding the number of a case indicates that it is pending before the Court, and I that it is pending before the Court of First Instance.

CHAPTER 1

The Treaties and the Institutions

The three communities

1.01 Since "the Common Market" or "the European Community" is normally spoken of as a single organisation, it is easy to lose sight of the fact that there are three distinct communities. First came the European Coal and Steel Community established in 1951 creating a common market in coal and steel, then in 1957 the European Economic Community and the European Atomic Energy Community were established to cover other areas of economic and industrial life. From the beginning these three bodies shared some common institutions, and since 1967 they have all been governed by the same institutions. (1)

1.02 This organisational unity conceals the continuing consequences of separation. The treaties governing each community remain distinct, and so therefore do the rules by which activity in each is regulated; the powers given by the treaties for the communities to legislate are also different and, to some extent, so are the procedures and remedies. Because coal, steel and atomic energy are however of limited concern, they will not often be encountered in practice, and detailed reference to them will not normally therefore be made. Eventual fusion of the communities themselves may result, and meanwhile the Court has held in *Case 328/85, Deutsche Babcock Handel v. Hauptzollamt Lübeck-Ost* (2) that EEC regulations can apply to steel products where there is no corresponding ECSC provision applicable, an indication of the "catch-all" character of the provisions of the EEC treaty.

1.03 As will become clear when the nature of the Community legal order is examined in Chapter 2, the **European Community**, as the three communities are now generally called, is not a loose international organisation like the EFTA, nor yet a full confederation. It is in a constant process of evolution, and in this process the Single European Act (the "SEA") of 1986 is the latest and most important landmark. The three base treaties are: the European Coal and Steel Community

(1) Treaty establishing a Single Council and a Single Commission of the European Communities—Brussels 8 April 1965.
(2) *Case 328/85* (not yet reported)—Times 12.1.1988.

1

Treaty (Paris, 18 April 1951); the European Economic Community Treaty (Rome, 25 March 1957); and the European Atomic Energy Treaty (Rome, 25 March 1957). (3)

The objectives of the Community

1.04 Articles 1–8c of the Treaty, as supplemented by the SEA, make it clear that European unity is the ultimate goal, with the fundamental principle in Article 7 of non-discrimination between nationals of the Member States. This is to be achieved by measures in the following areas: freedom of movement of goods within a customs union, a common agricultural policy, the free movement of persons, services and capital, a common transport policy, a common commercial policy, coordination of economic and monetary policies, and competition free from distortions and restrictions. Articles 8a–c provide for the completion of the internal market for movement of goods, services, persons and capital by 31 December 1992.

1.05 Although it is expressly declared that this date is not to give rise to automatic legal effects, the relevant provisions of the SEA facilitate the passing of the necessary legislation, and add specific new policy objectives in relation to research and development, and the environment. They also recognise European political co-operation as a formal objective. The institutions by means of which these aims are achieved are now considered.

The Council of Ministers

1.06 The **Council** is the principal governing body where ultimate political power still resides. It passes all major legislation, and settles the policies which determine how the Community is run. Meeting in closed session, it is composed of one representative from each Member State, who will be the minister of the national government most nearly concerned with the business under discussion. All draft legislation coming before the Council is prepared by the **Commission**, either on its own initiative or at the Council's request.

1.07 Since contentious political issues have often to be resolved, the system of voting which the Treaty provides for the Council is of

(3) These treaties have been much amended by accession treaties, the Single European Act (Luxembourg, 17 February 1986 and The Hague, 28 February 1986), the Merger Treaty (note (1) above), and by two budgetary treaties, Luxembourg 22 April 1970 and Brussels 22 July 1975.

importance. Under a political understanding known as the "Luxembourg compromise" reached in 1965, which seems still to be current, if any Member State considers an essential national interest to be at issue, the Council continues to discuss a matter until unanimity is reached. This procedure is not recognised in the Treaty, which does however prescribe cases in which unanimity is required, as, for example, to adopt legislation under Article 235 for which there is no specific authority elsewhere in the Treaty, or to take further steps towards alignment of taxation in the Community under Article 100A.

1.08   More frequently, however, either simple majority voting is prescribed, or voting is by qualified majority, when a system of weighting applies to give some Member States more votes than others. Thus, under Article 148, France, Germany, Italy and the United Kingdom have ten votes each, while Spain has eight, Belgium, the Netherlands, Greece and Portugal have five, Denmark and Ireland have three and Luxembourg has two. To determine which voting regime any matter falls within, reference must be made to the article of the Treaty under which it is proposed to act. It was held in *Case 68/86, United Kingdom v. Council* (4), that failure on the part of the Council to adhere to essential procedural rules laid down for the adoption of legislation rendered the legislation adopted in violation of those rules invalid. More detailed reference is made to the legislative process if it has a particular bearing on specific areas of Community law in the chapter concerned.

1.09   The **European Council** is very similar to the Council of Ministers but with some differences. Most important is that it consists only of heads of government and the President of the Commission, assisted by foreign ministers and a member of the Commission, and formulates policy on matters which are especially contentious, or which are not covered by the Treaty. The existence of this body, which grew up outside the framework of the Treaty, is now given formal recognition in Article 2 of the SEA. The European Council meets at least twice a year and may in practice also deal with Community business as such (in which case it constitutes itself as the Council of Ministers), or undertake the European co-operation in foreign policy provided for in Title III of the SEA.

1.10   Officials with the rank of ambassador, known as Permanent Representatives, operate as each Member State's principal working link with the Commission and, at the same time they provide, through the

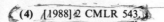
(4)   [1988] 2 CMLR 543.

Committee of Permanent Representatives, a kind of shadow Council with which the Commission prepares legislation or other proposals before they are considered by the Council itself. Also meeting behind closed doors, this body is staffed at working levels by the appropriate officials from each country depending on the matter under consideration, with the Permanent Representatives themselves participating only to consider the most important or sensitive issues. Coreper, as it is known after its French initials, is thus the forum in which legislation reaches its final form subject only to the settlement of policy questions in Council.

Parliament

1.11   The functions of this institution do not, as yet, correspond fully to those of national parliaments. Since 1978, it has been directly elected on a five year basis as a result of elections held at the same time throughout the Community (5). Political parties roughly corresponding to national political groupings are formed, but since membership of Parliament is incompatible with membership of a national government or of the Commission, no "ministers" sit as MEPs. There is a total of 518 members, of whom 81 are elected from UK constituencies. Parliament has three principal functions, none of which includes actually enacting legislation.

1.12   First, is the *scrutiny of draft legislation.* Under Articles 237 and 238, Parliament's consent is required for the admission of new members to the Community, or for the conclusion of association agreements between the Community and third countries. But all proposals for Community legislation are now in practice submitted to Parliament for an advisory opinion and, in those cases where the Treaty expressly provides for such consultation, failure to undertake it renders the legislation invalid: *Case 138/79, Roquette Frères v. Council* (6). Under Article 149 as amended by the SEA, this role is enhanced by a complex procedure for co-operation between Parliament, the Commission and the Council, designed to ensure Parliament's closer involvement in the legislative process.

1.13   Where this procedure is required, the Council adopts a "common position" on the proposed legislation submitted by the Commission, i.e. it either approves it by the required majority, or it unanimously amends it, but only after receiving the opinion of Parliament following the

(5)   Act concerning the election of the representatives of the European Parliament by direct universal suffrage: Brussels, 20 September 1976.
(6)   [1980] ECR 3333.

latter's first reading of the proposal. Parliament then gives a second reading to the proposal which, if it is then amended or rejected, has to go back to the Council. Where Parliament has rejected Council amendments to draft legislation, the Council can only disregard the rejection by acting unanimously. Where Parliament amends the proposal as transmitted to it by the Council, the Commission must resubmit the proposal to the Council after considering the amendments made by Parliament. The Council may then adopt, by the required majority, the proposal as resubmitted; may amend it, acting unanimously; or—in so far as they differ from the revised Commission proposal—it may, also acting unanimously, adopt the amendments proposed by Parliament.

1.14 Second, Parliament enjoys a real degree of *control over the budget* pursuant to Article 203. The budget is prepared by the Commission and submitted to the Council, but Parliament has the right to approve or modify it, which, depending on the type of expenditure involved, is subject to the Council's final decision. For expenditure which is obligatory under the Treaty (e.g. on the Common Agricultural Policy), Parliament may only change the proposed budget with the concurrence of the Council, but for other expenditure (which accounts for the greater part of the budget), it has the final say in case of disagreement with the Council, subject only to being restricted in the amount by which it can increase the expenditure proposed.

1.15 The procedure for settling the budget is again complex, making elaborate allowance for the interplay of Commission, Council and Parliament. It has more than once given rise to crises and even in one instance to litigation, when the 1986 budget was declared invalid. In *Case 34/86, Council v. Parliament* (7), the Court held that an attempt by Parliament to cut short an unresolved disagreement with the Council over the level of expenditure failed because Parliament could not lawfully declare the budget to have been adopted without the full procedure prescribed having been followed through.

1.16 Third, there is Parliament's overall role in *surveillance of the Commission* and also to an extent of the Council. The most drastic feature of this is found in the power in Article 144 to dismiss the Commission by passing a vote of censure on it, a power which has never in fact been used, although it has been threatened. It was held in *Case 302/87, Parliament v. Council* (8) that Parliament had no *locus standi* to challenge the legality of acts of either the Council or the Commission

(7) [1986] 3 CMLR 94.
(8) (Not yet reported)—Times 11.10.88.

under Article 173, although it was competent to bring an action against them for failure to act in accordance with the Treaty, or to intervene in cases before the Court generally. The normal method of parliamentary control is provided by questions to Commissioners, which can also by practice be addressed to the Council, and through the Committee on Petitions which investigates complaints about the Community administration. An annual report is presented by the Commission and debated in Parliament. Members of the Commission may attend to answer questions, or to take part in debates.

The Commission

1.17 The Commission is the Community's administration, or civil service, but it plays an autonomous role in a number of respects which gives it a quasi-political character which has no real equivalent at the national level. The Commission has four main functions: (i) it is responsible for promoting the interests of the Community as such; (ii) it administers the legislation contained in the Treaty and elsewhere, either directly or through the administrations of the Member States; (iii) it takes the initiative in making proposals to the Council for action or for legislation; and (iv) it enacts delegated legislation or adopts decisions which are legally binding on those to whom they are addressed.

1.18 *Promoting the interests of the Community* includes acting for the Community in international matters within the Community's competence and taking action against Member States to enforce compliance with Community law. It is also apparent in the rule that Commission proposals for legislation can only be modified by the Council acting unanimously, the Commission's role being to assure respect for the interests of all the states and thus of the minority (9). The Commission is answerable generally to Parliament for its guardianship of the Community interest.

1.19 *Administering the legislation* includes such matters as maintaining in effect the Treaty provisions on competition, the Common Agricultural Policy and the Customs Union. Usually, however, the bulk of the day-to-day administration remains at the national level under overall Commission supervision, a supervision which extends to ensuring that national legislation implementing Community provisions is adequate.

(9) Article 149.

1.20 *Proposals for legislation* in the form of draft texts for consideration by Parliament and the Council are initiated by the Commission, which also formulates general policy for consideration likewise. This function, as well as requiring a high degree of technical and legal expertise, involves the Commission in a political role as it pursues its duty of reconciling the interests of the Community as a whole with those of Member States.

1.21 This task is accomplished, firstly, by the preparation of initial draft texts in working groups of experts in which national representatives help to thrash out what will be acceptable and workable in each Member State; then there is the examination of the draft formally proposed by the Commission, by the Council and by Parliament, in the course of which the Commission's job is to achieve unanimous agreement, or at least a qualified majority for the proposal. The procedure, known as the "co-operation procedure" involving Parliament, specified in Article 149, may also involve consultation with the Economic and Social Committee.

1.22 The *enactment of legislation* by the Commission is usually pursuant to powers conferred by the Council in its own legislation, but the Commission is also specifically authorised to take binding decisions (e.g. in relation to competition by Article 90 and the legislation adopted under Article 87, or in relation to economic policy by Article 107). Article 10 of the SEA provides for a systematic regime to govern the delegation of legislative powers to the Commission. Meanwhile, the Commission has on occasion adopted legislation without having any explicit authority to do so where the Council had failed to act, and it was a matter of necessity for action to be taken.

1.23 The Commission itself consists of seventeen members appointed unanimously by the Member States, and they hold office for terms of four years. The president and six vice-presidents are appointed from among the commissioners on the same basis for terms of two years at a time. All appointments are renewable. Each state must have at least one person of its nationality as a Commissioner, but no state may have more than two such persons. In accordance with the Commission's role as guardian of the interests of the whole Community, the commissioners undertake not to seek or accept instructions from any Member State in the discharge of their duties. (10)

(10) Articles 10ff of the Merger Treaty—see note (1) above.

The Court of Justice

1.24 Under Articles 164–188, the Court consists of thirteen judges appointed by unanimous decision of the Member States, and of six advocates-general similarly appointed. Both are appointed for six year terms, which may be renewed. The President of the Court is elected by the judges from among their own number. Those eligible are persons satisfying the conditions necessary for appointment to the highest judicial offices in their respective countries, or who are "jurisconsults of recognised competence". Although there is no legal requirement to that effect, the judges are customarily representative of the Community's nationalities. The advocates-general provide an impartial comment on each case, which in practice is of great influence, being delivered after the parties have closed their submissions and before the judges retire to deliberate.

1.25 In 1988, the Court delivered judgement in 238 cases, taking between 18 and 24 months to dispose of them. It would be impossible for all the cases emerging in a Community of twelve Member States to be considered in plenary session and, under Article 165 of the Treaty, only those brought by a Member State or by an Institution are required to be so heard. Important references from national courts may also be heard by the full court, but the majority are heard by *chambers* of three or five judges constituted under rules of procedure.

1.26 Decision 88/591 (11) provides for two classes of case involving direct actions to be heard by the **Court of First Instance** established pursuant to Article 168a of the Treaty; these are cases involving Community officials, and actions against the Community institutions in the context of the competition policy. The new court will sit in chambers of three or five judges, but may also sit in plenary session. There is an appeal to the principal Court on a point of law, and the provisions regarding the appointment of judges mirror those for that Court. Article 168a allows the Council to define the jurisdiction of the new court from time to time, but not to include within it actions brought by the Member States or the Institutions, or references under Article 177. For simplicity, reference will be made hereafter simply to "the Court", but should be understood as including the Court of First Instance where appropriate.

127 The jurisdictions of the Court are divided between the original and the consultative. In its *original jurisdiction*, the Court hears cases brought against any of the Institutions or by them, or between Member States. Thus it deals with actions seeking the annulment of Commission decisions or the review of fines imposed under the competition policy,

(11)   OJ 1988 L319/1; see also OJ 1989 C215/1 for corrected text.

claims that legislation is invalid, and with staff cases against the Institutions. On the other side of the coin, are actions brought by the Commission against Member States (called "infringement proceedings") for declarations that they have failed to comply with Community law, for example in maintaining a restriction or in failing to implement a directive. Member States may also take proceedings against each other in reference to treaty obligations. (12)

1.28 In its *consultative jurisdiction*, the Court gives rulings on the interpretation to be given to the treaties, Community legislation and to Community conventions. These rulings are given in the context of proceedings before national courts, and at their request, in order to enable them to reach a conclusion on issues of Community law arising before them. (13)

1.29 The various judicial remedies available in Community law, both in the national courts and in the European Court, are examined in more detail in Chapter 2.

The Court of Auditors

1.30 The use of the term "court" in the title of this institution does not mean that it is in any way a law court in which litigation is conducted. It is an audit body, composed of twelve members chosen from among persons who are or have belonged to external audit bodies or who are "especially qualified" for the office: Articles 206–206a contain provisions similar to those which apply to the Court of Justice governing their appointment and tenure.

1.31 The Court of Auditors' function is to provide a complete and independent check on the financial activities of all the Community Institutions, including any organs established by them, and on the expenditure of Community money in the Member States—where it is to be accorded the collaboration of the national audit bodies. The Court's annual report, which is submitted to all the Institutions and published, contains the responses of the various administrations audited to the Court's comments on their affairs. There is an explicit obligation on the Court to assist Parliament in its duty of exercising control over the implementation of the budget, and the annual report guides the Council and Parliament in deciding on the discharge given to the Commission in respect of the implementation of each year's budget. (14)

(12)   Articles 169–179.
(13)   Article 177.
(14)   Articles 206a and 206b.

Other Institutions

1.32 The foregoing accounts for the principal bodies which govern the Community, but there is a constantly growing number of other organs which have a legally recognised role. They include organisations such as the European Investment Bank (15), the European Social Fund (16) and the European Regional Development Fund (17). These and others of the same kind have an operational function, while a further set of bodies led by the Economic and Social Committee (18) are consultative.

1.33 The **Economic and Social Committee's** role is to bring together representatives of all economic and social sectors to examine, at the request either of the Council or the Commission, proposals for legislation or other Community initiatives. The Committee may be consulted in any instance, and must be consulted where the treaty article under which action is being taken so provides. Article 49 on free movement of workers and Article 130a on the implementation of a Community environment policy are examples. A variety of more specialised consultative committees also exists, and provision for them will be found in the sectoral legislation concerned. Frequently, they have a particular role in approving delegated legislation by the Commission which, in the absence of their agreement, must be referred to the Council.

The Community's legal personality

1.34 Article 210 provides that the Community is to have legal personality, and Article 211 requires that it shall enjoy, in each Member State, the most extensive legal capacity accorded to legal persons by its law: the Community may aquire or dispose of all types of property, and be a party to legal proceedings. In *Maclaine Watson & Co Ltd v. Department of Trade and Industry* (19) it was held that the Community was not within the scope of the general immunity from action conferred on sovereign states under the State Immunity Act 1978. The Commission represents the Community in proceedings within the Member States, and in international agreements its function is to negotiate on behalf of the Community, but the agreements themselves are concluded by the Council: Article 228. Such agreements are binding upon both the Institutions of the Community and on the Member States.

(15)   Articles 129 and 130.
(16)   Article 123ff.
(17)   Article 130C.
(18)   Article 193ff.
(19)   (Not yet reported).

CHAPTER 2
Principles of Community Law

Character of Community law

2.01 Community law is not conventional international law establishing a code of conduct between sovereign states, but a system of law which has essentially the same features as national systems, in that it creates enforceable rights and obligations which all may invoke in legal proceedings. That some matters may only be the subject of declarations by the European Court that a Member State has failed to give effect to a Community law obligation, does not detract from the significance of the very large number of provisions which are as immediately binding on the individual as any provision of national law. Which Community provisions may be relied upon in national proceedings or impose obligations, and which may not, is discussed below under "Direct applicability and direct effect" (paras. 2.13ff).

2.02 The Treaty outlines the principal objectives which inform the system of Community law, namely the creation of a single market for goods, services, workers and capital in which there are no impediments or discriminations related to nationality, and no internal frontiers. These concepts underlie the whole structure of the Treaty's provisions, and constantly inform the way in which the Court addresses issues of interpretation of Community law coming before it.

The sources of Community law

2.03 The principal sources of Community law are the treaties and conventions made between the Member States, legislation or other acts adopted by Community Institutions by virtue of treaty provisions, the case law of the European Court, principles of law common to the Member States, and international agreements adhered to either by the Community itself or by the Member States generally (1).

(1) Regulations, directives and decisions are published in the "L" series of the Official Journal of the European Communities (OJ), and judgments of the Court are published in the European Court Reports (ECR): these and the full texts of the Treaties and Conventions are available from the Office for Official Publications of the EC in Luxembourg, and through HMSO or Alan Armstrong Ltd in the UK. This material is also widely available in a number of commerical publications, notably the Common Market Law Reports (CMLR) and its associated series.

11

2.04 The treaties evidently form the basis from which all else proceeds, and they have been itemised in Chapter 1; as indicated there, reference will normally be made only to the EEC Treaty and the treaties specifically amending it. The EEC Treaty remains the continuing legal and policy base, and is constantly being supplemented by further treaties or conventions as new states join the Community or as new areas become the subject of Community-wide agreement: examples are the accession treaties which have been made on the joining of each of the members since the original six and the Single European Act, which brings European political co-operation formally into the sphere of Community activity.

2.05 The legislation adopted under the Treaty may take the form either of regulations or directives.

2.06 Regulations may be made either by the Council or by the Commission, the former usually acting pursuant to a requirement in the Treaty and the latter under powers conferred by the Council. They take the form of detailed legislation which, in the majority of cases, stands on its own and needs no further legislation to make it immediately applicable. Article 189 states that regulations are to binding in their entirety and "directly applicable" in all Member States. This means in effect that they are like legislation enacted by a national parliament and, subject to what appears below on the question of interpretation and annulment, they can be treated as such. Since matters of criminal and civil enforcement are normally left within the province of the Member States, regulations may need to be supplemented by national provisions for those purposes.

2.07 Directives have, in principle, a different role. In Article 189 they are described as binding on the Member States as to the result to be achieved, but leaving to the national authorities the choice of form and methods. It is therefore to be expected that implementing legislation or administrative action will follow at the national level. Although it was originally argued that the Treaty intended them normally to be treated as a blueprint for national legislation, it will be seen below that they have acquired a much wider role. Like regulations, they are either made by the Council acting under a provision in the Treaty, or by the Commission acting under powers conferred by the Council.

2.08 A third category of legal act is the **decision**. This is binding upon the person to whom it is addressed. Examples of decisions are those taken by the Commission addressed to undertakings under Articles 85 and 86 (competition policy), or to Member States under Article 90 (its application to public undertakings). Decisions which impose a pecuniary obligation, such as a fine, are enforced through the civil procedure in the relevant Member State (2). Because they show the principles on which the competition policy is being applied, the Commission's decisions in that sphere are in practice treated as precedents and can, as such, be regarded as a subsidiary source of law.

2.09 There are other legally significant acts, as for example opinions of Parliament or a declaration by it that the budget has been adopted, but these do not add to the corpus of Community law as such. Still less do the recommendations or opinions which the Commission is authorised to give, or the various programmes or resolutions adopted by the Council or Commission, which are of merely political significance. Nonetheless, it is possible that they may be taken into account by the Court as being of relevance to the context of matters before it.

2.10 The role of the European Court in interpreting the treaties and Community legislation, and in building up what might be termed the "common law" of the Community has been very important. Strictly, there is no doctrine of *binding precedent*, but in practice the Court's concern for legal certainty has led it to follow precedent in much the same way as common law courts do. This trend has been encouraged by the fact that the Court's decisions consist of a single judgment, rather than a variety of judgments or speeches, with the result that clear judical doctrine is more easily established than it is in systems where decisions consist of a number of converging, though dissimilar, judgments.

2.11 It has been mentioned in Chapter 1 that the Court is assisted by Advocates-General. In each case, the Advocate-General assigned offers his reasoned submissions to the Court in addition to those of the parties, acting in the role similar to that of *amicus curiae*. These submissions may or may not be followed by the Court, but they will be regarded as authoritative where they are followed, when they often provide a helpful gloss on the rather terse language in which the Court's rulings are given.

2.12 The use of principles of law common to the Member States and of international agreements to which the states are parties, as sources of Community law, is illustrated below under "Human rights" (paras. 2.40ff).

(2) Article 192

Direct applicability and direct effect

2.13   These two concepts are frequently encountered in the Court's judgments and have sometimes caused confusion. **Direct applicability** is prescribed in Article 189 for regulations, though not for directives or decisions. It requires that the binding force of the Regulation as it stands must be acknowledged in each Member State's legal system without the need for its individual "reception" or validation by national law. This concept is provided for in the UK by section 2 of the European Communities Act 1972, which states:

> "**2.**—(1) All such rights, powers, liabilities, obligations and restrictions from time to time created or arising by or under the Treaties, and all such remedies and procedures from time to time provided for by or under the Treaties, as in accordance with the Treaties are *without further enactment* to be given legal effect or used in the United Kingdom shall be recognised and available in law, and be enforced, allowed and followed accordingly; . . ." (emphasis supplied)

2.14   By this formula, the direct applicability of regulations is assured in UK law. Direct applicability can thus be summarised as meaning that, while on occasion supplementary measures may need to be taken with regard to directly applicable acts—as for example, to provide penalties for non-compliance—they need not, and indeed must not, be re-enacted in national legislation but must be taken as law as they are. (3)

2.15   By contrast, directives, decisions and articles of the Treaty are not designed to be directly applicable but to be the subject of national legislative action to implement them (4). In a long sequence of judgments, however, the Court has held that both types of law may have **direct effect**. Direct effect means that a provision creates rights which may be relied upon by litigants in proceedings before national courts, and to which those courts must give effect. This is of course already the case with regulations which are designed to establish precise rules, but wherever the conditions requisite to enable any other text to have direct effect are present, the Court has held that it also will have such effect.

2.16   The development of this doctrine has owed much to the failure at various times either by Member States or by the Community Institutions to adopt measures in implementation of the Treaty, or of directives, by the required date. In such circumstances, the Court has held that it would be inconsistent with the binding effect of the Community legal

(3)   *Case 24/73, Variola* [1973] ECR 981; see also *Case 50/76, Amsterdam Bulb* [1977] ECR 137; [1977] 2 CMLR 218.

(4)   Administrative action alone is not sufficient: *Case 169/87, Commission v. France* [1974] ECR 359; [1974] 2 CMLR 216. See also para. 8.06 below.

system not to allow individuals to rely on provisions in so far as they establish clear, precise and legally complete obligations, leaving the judge no element of political evaluation or discretion beyond what is normal to the judicial process. This will not be the case where a time limit has been laid down for implementing action and it has not yet expired.

2.17 This principle may be illustrated by *Case 9/70, Grad v. Finanzamt Traunstein* (5). In that case, the plaintiff had argued before a national court that he should not be subject to tax legislation which was inconsistent with both a decision of the Council, and a directive relating to turnover taxes; the European Court held that the provisions of both these acts could in principle be relied upon by the taxpayer in so far as they had not been incorporated into national legislation. The Court has reached similar conclusions in a wide variety of cases in relation to Treaty provisions or directives which have not been implemented correctly, or at all.

2.18 There is, however, an important restriction on this doctrine in consequence of which the possibility of unimplemented legislation being directly effective cannot be raised except against the state (5a). This is the so-called "vertical" direct effect which is occurs when a provision is enforceable by a citizen in proceedings involving a Member State. It contrasts with the "horizontal" direct effect which a Regulation has, by virtue of the fact that it is a fully developed legislative text, in establishing rights and liabilities between individuals, as well as in relation to national authorities.

2.19 Thus in *Case 152/84, Marshall v. Southampton Area Health Authority* (6) the Court held that Directive 76/207 (7) could only be held to have direct effect as against the state, or a body to whom the state had delegated state functions; the Health Authority was a public body with such functions, and therefore fell within this definition. On the other hand, a wholly-owned state trading concern such as, at the time, Rolls-Royce or British Gas, was held not to. (8) It has been seen that in *Case 9/70, Grad v. Finanzamt Traunstein* that a decision was capable of having direct effect (9), and in *Cases 21–24/72, International Fruit Co v.*

(5)   [1970] ECR 825; [1971] CMLR 1.
(5a) But not by the State: *Case 80/86, Kolpinghuis Nijmegen* [1989] 2 CMLR 18.
(6)   [1970] ECR 723; [1986] 1 CMLR 688. See also *National Smokeless Fuels Ltd v. CIR* [1986] STC 300.
(7)   OJ L 45/19.
(8)   *Doughty v. Rolls-Royce* EAT [1988] CMLR 569; *Foster v. British Gas* CA (not yet reported).
(9)   *Case 9/70* [1970] ECR 825; [1971] CMLR 1.

Produktschap (10) it was held that international agreements concluded by the Community could also have such effect.

Supremacy and effectiveness of Community law

2.20 Community law which has direct effect takes precedence over national law. An inconsistent national provision therefore is automatically overruled by a Community provision, and this is so whether the national provision is enacted before or after the Community one. This rule, it may be objected, conflicts with the fundamental doctrine of UK constitutional law that no parliament can bind its successors, and that section 2 of the European Communities Act 1972, which accords precedence to Community law, may be repealed by any subsequent statute. While the possibility of the UK parliament deliberately legislating in opposition to Community law clearly exists, section 2(4) of the 1972 Act meanwhile suffices to incorporate in UK law the rule of supremacy, and it is presumed that the rule is not to be displaced except by a statute expressly repealing the section and making it clear that the obligations flowing from accession by the UK are abrogated.

2.21 Reference to section 2(4) of the European Communities Act will not in fact disclose any mention of the doctrine of Community precedence; it refers simply to past or future enactments having effect subject to subsection (1), which provides for the rights and obligations arising under the treaties to have effect in the UK. The supremacy of Community law is one such feature, and was established by the European Court as the necessary corollary of the existence of the new legal order, which presupposes an equal and consistent application of Community law in all the Member States, and without which the objectives of the Community cannot be achieved.

2.22 The leading case, which has been followed on numerous occasions, is *Case 6/64, Costa v. E.N.E.L.* (11), where it was claimed that the Italian legislature had, in the terms in which it had nationalised the electricity industry, acted in breach of the Treaty. Although the Italian government argued that such a breach could only be the subject of infringement proceedings leading to a formal declaration to that effect by the Court, it was held that as some of the provisions in question were capable of direct effect, they could override the national legislation and that, in such an eventuality, the national courts would be bound to give effect to the Community provisions, without more ado. As always in the case of

(10)   [1972] ECR 1219; [1975] 2 CMLR 1.
(11)   [1964] ECR 585; [1964] CMLR 425.

references from a national court, it was a matter for that court to decide, in the light of the European Court's interpretation of the Community law, whether the national legislation in issue did indeed conflict with it.

2.23 The rule of supremacy applies to all national law at odds with directly effective Community law, even if the national law is criminal in character. Thus in *Case 8/74, Procureur du Roi v. Dassonville* (12) criminal proceedings against importers of Scotch Whisky into Belgium, who had failed to satisfy a national requirement as to certificates of authenticity, had to be dismissed in the face of a ruling that the terms of the requirement were unnecessarily onerous, and amounted to a restriction in breach of Article 30. And in *Cases 266 & 267/87, R. v. Royal Pharmaceutical Society of Great Britain ex parte Secretary of State for Social Services* (13) it was held that rules of a professional body, which by law controlled the exercise of a profession by its members, could amount to "measures" within the meaning of Article 30 of the Treaty.

2.24 Any national legislation which is in fact incompatible with Community law must be repealed for the sake of good legal order, even though it is automatically superseded (14). Moreover, once an area of law has been made the subject of common Community legislation, the Member States may in general no longer legislate in respect of it, even if their legislation does not conflict with the Community provisions. Thus, in Case *60/86, Commission v. United Kingdom* (15) the UK was held to be in breach of the Treaty in adopting national requirements on vehicle lights in addition to those laid down in the harmonisation directive. By contrast, where the Community legislation did no more than co-ordinate national social security schemes, its existence was held not to preclude Member States from adding to its provisions: *Case 21/87, Borowitz v. Bundesversicherungsanstalt für Angestellte* (16).

2.25 It follows from the principle of Community law supremacy that national courts are under an obligation to take steps to ensure its *effectiveness* in terms of the remedies and procedures open to the litigant. It is for the national legal system to determine the procedures to be used, provided that they are no less favourable to the litigant than those governing the equivalent right of action on an internal matter: *Case 158/80, Rewe v. Hauptzollamt Kiel* (17). The obligation to give effect to

(12)   [1974] ECR 837; [1974] 2 CMLR 436.
(13)   [1989] 2 CMLR 751.
(14)   *Case 167/73 Commission v. France* [1974] ECR 359; [1974] 2 CMLR 216.
(15)   *Case 60/86* [1988] 3 CMLR 437; and see also *Case 216/84 Commission v. France* (not yet reported).
(16)   (Not yet reported). See *Case 165/88, ORO Amsterdam Beheer* (not yet reported) on the residual scope for national action in Community-occupied fields.
(17)   [1981] ECR 1805; [1982] 1 CMLR 449.

Community law in priority to national law, including Community law consisting of the directly effective provisions of a directive, was held in *Case 103/88, Costanzo* (18) to extend to public authorities, and not to be confined to the courts.

2.26 The consequences of this approach have been spelled out in a number of detailed respects. Thus, in the absence of Community measures, national limitation periods are *prima facie* applicable to the enforcement of Community rights, so long as it is not impossible in practice to exercise them (19); a ruling by the European Court that a provision is contrary to Community law does not reopen the limitation period, if it had already expired when the proceedings were commenced; (20) interest and rights of counter-claim and set-off are likewise governed by the relevant national provisions (21); remedies must be real and of value (e.g. not confined to nominal damages) (22); and there must be no ouster clauses whose effect is to prevent the national court evaluating whether or not the Community right has been respected. (23)

Interpretation

2.27 Article 190 requires that regulations, directives and decisions "shall state the reasons on which they are based". Thus, each piece of Community legislation is preceded by recitals, of the kind found in some commercial documents and in old English statutes. Their purpose is to enable the user to construe the text in accordance with the legislator's intentions. This approach to interpretation, sometimes referred to as the "teleological approach", is designed to be flexible and purpose-orientated, and generally avoids literal analysis. The context of the legislation and its purpose must be considered, and the meaning given to it which is in line with them (24). This is limited, however, by the need to ensure legal certainty: see for example *Case 122/80, Analog Devices* (25), where the Court would not adapt the interpretation of the Common Customs Tariff to take account of technological change, but left it to legislative action to provide for unforseen cases, citing the need to ensure legal certainty for traders.

(18) (Not yet reported).
(19) *Case 45/76, Comet v. Produktschap* [1976] ECR 2043; [1977] 1 CMLR 533.
(20) *Case 33/76, Rewe v. Landwirtschaftskammer* [1976] ECR 1989; [1977] 1 CMLR 533.
(21) *Case 130/79, Express Dairy v. IBAP* [1980] ECR 1887; [1981] 1 CMLR 451—and *Case 177/78, Pigs and Bacon Commission v. McCarren* [1979] ECR 2161; [1979] 3 CMLR 389.
(22) *Case 14/83, von Colson v. Land Nordrhein-Westfalen* [1984] ECR 1891; [1986] 2 CMLR 430.
(23) *Case 14/83, von Colson*, note (22) supra, and *Case 222/84, Johnson v. Chief Constable of the Royal Ulster Constabulary* [1986] 3 CMLR 240.
(24) *Case 292/82, Merck v. Hauptzollamt Hamburg-Jonas* [1983] ECR 3781.
(25) [1981] ECR 2781.

2.28 Following these principles through into the construction of United Kindom legislation, section 2(4) of the European Communities Act 1972 requires UK statutes to be so interpreted as to be consonant with governing Community legislation. The European Court has specifically stated that national legislation should be interpreted in the light of the wording and purpose of the directive. (23)

2.29 The House of Lords, in *Duke v. GEC Reliance* (26), has held that national legislation pre-dating a directive (and therefore not presumed to be passed to give effect to it), should not be strained so as to be consistent with the directive, and that the obvious meaning should be adopted; in that case, the result was that, since the defendant was not a public authority, the directive (though capable of direct effect) could not be relied upon and the inconsistent national law prevailed. In *Pickstone v. Freemans Plc* (27), however, the House construed statutory provisions purposively in order to give effect to the Community law they were intended to implement; and the court was willing, to achieve this objective, to take into account the statement in parliament of the minister who had moved the regulations inserting the provisions in the statute concerned.

2.30 In the context of a Community with twelve Member States, with a rather greater number of legal systems, and in the light of the Community's overall objectives, it is evident that there is a need to ensure that the law is interpreted uniformly throughout. This task is undertaken by the European Court through the mechanism of preliminary rulings given in response to requests by national courts under Article 177 of the Treaty. This jurisdiction ensures that national litigants can always seek to have questions of Community law resolved outside the sometimes distorting confines of the national legal system. In Directive 77/388 (28), on the harmonisation of value added tax, the expression "consideration" is used, and the Court has held in *Case 102/86, Apple and Pear Development Council v. Customs and Excise* (29) that, even though it is well known in English law, its use in the directive requires that its interpretation should be established on a Community basis.

2.31 Community legislation is published in the nine official working languages in the Official Journal of the European Communities. All texts

(26) [1988] 2 WLR 359.
(27) [1988] 3 WLR 265.
(28) OJ 1977 L 145/1.
(29) [1988] 2 CMLR 394.

are equally authentic, and in the event of divergence between them (or, strictly speaking, in every case), each must be interpreted in the light of all the others. Thus, in *Case 122/87, Commission v. Italy* (30), Italy had implemented Directive 77/388 (31) on value added tax by exempting veterinary services pursuant to a provision exempting the services provided by "medical and paramedical professions as defined by the Member State". This could arguably have included the case of veterinary services; every language version except the English and Italian, however, stated that the services in question were those provided "to persons", making the construction contended for by Italy implausible, and the Court therefore found against Italy. Applying United Kingdom legislation implementing the same directive, the Court of Appeal has referred to the French text in order to resolve an ambiguity in the English version: *Bell Concord Educational Trust v. Customs and Excise* (32).

Passing on

2.32 In the sphere of taxation (which includes customs duties and other levies), the Court has evolved a doctrine specifically to deal with claims for repayment of dues levied contrary to Community law in circumstances where a ruling to that effect may serve only to provide the taxpayer with a windfall. The principle, known as "passing on", provides that where the burden of a tax or levy which has been charged illegally has been passed on to the taxpayer's customers, Member States may deny him the right to repayment, notwithstanding a declaration by European Court of its unlawfulness. This exception may not however be hedged about with rules of procedure or evidence which make it virtually impossible for the taxpayer to show that the charge was not passed on, even if the same rules apply to purely national claims: *Case 199/82, San Giorgio* (33). The relevant United Kingdom provision in relation to value added tax is now contained in section 24 of the Finance Act 1989.

Nationality discrimination

2.33 The fundamental prohibition of discrimination on grounds of nationality, enunciated in Article 7 of the Treaty, applies to all areas of Community law. Its scope may be illustrated by *Case 186/87, Cowan v. French Treasury* (34), where a British tourist, who had been mugged in

(30) (Not yet reported).
(31) OJ 1977 L145/1.
(32) [1987] 3 CMLR 424
(33) [1983] ECR 3595; [1985] 2 CMLR 658.
(34) (Not yet reported).

Paris, was denied a payment in respect of his injuries by the French Criminal Injuries Compensation Board on the ground that he was neither a French national nor from a state which had a reciprocal arrangement with France in the matter. It was held that the tourist must be considered for compensation on the same basis as a French national, because he was entitled under Community law to go to another Member State to receive the (tourist) services supplied there (35). The corollary of that entitlement was the right to protection against the risk of assault, and to compensation in default, on the basis provided by the law of the state where the services were rendered.

2.34   In general, it may be said that any nationality discrimination will be contrary to Community law unless a specific authorisation for it can be found, as where Article 48(4) of the Treaty excludes employment in the public service from the provisions on free movement of workers. Discrimination which is the result of Community legislation may render the legislation liable to annulment, as in *Case 305/85, United Kingdom v. Commission* (36) where the Court declared invalid regulations on the calculation of sheep premiums which uniquely prejudiced United Kingdom producers.

Prospective overruling

2.35   The Court has recognised that, both in the tax sphere and elsewhere, the effect of declaring a measure to be contrary to Community law may be to upset retrospectively a large number of transactions which the parties to them had good reason to suppose were lawful. Article 174 states that if a regulation is annulled, the Court may decide which elements of it are nonetheless to be regarded as definitive. It has been held that this enables the Court to overrule the disputed act, while maintaining its effect in relation to past transactions. In the wider context of findings pursuant to an Article 177 reference that a national measure is unlawful, the decision may have effect only for the future, or in cases where a claim had already been brought at the date of the ruling (37). If such a limitation is to be adopted, however, it must be provided by the Court in its ruling on the case, and may not be sought subsequently (37).

Legitimate expectations

2.36   A doctrine similar to that known in English administrative law is recognised by the European Court. In *Case 120/86, Mulder v. Minister*

---

(35)   *Cases 286/82 & 26/83 Luisi and Carbone v. Ministero del Tesoro* [1984] ECR 377; [1985] 3 CMLR 52.
(36)   [1988] 2 CMLR 169.
(37)   *Case 24/86, Blaizot v. University of Liège* [1989] 1 CMLR 57.

van Landbouw, (38) the plaintiff had gone out of milk production for a limited period pursuant to a Community scheme under which he had received a compensating payment for doing so. A subsequent Regulation introducing milk quotas failed to make any provision for persons in his position, as a result of which, after the period for which he had agreed to leave production had expired, he was unable to obtain any quota allocation at all, and was forced out of the business permanently.

2.37   The Court held that the farmer had had a legitimate expectation that at the end of the period during which he had ceased production at the Community's instance, he would be in a position no less favourable than that he would have enjoyed had he not acceded to the scheme. The quota regulation was therefore held *pro tanto* invalid. But in *Case 161/88, Binder v. Hauptzollamt Bad Reichenall* (39) an importer was held not to have had a legitimate expectation of being able to import goods at 10.4% duty when the Official Journal showed that the duty was 13%, even though an official German Customs manual showed the lower rate, and the lower rate had actually been charged by the Customs office: the Court decided that the administration must recover the full duty.

Proportionality

2.38   The doctrine of proportionality is an example of the non-literal and purpose-orientated way in which Community law is interpreted. It requires that an action which it is sought to bring within the scope of a legal concept should be proportionate to its avowed objective. Frequent illustrations of this principle at work may be seen in the context of Articles 30 and 36. Article 30 prohibits, in trade between Member States, "quantitative restrictions" or measures having equivalent effect, but Article 36 allows exceptions from this rule where the restriction is, *inter alia*, justified on grounds of public health and is not a disguised restriction on trade.

2.39   Restrictions *prima facie* within Article 30 are often encountered in the absence of Community-wide health standards. In *Case 216/84, Commission v. France* (40), France had imposed an absolute ban on the import and sale of milk substitute products on the ground that they were less healthy than real milk products, and that consumer protection justified their prohibition. The Court held that, although consumer protection was a proper objective for a Member State to pursue for the purpose of the exceptions in Article 36, it could adequately be attained

(38) [1989] 2 CMLR 1.
(39) (Not yet reported).
(40) (Not yet reported).

by means of less drastic measures, such as sufficient labelling of products, leaving it open to consumers to make an informed choice. The absolute ban was out of proportion to the permitted objective, and declared illegal.

2.40 Although the European Convention for the Protection of Human Rights is not a Community treaty (it is a convention of the Council of Europe), it is regarded by the Court as important persuasive authority on the general principles of law which are accepted by all the Member States, and thus as a source of Community law itself. In a number of decisions this Convention has been influential, as has the general adherence of Member States' legal systems to particular principles of law. Thus in *Case 374/87, Orkem* and *Case 27/88, Solvay* (40a) the Court annulled Commission decisions, requiring undertakings to answer questions in the course of investigation into anti-competitive practices, on the ground that they sought to induce answers as to the intention of certain activity which would have been self-incriminatory.

2.41 In *Case 222/84, Johnson v. Royal Ulster Constabulary* (23), the plaintiff was denied continued full-time employment as a police reservist in consequence of a policy decision that women should not carry firearms. This decision was protected from challenge on the ground of sex discrimination by a provision in the Sex Discrimination (Northern Ireland) Order (41) covering any act done for the purpose of safeguarding national security, and providing that a certificate of the Secretary of State that an act was so done should be conclusive of the fact. Relying on the general principle stated in Articles 6 and 13 of the Convention, that the rule of law requires that all persons must be entitled to test the lawfulness of any action in a competent court, the European Court went on to hold that the provisions of the relevant directive (42) should be interpreted in the light of those principles, and that the purported ouster of judicial control was contrary to Community law.

Enforcement in the English courts

2.42 It has already been emphasised that it is an essential characteristic of Community law that directly effective provisions may be relied upon in national courts in the same way as national statutes can. The corollary of this, and of the facility for any court or tribunal to make a reference to the European Court, is that all courts have a duty to apply Community law themselves, even if it means recognising that a provision of national

(40a) (Not yet reported).
(41)   SI 1976 No. 1042 (NI 15).
(42)   Directive 76/207 1976 OJ L 39/40.

law is invalid—and there must be no rule or practice reserving such a decision to a particular court or courts (43).

2.43 In principle therefore issues of Community law may be raised in the course of any proceedings before an English court or tribunal, whether they involve the state or are between private parties. Community law creates no new remedies for use in national courts, and no special procedural steps are necessary in order to raise a Community law matter. (44) The normal English law remedies are available, though to a limited extent they may be modified by substantive Community law e.g. by the rule against ouster provisions discussed under the previous heading, or the Court's doctrine of "passing on" in claims for recovery of sums wrongfully charged by the state. Attention may be drawn however to two classes of remedy, and their interaction with Community rights.

(i) *Judicial review*

2.44 Judicial review will be granted for any breach by a public authority of Community law as for national law (45). In *R. v. Inland Revenue Commissioners ex parte Imperial Chemical Industries* (46), the plaintiff successfully sought judical review of an arrangement between the Inland Revenue and one of its competitors, in relation to the taxation of oil exploration activities, on the ground that the arrangement was unduly favourable and amounted to an illegal state aid.

(ii) *Tort*

2.45 Actions in tort based upon or related to a breach of Community law may also be available, and two possibilities in particular exist of proceedings in tort: for the tort of *breach of statutory duty* (to give effect to Community law under section 2 of the European Communities Act 1972, or treating a duty imposed by Community legislation as analogous to one imposed by a UK statute), or for the little used tort of *misfeasance in a public office.*

2.46 The House of Lords has recognised that a contravention of Article 86 (on abuse of a dominant position in the market) may give rise to a cause of action for breach of statutory duty, and to a right to damages and/or an injunction; *Garden Cottage Foods v. Milk Marketing Board* (47), Likewise, it was held in *Cutsforth v. Mansfield Inns Ltd* (48) that an

(43) *Case 106/77, Simmenthal* [1978] ECR 629; [1978] 3 CMLR 263.
(44) *Case 158/80, Rewe v. Hauptzollamt Kiel* [1981] ECR 1805; [1982] 1 CMLR 449.
(45) *Bourgoin v. Ministry of Agriculture* [1985] 3 WLR 1027 CA
(46) [1987] 1 CMLR 72.
(47) [1984] AC 130.
(48) [1986] 1 All ER 577

injunction could be obtained to restrain a breach of Article 85. The state will be a prospective defendant where national legislation is passed or government action is taken in contravention of Community law. In *An Bord Bainne v. Milk Marketing Board* (49), the Court of Appeal held that the Crown was not liable in damages for a breach of Community law occasioned by legislative or quasi-legislative acts, or administrative action involving the exercise of discretion.

2.47 The situation where the private law regime of damages may also apply to government action, however, was illustrated in *Bourgoin v. Ministry of Agriculture* (45). In that case, the Minister of Agriculture withdrew a general import licence permitting the importation of turkeys just before the 1981 Christmas season on the pretext of stopping the spread of Newcastle disease. The European Court subsequently held that the ban was more severe than was genuinely necessary to check the disease and was contrary to Article 30. Although the judgment was delivered in July 1982, the Minister did not reissue the licence until November 1982, too late for the 1982 Christmas season's business.

2.48 The plaintiffs, French turkey producers, and importers in the UK, sought damages for the tort of misfeasance in a public office, alleging that the Minister's act was knowingly illegal and calculated to inflict economic damage on them by giving an unfair advantage at a crucial time to UK producers. On trial of the preliminary question of law, the Court of Appeal held that if the allegations were proved, then liability in damages would result, even though the acts complained of were public law governmental actions in the classic sense of the term. But it should be noted that for such liability to exist, there will need to have been a deliberate and conscious violation of Community law calculated to cause loss or damage.

2.49 A further limitation on state liability in national actions for damages was laid down by the Court in *Cases 106-127/87, Asteris v. Hellenic Republic* (50). The plaintiffs were producers of tomato concentrate who claimed to have suffered loss as a result of the annulment of Regulation 1615/83 (51) by the Court (52), and had failed in an action against the Commission (53) to recover damages under Article 215 of the Treaty (see below). The Court held that actions against national authorities for damages in respect of acts done in the application of Community law could be maintained without conflict with Community

(49) *An Bord Bainne v. Milk Marketing Board* CA [1984] 2 CMLR 584.
(50) (Not yet reported).
(51) OJ 1983 L 159/48.
(52) *Case 192/83 Greece v. Commission* [1985] ECR 2791.
(53) *Cases 194–206/83 Asteris v. Commission* [1985] ECR 2815.

law, but could not be brought on the same grounds as an action brought against the Community itself under Article 215 of the Treaty, which the European Court alone would have jurisdiction to entertain.

Enforcement and penal sanctions

2.50 With few exceptions (principally in relation to the competition policy), Community law does not prescribe criminal type sanctions for its non-observance. Article 5 requires Member States to "take all appropriate measures, whether general or particular, to ensure fulfilment of the obigations arising out of this Treaty. . ." It is therefore for national legislation to give criminal "teeth" to Community provisions, and this is provided for on a general basis by section 2 of the European Communities Act 1972 which permits Ministers to make delegated legislation to give effect to Community obligations generally. This includes a power to create criminal offences, as well as a general power to enact implementing or amending legislation.

2.51 This provision may be used where the enactment of specific primary legislation to implement a Community measure would be unduly cumbersome; but does not of course preclude such legislation, which may indeed be necessitated by the restrictions in Schedule 2 on the section 2 powers. The restrictions involve a prohibition on (a) imposing or increasing taxation, (b) retrospective legislation, (c) subdelegation i.e. authorising another Minister or body to enact delegated legislation, and (d) creating new criminal offences punishable by more than two years' imprisonment. It should be noted, however, that the Court has held in *Case 63/83, R. v. Kirk* (54) that Community legislation entailing a retrospective criminal liability is contrary to the general principles of Community law. National criminal provisions undergirding such legislation are therefore likely themselves to be unenforceable.

Proceedings before the European Court

2.52 The European Court's jurisdictions, which are both original and consultative, fall under five distinct headings. First, in relation to the enforcement of Treaty obligations by the Commission or by Member States (Articles 169 and 170), second, for annulment of a Community act (Article 173), thirdly, for failure by the Commission or the Council to adopt a measure required by Community law (Article 175), fourth in

(54) [1984] ECR 2689; [1984] 3 CMLR 522. In *Case 68/88 Commission v. Hellenic Republic* (not yet reported), Greece was held to be in breach of Article 5 for not having prosecuted frauds against Community agricultural levies.

relation to the non-contractual liability of the Institutions (Articles 178 and 215) and, fifth, for preliminary rulings on questions of Community law at the instance of national courts (Article 177). The position of the Court of first Instance is refered to in Chapter 1.

2.53 In its *original jurisdiction*, the Court hears cases brought against any of the Institutions or by them, or between Member States. Thus it deals with actions seeking the annulment of Commission decisions or the review of fines imposed under the competition policy, claims that legislation is invalid, and with staff cases against the Institutions. On the other side of the coin are actions brought by the Commission against Member States (called "infringement proceedings") for declarations that they have failed to comply with Community law, for example in maintaining a restriction, or in failing to implement a directive. Member States may also take proceedings against each other in reference to Treaty obligations. (55)

2.54 Parties other than member States and Community Institutions have very limited rights before the Court in its original jurisdiction. First, an individual or a corporation may bring proceedings under Article 173 against the Commission or the Council claiming that a decision of direct concern to them (or a regulation if it satisfies the same condition) should be annulled (56). An example of challenges under this heading occurs in connection with anti-dumping regulations. In *Case 260/85, Tokyo Electric Company Ltd v. Council* (57), a Japanese company sought annulment of such a regulation which, it claimed, discriminated in favour of a competitor who was not affected by it: it was held that, even if this could be shown to be the case, it would not be a ground for annulment of legislation validly adopted in so far as the plaintiff was concerned.

2.55 The action must be brought within two months of publication or notification and may only succeed on grounds of (i) lack of competence; (ii) infringement of an essential procedural requirement; (iii) infringement of the Treaty or any rule of law relating to its application, or (iv) misuse of powers. In *Case 294/83, The Greens v. European Parliament* (58), the Court held that action under Article 173 could also be taken for annulment of acts of the Parliament, even though Parliament is not mentioned as a possible defendant in the Article.

(55) Articles 169–179.
(56) *See Cases 16 & 17/62, Confédération Nationale des Fruits et Légumes v. Council* [1962] ECR 471; [1963] CMLR 160. But the European Parliament may not do so: *Case 302/87, Parliament v. Council* (not yet reported).
(57) [1989] 1 CMLR 169.
(58) [1987] 2 CMLR 343.

2.56 There is no right on the part of an individual to challenge the validity of general legislation by direct action under Article 173, and in any proceedings under that Article an individual plaintiff must show that the decision or regulation is "of direct and individual concern" to him (59). Article 184 by contrast entitles any party to plead the general invalidity of a regulation (60) in proceedings before the Court, notwithstanding the two month time limit under Article 173 having elapsed, by invoking any of the four grounds mentioned in that Article. There is therefore in effect a separate and much wider ground of challenge to Community legislation always open to the litigant in any proceedings which are before the European Court, either in its original jurisdiction or on a reference for a preliminary ruling.

2.57 Under Article 175, there is a right for anyone to take action against an Institution for failure, contrary to the Treaty, to address to that person "any act other than a recommendation or an opinion". This could be the case for example in connection with the Commission's powers in relation to the competition policy. Articles 178 and 215(2) confer jurisdiction on the Court to deal with actions against the Community for non-contractual liability for damage caused by the Institutions or their servants "in accordance with the general principles common to the laws of the member states". This jurisdiction may not be replicated at the national level by means of actions against national authorities in national courts (50). Contractual liability is governed by the proper law of the contract, and is within the jurisdiction of the appropriate national court.

2.58 A little-used jurisdiction permits the Council, the Commission or a Member State to seek a ruling from the Court on the compatibility with the Treaty of a proposed agreement between the Community and third countries or international organisations. (61)

2.59 The Court's *consultative jurisdiction* is of the widest practical importance from the point of view of the individual affected by Community law. It arises under Article 177, and exists to enable the uniform application of Community law by providing national courts with the means of clarifying points which emerge in proceedings before them in relation to: (a) the interpretation of the treaties; (b) the validity and interpretation of acts of the institutions (such as legislation), and (c) the interpretation of the statutes of bodies established by the Council. In a

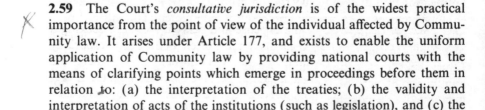

(59)   See e.g. *Case 25/62, Plaumann v. Commission* [1963] ECR 95; [1964] CMLR 29.
(60)   Or certain other legal acts: *Case 92/78, Simmenthal v. Commission* [1978] ECR 1129; [1980] 1 CMLR 25.
(61)   Article 228.

number of other cases, a similar jurisdiction has been conferred on the Court, for example by the 1968 Civil and Commercial Judgments Convention and by the European Patent Convention.

2.60 Proceedings involving the European Court, whether in its original jurisdiction or on a reference, are governed by the Court's consolidated rules of procedure (62). They contain an outline of the stages of the procedure, time limits for service of documents and details of parties to be served, provisions with regard to witnesses and taking evidence on commission, interim measures, costs and enforcement. In general it may be said that much more emphasis is placed upon the written stage than in the UK, and that it is at this stage that the main presentation of the case normally occurs.

2.61 The rules provide a wide degree of privilege for the papers and persons of lawyers acting in proceedings. The Institutions and the Member States may be represented by an "agent" appointed for the purpose (in practice usually a legally qualified person) and other parties by a lawyer admitted to practise before the courts of a Member State. In so far as England and Wales is concerned, this means a barrister, or a solicitor if he could have appeared in the national proceedings or there are no national proceedings involved.

References under Article 177

2.62 Preliminary rulings by the European Court *may* be sought by "any court or tribunal" (which does not include an arbitrator (63)) in a Member State which considers a reference necessary to enable it to give judgment. A reference *must* be made by any court or tribunal against whose decisions there is no judical remedy; i.e. in most cases in the U.K., the House of Lords, but the Court of Appeal if leave to appeal to the House of Lords is refused. (64)

2.63 Weighing up whether the expense and delay involved in seeking a preliminary ruling would be justified may often be difficult, especially where relevant issues of fact are to be contested. Save where the reference is obligatory, this is a matter for the national court's discretion: *Cases 98, 162 & 258/85, Bertini* (65). Guidance on the exercise of this discretion has been given by the Court of Appeal in *H. P. Bulmer*

(62)   See OJ 1974 L350/1 & 29, as last amended in OJ 1987 L 165/3 & 4 and OJ 1989 L 241/1.
(63)   *Case 102/81 Nordsee v. Reederei Mond* [1982] ECR 1095.
(64)   *Hagen v. Fratelli* [1980] CMLR 253.
(65)   [1986] ECR 1893; [1987] 1 CMLR 774.

Ltd v. J. Bollinger SA (66), where the principles to be followed were laid down. They include that no reference should normally be made unless the facts have been ascertained or agreed, or if the point raised is clear and free from doubt, whether or not the European Court has previously ruled on it. It has subsequently been held, however, that courts should be hesitant in reaching the conclusion that there is no doubt (67) and that, in an appropriate case, magistrates may refer at the close of the prosecution case, if a submission of no case to answer based on an issue of Community law necessitates it. (68)

2.64 Ultimately, the European Court has jurisdiction to decide when, as a matter of overriding Community law, a reference under Article 177 should be made, and it has given guidance itself from time to time emphasising the wide measure of freedom which national courts have to make use of the procedure. In *Case 283/81, CILFIT v. Ministry of Health* (69), the Court has, in the context of the situation in which reference is *prima facie* obligatory (because proceedings are before a court of final resort), indicated those cases in which a reference is not called for: where the Community issue is irrelevant; where it has already been the subject of a ruling, and where there is no room for reasonable doubt about its meaning—the so-called doctrine of the *acte clair*. It should be noted, however, that only the European Court may declare a Community act invalid: *Case 314/85, Foto-Frost v. Hauptzollamt Lübeck-Ost*. (70)

2.65 The provisions of RSC Order 114 deal with references from the High Court and the Court of Appeal to the European Court, while references from other courts or tribunals will be governed in procedural terms by such courts' own rules. While a reference is made by the national court or tribunal (not by the parties) and is in its discretion, it will be normal for the terms of the reference to be settled by agreement between counsel and the court. No reference can be made after a court has given judgment, even though the order of the court has not yet been drawn up, nor if the possibility of an appeal no longer exists (71). The effect of a reference is to stay the national proceedings, unless the court otherwise orders. (72)

(66)   [1974] Ch 401.
(67)   *R. v. Pharmaceutical Society of Great Britain* [1987] 2 CMLR 769
(68)   *R. v. Plymouth Justices ex parte Rogers* [1982] QB 863.
(69)   [1982] ECR 3415; [1983] 1 CMLR 472.
(70)   [1988] 3 CMLR 57.
(71)   *Magnavision v. General Optical Council* [1987] CMLR 262.
(72)   RSC O. 114 r. 4

2.66 In *Portsmouth City Council v. Richards* (73) an injunction restraining breaches of the criminal law was upheld, even though a reference to the European Court was pending to test the legality of the offence provisions. Similarly, the House of Lords held in *R. v. Secretary of State for Transport, ex parte Factortame Ltd* (74) that a United Kingdom statute—the Merchant Shipping Act 1988—must be given effect pending a reference under Article 177. In that case, the House referred to the Court the question of what interim protection Community law required should be given to a party claiming the benefit of it while a reference is pending. However, in parallel infringement proceedings brought by the Commission also calling in question the Act's compatibility with Community law, the Court did grant an interim injunction against the United Kingdom suspending the operation of the nationality provisions of the legislation in so far as they affected those who had established rights under the law immediately prior to the new statute coming into force. (75)

(73) CA (not yet reported).
(74) *R. v. Secretary of State for Transport ex parte Factortame* (not yet reported—now *Case 221/89* in the European Court).
(75) *Case 246/89 Commission v. United Kingdom*, Order dated 10 October 1989 (not yet reported).

CHAPTER 3

Free Movement of Goods within the Community

Objectives

3.01 Article 2 of the Treaty states briefly the objectives of the Community, which are set out at greater length in the Preamble to the Treaty, and specifies two courses of action for the attainment of these objectives: by establishing a common market and by progressively approximating the economic policies of Member States. It is clear that the Treaty considers the establishment of the common market as the more urgent of the two, while in *Case 167/73, Commission v. France* (1) the Court held that the establishment of the common market refers to all the economic activities of the Community, and that the basis of the common market was the free movement of goods, persons, services and capital.

3.02 Article 3 states that for the purposes set out in Article 2 the activities of the Community shall include, *inter alia*, the elimination as between Member States of customs duties and of quantitative restrictions on the import and export of goods, and of all other measures having equivalent effect; and the establishment of a common customs tariff and of a common commercial policy towards third countries (see Chapters 4 and 5). It is thus apparent that the free movement of goods is the basic part of a real common market. The part of the Treaty dealing with free movement of goods contains detailed and specific rules, while other parts often go no further than to supply guidelines.

3.03 The two chapters of the Treaty dealing with free movement of goods are headed "Customs Union" and "Elimination of Quantitative Restrictions Between Member States". Article 9 provides that the Community shall be based on a customs union which shall cover all trade in goods, and which shall involve the prohibition between Member States of customs duties on imports and exports and of all charges having equivalent effect and the adoption of a common customs tariff in their relations with third countries. This distinguishes a customs union from a free trade area in that a free trade area has no common customs tariff and no common rules of customs administration.

(1)   [1974] ECR 223; [1974] 1 CMLR 309.

Free circulation

3.04 The provisions relating to elimination of customs duties and the elimination of quantitative restrictions between Member States apply both to products originating in Member States and to products coming from third countries which are in **free circulation** in Member States. The term "goods" has been defined by the Court in *Case 7/68, Commission v. Italy* (2) as meaning products which can be valued in money, and which are capable of forming the subject of commercial transactions. Coins which are in the form of legal tender do not fall within the definition: *Case 7/78, R. v. Thompson*. (3)

3.05 Article 10 enlarges Article 9 by saying that products coming from a third country shall be considered to be in free circulation in a Member State if the import formalities have been complied with and any customs duties or charges having equivalent effect which are payable have been levied in that Member State, and if they have not benefited from a total or partial drawback of such duties or charges. This definition enabled the Court to hold in *Case 119/78, SA des Grandes Distilleries Peureux v. Directeur des Services Fiscaux* (4) that the provisions of Article 30 relate not only to goods from other Member States, but also to goods of third country origin but in free circulation in a Member State. No import licence may be required for the importation into one Member State of goods of third country origin which are in free circulation in another Member State. But the country of final destination of the goods may require an indication of the country of origin of the goods: *Case 41/76, Donckerwolke*. (5)

3.06 Article 10(2) requires the Commission to determine the methods of administrative co-operation to be adopted for the purposes of applying Article 9(2), taking into account the need to reduce as much as possible formalities imposed on trade. These formalities have been gradually reduced. Directive 83/643 (6) has limited the inspection and formalities at Community borders. Regulations 678/85 (7) and 679/85 (8) provide for a single Community customs document (known as the Single Adminstrative Document) and other simplifications for trade within the Community.

(2) [1968] ECR 423; [1969] CMLR 1.
(3) [1978] ECR 2247; [1979] 1 CMLR 47.
(4) [1979] ECR 975; [1980] 3 CMLR 337.
(5) [1975] ECR 1921; [1977] 2 CMLR 535.
(6) OJ 1983 L359/8.
(7) OJ 1985 L79/1, as last amended by Reg 2793/86 OJ 1986 L263/74.
(8) OJ 1985 L79/7, as last amended by Reg 1062/87 OJ 1987 L107/1.

Customs duties and equivalent charges

3.07 Article 12 plays an essential part in the creation of the customs union since it prohibits Member States from introducing between themselves any new customs duties on imports or exports or any charges having equivalent effect, and from increasing those which they already apply in their trade with each other. The Article introduces the concept of "charges having equivalent effect". This concept has been given a wide interpretation by the Court which, in an early developement of the law, held in *Cases 2 & 3/62, Commission v. Luxembourg and Belgium* (9) that a charge falls within the definition if, whatever its name, it amounts to a charge imposed unilaterally, either at the time goods are imported or at a later time, which directly affects goods imported from a Member State but not similar domestic goods, so that it increases the price of the goods and has thus the same consequences on the free movement of goods as a customs duty.

3.08 As a general rule a charge imposed on goods at the time they cross the border, and not authorised by the Treaty, amounts to a charge having equivalent effect: *Cases 2 & 3/69, Sociaal Fonds voor de Diamantarbeiders v. Brachfeld et al.* (10) Statistical fees levied at the time imported goods were declared for statistical purposes have been held to be such a charge: *Case 24/68, Commission v. Italian Republic* (11). Likewise, charges for customs administration within the obligatory opening hours laid down by Directive 83/643 (12) are forbidden: *Case 340/87, Commission v. Italy* (13). The same principle is applied to charges levied on exports, where the prohibition is contained in Article 16.

3.09 The prohibition of such charges applies even if the charge is imposed as payment for a service actually rendered, such as a sanitary inspection of animal products, when no charge or a smaller charge is imposed for the inspection of products not imported or destined for export: *Case 87/75, Bresciani v. Amministratione Italiana delle Finanze* (14). In *Case 26/62, Van Gend en Loos v. Nederlandse Administratie der Belastigen* (15), it was held that the absolute and binding terms of Article 12, which requires no specific implementation, create rights directly enforceable by nationals of the Member States.

 (9) [1962] ECR 425; [1963] CMLR 199.
(10) [1969] ECR 211; [1969] CMLR 336.
(11) [1969] ECR 193; [1971] CMLR 611.
(12) OJ 1983 L359/8, as last amended by Dir 87/53 OJ 1987 L24/33.
(13) (Not yet reported).
(14) [1976] ECR 129; [1976] 2 CMLR 62.
(15) [1963] ECR 1; [1963] CMLR 105.

3.10   Article 13 provided for the progressive abolition of customs duties and charges having equivalent effect in accordance with the timetable set out in Article 14 or by virtue of Article 15. On 1 July 1968 the original six Member States abolished all duties on industrial goods (Decision 66/532) (16). This has now been accomplished for all the subsequent Member States except Spain and Portugal, for whom a transitional period ends on 1 January 1993—see Chapter 4. Article 16 called for the abolition of customs duties on exports and charges having equivalent effect by the first stage envisaged by Article 14. Article 17 applied Articles 9 to 15 to customs duties of a fiscal nature. These customs duties were intended not to protect domestic producers but had a revenue gathering object: they have now been converted in the United Kingdom to excise duties *prima facie* compatible with the internal taxation requirements of Article 95—see Chapter 11.

Quantitative Restrictions on Intra-Community Trade

3.11   The major objective of the Treaty is the free movement of goods in the Community and this involves, in addition to the abolition of customs duties, the abolition of all impediments to imports and exports within the Community. This objective is given effect in Articles 30 to 37 of the Treaty, which provides that quantitative restrictions on imports or exports, and all measures having equivalent effect, shall be prohibited between Member States. Community law envisages a broad meaning for the term "measures", to include any instruments issuing from a public authority which, while not legally binding on the addressees, cause them to pursue certain conduct. In *Case 249/81, Commission v. Ireland* (17) a "Buy Irish" campaign funded by the government was held to be capable of infringing Article 30. These Articles have direct effect since the end of the transitional period: *Case 74/76, Ianelli & Volpi v. Meroni* (18).

3.12   The jurisdiction of the Court has established very wide parameters in interpreting the concept of measures having equivalent effect to quantitative restrictions, and directives which were enacted under Article 33(7) to give effect to Article 30 have been overtaken by the Court's decisions. In *Case 8/74, Procureur du Roi v. Dassonville* (19) the Court stated that "All trading rules enacted by Member States which are capable of hindering, directly or indirectly, actually or potentially intra-

---

(16)   O.J. 1966 2971.
(17)   [1982] ECR 4005, [1983] 2 CMLR 104; contrast *Apple and Pear Development Council v. Lewis* [1983] ECR 4083, [1984] 3 CMLR 733.
(18)   [1977] ECR 557; [1977] 2 CMLR 688.
(19)   [1974] ECR 837; [1974] 2 CMLR 436.

Community trade are to be considered as measures having equivalent effect to quantitative restrictions." In that case the Belgian rule requiring a British Customs certificate of origin for Scotch whisky imported into Belgium after being in free circulation in France was found to be such a measure. A requirement by Belgium allowing for certified copies of the certificate or origin was however lawful: *Case 2/78, Commission v. Belgium.* (20)

3.13 As a general principle, all rules that hinder trade between the Member States are prohibited by Article 30: *Case 119/78, SA des Grandes Distilleries Peureux v. Directeur des Services Fiscaux* (21). Thus the Court starts with the presumption that health checks are contrary to the prohibition—*Case 4/75, Rewe v. Zentralfinanz* (22). *Case 155/73, Sacchi* (23) indicated that even measures not directly connected with the import or export of goods may violate Article 30: there the Court considered the practice by Italian radio and television authorities of choosing advertisements which would hinder the promotion of non-Italian goods.

3.14 The Court also held that a restriction on the total production of goods could fall within the prohibition of Article 30 where the country imposing the restriction was the only producer of any consequence: *Case 190/73, Officier van Justitie v. van Haaster* (24). And in *Case 56/87, Commission v. Italy* (25) it was held that rules fixing the prices of pharmaceutical products which were likely to favour domestic products to the detriment of imported ones were contrary to Article 36. Article 31 prohibits all new quantitative restrictions and equivalent measures. This Article has direct effect: *Case 13/68, Salgoil v. Ministry of Foreign Trade* (26). All these prohibitions apply to intra-Community trade. It was held in *Case 225/78, Procureur v. Bouhelier* (27) that they did not apply in trade with third countries, to the extent not inconsistent with the Community commercial policy.

3.15 Article 34 prohibits quantitative restrictions on exports between Member States, and all measures having equivalent effect. It has direct effect: *Case 83/78, Pigs Marketing Board v. Redmond* (28). Export

(20) [1979] ECR 1761; [1980] 1 CMLR 216.
(21) [1979] ECR 975; [1980] 3 CMLR 337.
(22) [1975] ECR 843; [1977] 1 CMLR 599.
(23) [1974] ECR 409; [1974] 2 CMLR 177.
(24) [1974] ECR 1123; [1974] 2 CMLR 521.
(25) [1989] 3 CMLR 707.
(26) [1968] ECR 453; [1969] CMLR 181.
(27) [1979] ECR 3151; [1980] 2 CMLR 541.
(28) [1978] ECR 2347; [1979] 1 CMLR 177.

restrictions are not very much in evidence, but the Court has intervened in cases where the access of individual traders to the export market is being limited—see for example *Case 177/78, Pigs and Bacon Commission v. McCarren & Co Ltd* (29), or where there are licensing requirements, even where the licensing is automatic, because the inconvenience and delay of the licence requirement is itself a restraint on trade: *Case 68/76, Commission v. France.* (30)

The permitted restrictions—Article 36

3.16 Article 36 lays down exceptions to the requirement for the abolition of quantitative restrictions and measures having equivalent effect between Member States. The task of particularising the scope of the exceptions to Articles 30 to 34, which Article 36 allows, falls largely to the Court to undertake on a case by case basis. The Article provides that the provisions of Articles 30 to 34 do not preclude prohibitions or restrictions on imports, exports or goods in transit justified on the grounds of: (a) public morality, public policy or public security; (b) the protection of health and life to humans, animals and plants; (c) the protection of national treasures possessing artistic, historic or archeological value; or (d) the protection of industrial and commerical property.

3.17 Such prohibitions or restrictions must not, however, constitute a means of arbitrary discrimination or a disguished restriction on trade between Member States. The Article has to be interpreted strictly: *Case 29/72, Marimex v. Ministry of Finance* (31), and may not be used to by-pass specific provisions in Articles 30 to 34. The last sentence of the Article makes it clear that every prohibition has to be reasonable and justified, and much use is made by the Court in applying this provision of the principle of proportionality referred to in Chapter 2. Article 36 cannot be used in relation to subjects not specified in the Article itself: *Case 113/80, Commission v. Ireland.* (32)

3.18 A very frequently cited case on Article 36 is *Case 120/78, Cassis de Dijon* (33), in which the Court held that Germany was not entitled to prohibit the import of the drink cassis, which was being lawfuly marketed in France, on the ground that its alcoholic content was less than 25%; no detriment to public health existed, and consumer protection could be adequately be provided for by labelling. The Court there

(29) [1979] ECR 2161; [1979] 3 CMLR 389.
(30) [1977] ECR 515; [1977] 2 CMLR 161.
(31) [1972] ECR 1309; [1973] CMLR 486.
(32) [1981] ECR 1625; [1982] 1 CMLR 706.
(33) [1979] ECR 649; [1979] 3 CMLR 494.

recognised that the Article could legitimately be invoked to justify measures genuinely needed for consumer protection or the effectiveness of fiscal supervision. These measures must of course apply to both imported and domestic products without any discrimination. The Court has had to apply the principles of Article 36 in a large number of cases which, following the four main categories in the Article, may be illustrated as follows.

(a) *Public morality, public policy and public security*
   Case 34/79, R. v. Henn and Darby (34) upheld a prohibition on the importation of obscene articles on the basis of the reference to public morality, and the content of this concept is for each Member State to determine. The Court appears to have left more discretion to Member States when it comes to restrictions on trade due to the concept of public policy where the protection of domestic products does not come into play. Restrictions on export and import protecting coinage are valid: *Case 7/78, R. v. Thompson* (3) There are, however, indications that the Court's decisions move in response to general changes of climate, as where the maintenance of essential supplies was considered a matter of public security in *Case 72/83, Campus Oil Ltd v. Minister for Industry* (35). In *Case C145/88, Torfaen BC v. B&Q Plc* (35a), the United Kindgom's Sunday trading restrictions were held to be *prima facie* compatible with Article 30.

(b) *Protection of life and health*
   The validity of rules governing public health is recognised by the Court, but measures for the protection of public health should not be allowed to interfere with imports or exports unless genuinely necessary: *Case 104/75, De Peijper.* (36)
   Case 788/79, Gilli and Andres (37) and *Case 193/80, Commission v. Italy* (38) illustrate the Court's attitude: in these cases, the Court considered contrary to Article 30 Italian legislation requiring that only vinegar made from wine should be sold as "vinegar", reasoning that since vinegars made from other argicultural products were not harmful to health, comsumers' interest could be protected by the listing of ingredients.
   To avoid the prohibition of the Article, a national measure alleged to protect health must constitute a "seriously considered health policy": *Case 40/82, Commission v. United Kingdom* (39), and the burden of

(34) [1979] ECR 3795; [1980] 1 CMLR 246.
(35) [1984] ECR 2727; [1984] 3 CMLR 544.
(35a) (Not yet reported).
(36) [1976] ECR 613; [1976] 2 CMLR 271.
(37) [1980] ECR 2071; [1981] 1 CMLR 146.
(38) [1981] ECR 3019.
(39) [1982] ECR 2793; [1982] 3 CMLR 497.

showing that the measure is necessary for the protection of health, and goes no further than is needed for that purpose, lies on the Member State: *Case 227/82, van Bennekom* (40). A minor burden or a rule aimed at prevention of alcoholism is not considered unlawful; *Case 75/81, Blesgen v. Belgium* (41). Where Community measures to harmonise provisions on health protection have been adopted, recourse to Article 36 is no longer possible: *Case 190/87 Handelsonderneming Moormann BV* (42).

Where a product is lawfully marketed in a Member State there is a presumption that there is an adequate guarantee of its quality and safety, especially where the exercise of the profession concerned in its marketing is already governed by Community legislation. Thus a ban on private import from France to Germany of a medicinal product lawfully purchased in France (for a quarter of the German price), and available at pharmacies without prescription in Germany, was held not to be justified on public health grounds in *Case 215/87 Schumaker* (43).

Fees may be charged to reflect the actual cost of carrying out such checks as are provided for in the Community legislation: *Case 18/87, Commission v. Germany.* (44)

(c) *Protection of national heritage*

Case 7/68, Commission v. Italy (45) shows that concern for the protection of objects of historic, artistic or archeological value does not enable a Member State to impose a tax on the export of such objects.

(d) *Protection of intellectual property*

The cases under this subheading are largely concerned with the interrelation between national intellectual property law and competition law, and the principles of Article 36, and are referred to in Chapter 14. Here the Court has tended to be readier to accept the need for national restrictions to be maintained pending harmonisation of legislation at Community level.

State monopolies

3.19 Concluding the section of the Treaty on free movement of goods is Article 37 with its requirement that commercial state monopolies must not operate to discriminate between nationals of different Member States in regard to the conditions under which goods are procured and marketed. This has particular relevance to restrictions on importation,

(40) [1983] ECR 3883; [1985] 2 CMLR 692.
(41) [1982] ECR 2111; [1983] 1 CMLR 431.
(42) (Not yet reported).
(43) (Not yet reported).
(44) (Not yet reported).
(45) [1968] ECR 423; [1969] CMLR 1.

whether they take the form of exclusive rights to import certain products or of charges or levies on such goods. The article applies not only to state undertakings as such, but also to any body through which a state "supervises, determines or appreciably influences" imports or exports, or any body to which a monopoly is delegated by the state. It does not apply to monopolies of services maintained by states: *Case 30/87, Bodson v. Pompes Funèbres* (46).

3.20 Monopolies themselves are not affected and may continue, but any form of intra-state impediment to trade associated with them has been illegal since the end of the transitional period in 1970 and liable to be set aside in litigation before national courts: *Case 59/75, Pubblico Ministero v. Manghera* (47). Thus quotas or duties (however described) are prohibited, and products of the kind in question coming from another Member State must be capable of both importation and marketing on the same commerical terms as the products dealt in by the state monopoly. Inconsistent with these requirements are: an exclusive right to import a particular product: *Case 59/75, Manghera* (47); a price adjustment designed to place the imported product on the market at the same price as those marketed by the monopoly: *Case 91/75, Hauptzollamt Göttingen v. Miritz* (48); and marketing a product with the assistance of public funds so as to undercut comparable imported products: *Case 91/78, Hansen v. Flensburg Customs Office* (49).

3.21 The only exceptions now permitted to the right to free movement of goods are those specified in Article 36—public morality, public policy, or public security etc. Article 37(4) does, however, provide that in the case of agricultural products measures may be taken to ensure equivalent safeguards for the employment and standard of living of producers affected, though this does not justify any measure which would infringe the Article's policy. It should be noted however that Article 37 does not apply in the case of imports from outside the Community, but only to trade between Member States: *Case 91/78, Hansen v. Flensburg Customs Office* (49).

Community transit

3.22 A complex of Regulations based on Regulation 222/77 (50) defines the conditions under which goods may pass through internal

(46) (Not yet reported).
(47) [1976] ECR 91; [1976] 1 CMLR 557.
(48) [1976] ECR 217.
(49) [1979] ECR 935; [1981] 1 CMLR 331.
(50) OJ 1977 L38/1, as last amended by Reg. 1674/87 OJ 1987 L157/1.

Community borders without full customs examination or payment of duties and taxes. The scheme operates in two parts. First comes internal Community transit, for goods already in free circulation in the Community; secondly, there is an external Community transit regime applicable to goods imported from third countries and not yet in free circulation, and to goods which have been in free circulation but which have been entered for export from the Community with a view to receiving export refunds or subsidies under the Common Agricultural Policy. The Community transit system is only applicable where carriage through more than one Member State is involved.

3.23 The external transit system operates in relation to third country imports, so that the duties and taxes chargeable on entry to the Community are paid when the goods have reached their final destination within the Community, passage through Member States *en route* being assured without further formality upon presentation of the Community transit documentation. This documentation is issued, and the goods are sealed, at the customs office where the Community transit journey commences, with the arrival office verifying the goods and documentation, and confirming the position to the first office once the goods have been entered and duty paid. The bond guaranteeing payment of duties is then discharged.

3.24 The internal transit scheme enables goods to pass through Member States on the basis of documents issued on departure, together with a bond guaranteeing the payment of taxes etc., falling due. When the goods reach their destination, and are cleared by customs there, a notice is returned to the office of departure confirming that the transit operation has been completed satisfactorily, and their liability to taxes discharged. In both this and the external transit regime, there are arrangements to permit the acceptance of block guarantees for all Community transit business effected by individual merchants, and for certain types of traffic to be authorised without guarantees. Detailed rules are laid down with regard to the amount, terms and discharge of the guarantees.

3.25 Community transit declarations are now part of the Single Administrative Document for customs purposes (51). Two general implementing regulations have been adopted by the Commission, Regulations 1062/87 and 2823/87 (52). They allow for simplified systems for con-

(51) See Regulation 678/85 OJ 1985 L79/1, and Reg 679/85 OJ 1985 L79/7, as last amended by Reg 1062/87 OJ 1987 L107/1.
(52) OJ 1987 L107/1, as last amended by Reg. 1159/89 OJ 1989 L119/100 and OJ 1987 L270/1.

tainerised traffic and rail freight, and for approved undertakings to use pre-stamped official forms, and to substitute commerical documents for certain parts of the forms. Provision is also made for the use of form T5 for the purpose of end-use requirements in Community legislation, and for the issue of Community documents to permit transit from one Member State to another through a third country using a TIR carnet.

3.26 Specific provision has been made by regulation in relation to a number of European third countries with which Community Transit agreements have been entered into, in particular Austria and Switzerland. As regards goods coming from or going to destinations outside the Community, the TIR Carnet system or the Rhine Manifest (used for barge traffic on the River Rhine), if applicable, will remain operative (53).

(53) Regulation 3237/76 OJ 1976 L368/1, as last amended by Reg. 3020/81 OJ 1981 L302/6.

CHAPTER 4

The Customs Union

Role and purpose

4.01 Article 9 prescribes that the Community is to based on a customs union covering all trade in goods. It has been seen in Chapter 3 that the existence of a customs union makes possible the establishment of an internal free trade area, developing into a single market. Looking outwards, the customs union makes possible the Community's common commercial policy towards third countries, developed in the context of action under Articles 113 and 238. The external Community Customs Union is therefore already largely complete, and operating through the Customs administrations of the Member States who (save in so far as they are concerned with matters such as prohibited imports, or with internal taxes) act as the Community's agents in applying the Common Customs Tariff and Community customs law.

4.02 The area of customs law has accordingly had to be the subject of much Community activity and a large part of the existing legislation now in force in the Community consists either of Community legislation or the Treaty, or of national legislation governed by Community directives. Over the life of the Customs Union, there has been a steady trend towards the use of regulations instead of directives, thereby increasing the proportion of directly applicable Community law. This helps to avoid the trading distortions which can result from disparate national legislation. Whether directives or regulations are used, the broad pattern is for a Council enactment to constitute the primary source of the law and for Commission enactments (often very numerous) to provide detailed implementation.

The Community customs territory

4.03 The customs territory of the Community, by reference to which the rules on free movement of goods and the Common Commercial Policy both operate, is defined in Regulation 2151/84 (1). It *includes* the territories of all the Member States as defined in their own constitutions *plus*: the Austrian territories of Jungholz and Mittelberg (with Germany), Monaco (with France), San Marino (with Italy), the Channel

(1)   OJ 1984 L 197/1, as last amended by Reg 4151/88 OJ 1988 L 367/1 .

Islands and the Isle of Man (with the United Kingdom) (2), and the territorial sea and airspace of each Member State; but *minus* Heligoland and Busingen (from Germany), the non-European territories of the Netherlands and France, the Faroe Islands and Greenland (from Denmark), Livigno, Campione d'Italia and part of Lake Lugano (from Italy), the Canary Islands, Ceuta and Melilla (from Spain). Gibraltar is not part of the customs territory. (3)

4.04   Excluded from Community customs provisions, pending the introduction of Community legislation, are supplies and materials for offshore rigs or platforms, and for boats, within any Member State's territorial sea. The continental shelf is outside the Community customs territory, although certain rules on origin take account of it. (1)

The Common Customs Tariff

4.05   The Common Customs Tariff (CCT) has replaced national customs tariffs, and contains a comprehensive categorisation of goods together with the rates of duty chargeable. The tariff is subject to amendment throughout the year, but is consolidated and reissued annually. In the case of goods covered by the treaties governing the European Coal and Steel Community, the national tariffs remain in force, albeit on a harmonised basis, but details of the position in relation to coal and steel are given in the CCT for ease of reference. During the transitional period following their accession, ending on 1 January 1993, Spain and Portugal continue to use their national tariffs, and special provisions apply to trade involving those countries. (4)

4.06   The CCT in its present form was first laid down in Council Regulation 2658/87 (5) and based on the Combined Nomenclature adopted in an international convention sponsored by the Customs Cooperation Council (CCC), signed in June in 1983. Regulation 2886/89 (6) amends the Combined Nomenclature classifications and the CCT with effect from 1 January 1990. The Community is a party to the convention, which is expected in due course to be adopted by the great majority of countries. The CCC has a Nomenclature Committee which

(2)   See Protocol 3 to the Act of Accession of the United Kingdom, Denmark and Ireland for the general conditions of application of Community law to the Channel Islands and the Isle of Man.
(3)   See Article 28 of the Act of Accession of the United Kingdom etc., for its status within the Community generally.
(4)   Act of Accession of Spain and Portugal.
(5)   OJ 1987 L 256/1.
(6)   OJ 1989 L 282/1.

offers classification opinions in cases of doubt, and prepares explanatory notes on the nomenclature. Neither of these has binding force in the Community, but the Court will treat them as persuasive authority in the absence of any relevant Community material.

4.07 At Community level, there also exists a Nomenclature Committee whose functions are to approve delegated legislation proposed by the Commission on classification matters, to give classification opinions in cases referred to it and to prepare explanatory notes on the nomenclature. Regulation 2658/87 (5) provides general rules for the interpretation of the Combined Nomenclature and for the Commission, after consulting the Nomenclature Committee, to adopt clarification regulations where necessary. Generally, the Committee's opinions and explanatory notes, even where they are strictly non-binding, are respected in practice and are published in the C (information) series of the Official Journal. The present Combined Nomenclature has been in force since 1 January 1988, and within its 13,500 subdivisions it allows for all the Community's needs in relation to duties, levies and trade measures, as well as the compilation of statistics.

Rates and quotas

4.08 The tariff is amended globally each year with effect from 1 January by a regulation adopted within the framework of the common commercial policy and the common agricultural policy, and throughout the year in numerous detailed regulations. In general, the duties on agricultural products are higher than those on industrial products. The duties may be *ad valorem*, as a percentage of the value of the goods, specific, i.e. a sum fixed by reference to the weight, volume or number of the goods, or a combination of the two. The amount payable is indicated opposite each subdivision in the tariff.

4.09 Within the framework of the duties laid down in the tariff, the common commercial policy requires the application of a variety of quotas designed to meet particular sectoral or even national needs. Thus a *tariff quota* opened for specified goods enables a limited quantity of goods to be imported at reduced or nil rates of duty; an unlimited quantity of the same goods may be imported at the normal rate of duty. In a less rigid version of this regime, *tariff ceilings* allow import at reduced or nil rates of a fixed quantity of goods, but remain in force until revoked or the expiry of the period of the concession rather than, as in the case of tariff quotas, until the strict limit has been reached. *Quantitative quotas* allow the import of a fixed quantity of goods at the rates shown in the tariff, notwithstanding a prohibition on their import otherwise.

4.10 Quotas are usually allocated to the Member States, which administer their allocations, with a reserve sometimes being held by the Community. This fragmentation of the quotas is likely to cease following the establishment of the internal market, and to be replaced by exclusive Community management such as occurs already in the case of tariff ceilings, where the Commission monitors the import of the goods concerned until the overall limit is reached and then re-establishes the normal rates of duty. The opening, conditions and termination of quotas are the subject of Council or Commission Regulations. In *Case 51/87, Commission v. Council* (7), however, the Court annulled a regulation dividing quotas into national shares on the ground that the Council had not been justified in rejecting Commission proposals for Community management of the quotas.

Reliefs

4.11 A number of reliefs from duty on a standard basis are available on the conditions laid down in Regulation 918/83 (8). Under this regulation, customs duty and agricultural levies on import or export are relieved, but not value added tax or excise duty which are the subject of separate provisions. (These internal taxes, though levied on import into the United Kingdom *as* customs duties, are subject to Community control only through the Directives and Treaty provisions on taxation.) The provisions of Regulation 918/83 are lengthy, detailed and have been much amended, with the individual reliefs provided for being subject to a variety of limitations.

4.12 Among the headings under which relief is available are: small non-commercial consignments not exceeding given value limits, with quantity limits for tobacco, alcohol and perfume; goods in passengers' personal baggage of a non-commercial character not exceeding specified value limits, again with quantity limits for tobacco, alcohol and perfume; scientific, educational or cultural items, in some cases only where not obtainable within the Community; goods imported for charities, handicapped persons or catastrophe victims; the household goods of persons transferring their normal residence to the Community from a third country either generally or, subject to slightly different conditions,

(7) (Not yet reported).
(8) OJ 1983 L 105/1, as last amended by Reg. 4235/88, OJ 1988 L 373/1. See also Reg. 3301/74 OJ 1974 L 354/55.

on marriage or establishing a secondary residence in the Community; students' personal belongings; inherited goods; plant and equipment transferred by a business migrating into the Community; samples, publicity material, goods for exhibitions or for examination, analysis or tests.

4.13 There is a number of reliefs more relating to medical, agricultural and other purposes to which space precludes reference. It should be noted that Article 131 of Regulation 918/83 (8) provides for the drawback of the relief if conditions to which it is subject are not complied with, and places the burden of proof on the importer. Member States' freedom to allow further reliefs in certain areas, notably in relation to medical research and diplomatic imports, is preserved, and a Reliefs Committee, similar to the Nomenclature Committee, is established to approve legislation by the Commission resolving difficulties of application which arise.

Temporary importation

4.14 A wide range of reliefs is available to avoid payment of duty in the event of importation being followed by re-export. In these circumstances, the duty payable on import into the Community is relieved, either in total or in part, subject only to becoming payable in the event of the conditions attaching to it not being complied with. In general, the permitted period of temporary import may not exceed twenty-four months, but in a number of cases will be much shorter. A bond or guarantee for the payment of the duy relieved is usually required against the eventuality of its becoming payable due to failure to comply with conditions.

4.15 The temporary import is concluded by export within the permitted period, by the goods being placed in an approved warehouse or a free zone with a view to export, by destruction of the goods under customs control or by their being placed under one of the various customs regimes discussed later. Alternatively, the goods may be allowed to be released into free circulation on payment of the duty. If duty becomes payable, it is based on that normally payable on the goods at the time of actual import.

4.16 The main legislation is contained in Regulation 3599/82 (9), which allows for either part or total relief. *Part relief* is available for any

(9) OJ 1982 L 376/1; as last amended by Reg. 1620/85, OJ 1985 L 155/54.

goods not allowed full relief, and is on the basis that 3% of the duty will be payable for every month, or part of a month, during which the goods are inside the Community; certain goods specified in the regulation are excluded altogether. *Total relief* is available, subject to conditions, in respect of a wide variety of goods listed, of which the following are the main examples:

(a) certain business or professional equipment belonging to an individual or company operating temporarily within the Community;

(b) materials for demonstration or use at an exhibition or fair;

(c) certain teaching and scientific materials;

(d) medical and laboratory materials for hospitals;

(e) materials for the relief of catastrophes;

(f) packaging or containers (10);

(g) the personal belongings of travellers;

(h) goods for testing, experiment or demonstration;

(i) at a Member State's discretion in individual cases, any import with no economic significance.

Origin of goods

4.17 In order to apply the terms of the common commercial policy with regard to preferences for goods from certain countries, or restrictions on goods from other countries, the concept of origin is laid down in Community legislation. It is designed to establish the country (or customs territory) in which goods originated, rather than where they were sent from. In the application of the Common Customs Tariff, this notion is essential in enabling Community industries to be protected, or overseas industries to be assisted. Following from the 1973 CCC Kyoto Convention on Simplification, the Community legislation is primarily to be found in Regulation 802/68 (11), containing a general definition which is often given further precision by regulations applicable in particular sectors.

4.18 The basic concept is applicable alike both to exports from the Community and imports to it. It treats as originating in a customs territory goods which are either wholly obtained or produced there, or goods which are derived from materials whose last economically justified and substantial processing took place in it. The concept of goods being *wholly obtained* in an area is for the most part self-explanatory, but it includes: products mined or grown in the territory; products obtained from living animals born or reared in the territory; products of hunting

(10) See also Reg. 2096/87 OJ 1987 L 196/4.
(11) OJ 1968 L 148/1, as last amended by Reg. 3860/87 OJ 1987 L 363/30.

or fishing; sea products from boats (including factory ships) registered in and flying the flag of a country; and products from the sea or its subsoil over which the country has exclusive rights of exploitation.

4.19   Also treated as originating in a country are goods derived from materials *substantially processed* there. This refers to the last substantial processing which is economically justified, by a business equipped for the purpose, resulting in a new product or constituting a major stage of manufacture. The position with regard to oil products has not yet been the subject of legislation. It will be seen that the approach is to identify the place of origin by reference to an economic reality test, and it is specifically provided, in an anti-avoidance clause, that origin status is to be denied where processing or manufacture has been carried out in a particular place solely to take advantage of the Community origin provisions.

4.20   There are numerous deeming regulations to provide certainty in particular areas of trade which are adopted by the Commission with the approval of the Origin Committee, or by the Council in the context of third country preferences. The Court has not always upheld the terms of these regulations, requiring that the criterion of objectivity should be strictly adhered to. In *Case 385/85, SR Industries v. Administration des Douanes* (12), however, it was held that a stricter concept of origin might be adopted in the context of generalised trade preferences.

4.21   Certificates of origin are prescribed generally in Regulation 553/81 (13), and given on export from the Community by authorities authorised for the purpose (frequently chambers of commerce). In the case of imports, the Community cannot, save where so provided in Community agreements with third countries, insist on the exporting state using the prescribed forms, but the regulation remains applicable in regard to the information which must be furnished on import, and which the importer must therefore procure from the exporting authorities.

4.22   Where, under the safeguard for national interests provisions of Article 115, a Member State is authorised to take restrictive measures against certain imports, the same concepts of origin are applied; it should be noted however, that the Court has held that in intra-Community trade, a state may not demand of an importer more information

(12)   [1988] CMLR 378.
(13)   OJ 1981 L 59/1.

with regard to the origin of goods already in free circulation in the Community than he could reasonably be expected to know: *Case 41/76, Donckerwolcke v. Procureur de la République.* (14)

4.23 The Community has concluded a wide network of trade agreements with third countries which carry with them refinements of the general origin rules. The relevant legislation is extensive and complex, being contained in regulations based on the various agreements or conventions and the decisions of the committees established under them. The groupings include the EFTA countries, the countries with which there are special trade or association agreements, developing countries benefiting from the generalised system of preferences and the African, Caribean and Pacific countries covered by the Lomé convention. The EFTA agreements provide for reciprocal acceptance of certificates of origin and for simplified procedure in certain circumstances, and make provision for mutual assistance between customs administrations in verifying claims of origin. The other groupings are also subject to detailed modifications of the general rules.

Valuation

4.24 In order to establish the amount of customs duty to be paid on goods, it is necessary to have rules to establish their dutiable value. These, based on the provisions of Article VII of the GATT, are primarily contained in Regulation 1224/80 (15) which applies to all customs duties (including those payable on coal and steel products and Euratom goods), but not necessarily to national taxes levied on import—such as value added tax and excise duty. The fundamental conept of the legislation is that goods should be given their actual commercial value, at the place of introduction into the Community, by reference to the price paid for them on an arm's length sale on export.

(i) *Arm's length sales*
4.25 Where a sale on export to the Community does take place, and the parties are unconnected (as defined), the way is open for the sale price to be taken as the value for customs purposes. This is the basic method of valuation, referred to as the *transaction value.* A number of further requirements have however to be satisfied: (a) the buyer must be free to use or dispose of the goods without restrictions save those imposed by law, those relating to the area in which the buyer may

(14) [1976] ECR 1921.
(15) OJ 1980 L 134/1, as last amended by Reg. 1055/85 OJ 1985 L 112/50.

operate or any which have no substantial effect on value; (b) no further payment must be due to the seller with reference to the subsequent resale or hire of the goods; and (c) no part of the consideration may be unquantifiable—in this connection, expenditure by the buyer on his own account, e.g. on advertising, is disregarded, even though it may be of indirect benefit to the seller. To the sale price, there are additions and subtractions which, if applicable, must then be made.

4.26 If borne by the buyer, there must be *added*: if not included in the sale price, sale commission or brokerage and the cost of packaging; the cost of certain free or reduced price goods or services provided by the buyer and used for the goods; royalties or licence fees payable on sale of the goods (reproduction or distribution fees are not added, and may be subtracted if included in the invoice); the value of any payments to the seller from resale or hiring of the goods; the cost of transport and insurance up to the Community frontier, and loading and handling charges to the same point.

4.27 To be *subtracted* from the sale price if included in it are: customs duties, taxes and customs clearance charges; transport following import; the cost of instalation or maintenance following import; reproduction fees; purchase commissions; interest payments, and price reductions allowed by the seller. All other costs are disregarded, including unloading and storage (including the cost of warehousing where the goods are warehoused under a special scheme for that purpose—see below). There are special provisions relating to computer software.

(ii) *No arms' length sale*
4.28 Where the parties to the export sale are connected, the transaction value may still be used as the base for valuation if the importer can prove that the connection has had no influence on it. If he cannot do this, or if there was no sale, e.g. the goods were leased or gifted, or if they are released after a period in warehouse, various alternative methods of valuation are used in the order in which they must be resorted to; they constitute in effect, a "best evidence" rule under which in order to rely on any one method, the importer has to show that the evidence to operate any of those earlier in the order of preference cannot be had. The alternatives may themselves of course only be used where it is shown that the basic method described above is not possible. The order of preference is as follows.

4.29 (1) *Sale price of identical goods.* The circumstances must be as near as possible to those in the basic method, especially in regard to the timing of the export sale to the Community, the type, quantity and quality of the goods, and must have been accepted by customs in a case which has actually occurred.

(2) *Sale price of similar goods.* The goods must have been produced in the same country as the goods to be valued, have the same use and be in commercial terms interchangeable with them.

(3) *Deductive method.* This proceeds on the basis of working backwards from the unit resale price of the goods in the importing country (or of identical or similar goods). Thus an appropriate profit margin is deducted, together with all other admissable taxes or costs on import.

(4) *Constructed value.* This method may, at the importer's option, be reversed with the previous method in order of preference. It consists of building up the value of the goods from their constituent elements of cost, plus a margin for profit. It involves the production of the manufacturer's accounts, and agreement to checking of the information by the customs authorities of the exporting state.

(5) *Default method.* This is a last resort using reasonable accounting practices on the basis of the principles contained in Article VII of the GATT. In practice it usually involves a large element of negotiation with Customs, but the importer has a right to a written statement of the basis of the valuation which, at the end of the process, Customs adopt.

4.30 It was held in *Case 357/87, Schmid v. Hauptzollamt Stuttgart-West* (16) that, since packagings are chargeable to duty at the rates applicable to the goods they contain, where returnable packings are not returned and compensation is paid to the sender, the compensation is part of the cost of the goods for the purposes of Regulation 1224/80 (15). In that case, the packagings consisted of beer barrels, bottles and crates, payment for the non-return of which was assessable to duty, and made the subject of a post-clearance recovery under Regulation 1697/79. (17)

4.31 Regulation 1766/85 (18) provides for the rate of exchange to be used—usually that of the country of import at the time of importation. The Customs Valuation Committee approves detailed regulations made by the Commission to clarify particular matters arising in the course of applying the principal legislation. Regulation 1496/80 (19) prescribes the form for declaring particulars relating to customs value. A declaration is not necessary for imports whose value is below 3,000 European currency

(16) (Not yet reported).
(17) OJ 1979 L 197/1.
(18) OJ 1985 L 168/21.
(19) OJ 1980 L 154/16, as last amended by Reg. 3272/88 OJ 1988 L 291/49.

units (ECU), unless required by the Customs authorities. The point in time by reference to which valuation takes place is that prescribed in the rules of any special customs procedure applicable, or on the entry of the goods for free circulation.

4.32 A large number of Commission regulations supplements the main texts, among the more important being the following: Regulation 1577/81 (20) on simplified procedures in relation to the valuation of perishable goods, Regulation 3158/83 (21) on the incidence of royalties and licence fees, and Regulation 5333/89 (22) on the use of unit values for the valuation of perishable goods.

Warehousing and free zones

4.33 The system for customs warehousing of goods is designed to allow goods to be imported into the Community customs territory, and yet for many of the consequences of importation, notably the obligation to pay duty and levies, to be held in suspense. The goods may not normally remain in warehouse for more than five years and must be entered in the normal way; they may not be processed and will be subject to various checks by Customs to ensure that there is no abuse. Warehouses may be owned by the Customs administration itself, but are normally privately owned and subject to Customs approval before they can be used for this purpose.

4.34 The principal legislation governing the warehousing scheme is now contained in Regulation 2503/88 (23), to replace Directive 69/74. Goods may be released for free circulation in the Community, placed under a specific customs regime (such as inward processing) or be re-exported. In the first case, they will be liable to duty at the date of their release at the rates then prevailing, with rules to ascertain the value to be taken into account in the various situations which may obtain. While in the warehouse, goods may be subject to normal handling operations. Alternatively, they may be sold while remaining in the warehouse without incurring liability to duty. If the goods are removed illicitly, duty is payable, but no duty is payable if they are lost by reason of *force majeure*, accident or deterioration.

4.35 Under Regulation 4151/88 (24), customs entry procedures may permit the temporary warehousing of goods in approved premises before

---

(20)   OJ 1981 L 154/26, as last amended by Reg 3773/87 OJ 1987 L 355/19.
(21)   OJ 1983 L 309/19.
(22)   OJ 1989 L 59/13.
(23)   OJ 1988 L 225/1.
(24)   OJ 1988 L 367/1.

they are finally cleared for release or entry to a particular customs scheme. In the case of imports arriving by sea, this may last up to 45 days from first entry being made; where the goods arrive by land or air, the maximum delay is 20 days. In either case, a longer period may be permitted by Customs which "shall not however exceed genuine needs which are justified by the circumstances". Only normal handling to maintain the condition of the goods is allowed. Goods which are not, within the time limits, definitively entered for free circulation, placed under a customs procedure or re-exported, may be sold or stored at the importer's expense.

4.36 Similar in concept to customs warehouses are free zones or, as they are called in some states, free ports. They consist of small enclaves in the Community's customs territory inside which goods are treated as not having entered the Community, at least for the purpose of payment of duties and agricultural levies, or of any quantitative restrictions applicable. Goods may thus be imported to them without regard to the Community tariff regimes normally applicable, and they may remain without time limit. The goods may be the subject of normal handling, be destroyed, be entered for inward processing or may be subject to certain other actions. They may not however be consumed within the free zone, and when they are released into free circulation they are dutiable as at that date and in the condition in which they then are, the costs of storage being disregarded. The legislation is contained in Regulation 2504/88 (25), to replace Directive 69/75.

Inward processing

4.37 The inward processing scheme established under Regulation 1999/85 (26) allows the import free of duty of goods from third countries in order to be processed within the Community and subsequently re-exported outside it in the form of compensating products; provision is also made for the remission or repayment of duties on goods which have been released into free circulation but which undergo processing and re-export in the same way. The goods covered by the scheme may include those which are necessary or useful for the processing operation, but which themselves cease to exist in the course of it. The operation must be approved by Customs if the goods are above a certain value limit per importer per annum, when it must be shown that the processing will create the best conditions for the export of the compensating

(25)   OJ 1988 L 225/8.
(26)   OJ 1985 L 188/1.

products and that the essential interests of Community producers will not be prejudiced.

4.38 The scheme therfore has an important discretionary element and is intended to serve the Community economy's needs; it is accordingly restricted to persons established within the Community. Regulation 1999/85 (26) lays down a number of criteria on the basis of which the economic judgment is made whether to permit the use of the scheme. The goods exported will be compensating products, which are defined as products incorporating the imported item, either in the same state or after processing, or incorporating similar products obtained in the Community and equivalent to the imported ones. Where equivalent products are used in exported compensating products, the import of the goods to replace the equivalent goods may be subsequent; thus, the use of immediately available Community goods, rather than waiting for goods to be imported under relief, is not penalised and exports are facilitated.

4.39 The importer must furnish all relevant information and, if requested, give security for the duty which will become payable if the terms of the scheme are not complied with. The national authorities will determine the period within which the operation must be completed and the compensating products exported (or in some cases they may instead be placed in a warehouse, in a free zone or destroyed etc); permission can be given for the goods to be released into free circulation, though normally only on payment of the duty which has been suspended. Any duty thus payable (or payable if the conditions of the scheme are not complied with) is normally based on the liability as at the date of entry for inward processing, but in some cases the compensating products may be dutiable. Detailed implementation is provided by Regulation 3677/86. (27)

Outward processing

4.40 This is the converse of inward processing, and provides the means by which goods in free circulation within the Community can be exported to be processed, adapted or repaired outside the Community, and re-imported wholly or partly free of duty. It applies equally to goods originating in the Community and to those which have previously been imported (but not those which have attracted an export refund or remission of import duty), and it may also be applied to goods which have undergone inward processing. Like inward processing, the import to and export from the Community may take place in different Member States. In this scheme, it is also necessary for it to be established that its

(27) OJ 1986 L 351/1, as last amended by Reg 1325/89 OJ 1989 L 133/6.

use will not prejudice the essential interests of Community undertakings in the same field; it is only open to businesses established within the Community, and security for the duty may be required.

4.41 Where it is proved that goods have been repaired in a third country free of charge pursuant to a contractual guarantee, or on account of a fault in manufacture, there is total exemption from duties on re-import. In other cases, the relief is calculated by crediting against the duty payable on the import of the compensating products from the country where processing has taken place, the duty which would be payable on the import of the goods themselves from the same country. For this purpose, the duty is based on the quantity and classification of the goods at the point at which they are accepted for outward processing, while the rate and valuation to be taken into account are those applicable when the goods are reimported in the form of compensating products.

4.42 The principal legislation is now contained in Regulation 2473/86, (28) which also covers the temporary export of goods for repair or replacement. The imported product may enter free of charge as a replacement under a contract guarantee or on account of a defect in manufacture. In other cases, in order to qualify for this relief, the imported item must be classed under the same tariff subheading as that which is exported in exchange, be of the same quality and have the same technical characteristics. The import must normally be within the time limits laid down by the customs administration. Permission may be given for the import to *precede* the export of the faulty item, so long as the latter goes out within twelve months of the import. Both for this and for outward processing generally, there are detailed implementation regulations adopted from time to time by the Commission with the approval of the Customs Processing Committee.

Processing before release for free circulation

4.43 Regulation 2763/83 (29) allows for the processing of goods under customs control before assessment to and payment of duty on import. This facility is limited to the processes listed in the annex to the regulation and to persons established within the Community, offering such security for duty as the customs administration may require. It is subject to it being economically impossible to reverse the process, to the effect not being to circumvent the origin rules and quantitative restrictions applicable to the goods before transformation and, reminiscent of

(28) OJ 1986 L 212/1: Reg 1970/88 OJ 1988 L174/1 deals with triangular traffic and outward processing under the standard exchange system.
(29) OJ 1983 L 272/1, as last amended by Reg 2369/89 OJ 1989 L 225/5.

the inward processing regime, to the operation being conducive to establishing or maintaining a Community industry undertaking such work without prejudicing the interest of Community producers of similar goods. The goods resulting are dutiable on their release into free circulation at the rates then prevailing for such goods.

Returned goods

4.44 Goods which have been exported and are returned to the Community because they are rejected by the buyer, or cannot otherwise be utilised, may be readmitted free of duty, if they were in free circulation before export. The normal time limit for this is three years, or twelve months for agricultural products (which will not be eligible if export subsidies have been paid, unless they are repaid and proof that the goods could not be used in the third country is furnished). The person reimporting need not be the same as the exporter. Regulation 754/76 (30) governs the scheme, and prescribes in detail the reasons for which a return of goods may be recognised, which vary according to whether the goods have benefited from agricultural subsidies or not.

Dumping and export subsidies

4.45 Dumping is the practice by which goods are imported at a price lower than their price on the domestic market of the exporting country. It must be distinguished from the import of goods at a price lower than that at which they are or can be produced within the Community e.g. because the exporting country enjoys lower production costs or a higher degree of efficiency in its industry. Dumping may be the object of antidumping duties if it is considered that it gives rise to significant prejudice to an existing or possible Community-based industry.

4.46 The basic legislation is contained in Regulation 2176/84 (31), although there are often specific anti-dumping clauses in third country trade agreements, which will take precedence over the general rules. A provisional duty is imposed by the Commission, while a definitive duty may be imposed only by the Council; the Commission may accept undertakings from exporters in lieu of imposing duties.

4.47 The regulation makes provision for the ascertainment of the domestic selling price where there are no domestic sales of the goods, or where the domestic sales do not take place on a normal commercial basis, as where domestic sales are to a captive market or consistently at

(30)   OJ 1976 L 89/1 as last amended Reg. 1147/86 OJ 1986 L 105/1.
(31)   OJ 1984 L 201/1, as last amended by Reg 2423/88 OJ 1988 L 209/1.

less than cost. Also covered are cases where the dumped product is routed through a third country, and cases in which the price differential is concealed until an arm's length sale within the Community takes place, for example by reason of arrangements between the exporter and the importer. Formulae for calculating the dumping margin are laid down, with special provisions in the case of state trading countries where there is no market economy.

4.48 The same regulation provides for the imposition of countervailing duties on entry to the Community in the case of products the subject of aids or subsidies in the exporting country. There must, in this case also, be significant prejudice to a Community industry before the powers can be invoked. An illustrative (but not exhaustive) list of subsidies is given, including favourable transport charges, remission or repayment of direct taxes or social security contributions related to exports, remission or repayment of indirect taxes on exported goods of an amount greater than that charged on the same goods internally, and preferential export credit guarantees or loans.

4.49 A special case of dumping is encountered when, in order to circumvent the legislation, goods are imported in parts and then assembled or otherwise subjected to manufacturing processes within the Community and sold at prices which would have attracted the anti-dumping provisions had the finished goods been imported. Anti-dumping duty may be imposed on the finished product leaving the factory in the Community, at the anti-dumping rate applicable to the finished product but by reference to the c.i.f. value of the parts imported for assembly in this way.

4.50 Three conditions must also be satisfied: (i) that the assembly is carried out by a person connected with an exporter of like products subject to anti-dumping duty; (ii) that the assembly has started or substantially increased after the anti-dumping investigation leading to the duty in (i) had commenced; and (iii) that the value of the parts or materials used in the finished product which have come from the country concerned is at least 60% of that of all the parts and materials used. It will be seen that this is essentially a supplementary provision which will only be of significance in the context of anti-dumping measures of the normal kind.

Co-operation between customs authorities

4.51 Much of the legislation in this sphere, while previously contained in directives, is now in the form of regulations, which need little in the way of national provisions to supplement them. This is part of an explicit policy to give as close a degree of uniformity to customs law throughout the Community as possible, in view of the fact that the Customs Union is one of the Community's foundations and needs to function in the same way throughout, in order to avoid distortions to trade and business patterns (32). Although it is too soon for a Community customs administration to have emerged, particularly in view of the number of non-Community matters still the responsibility of the national administrations, there is now close collaboration between the twelve Member States.

4.52 The first form this takes is prescribed by Regulation 1468/81 (33) which, following a number of earlier provisions, provides for officials of each state to liaise, and to offer assistance to each other in investigating fraud, including the creation *ad hoc* of Community-wide enquiry teams which may also conduct investigations in third countries. It covers customs duties and agricultural levies.

4.53 Directive 76/308 (34) provides, in contrast to the traditional rule of law to the contrary, that any Member State must, on request by another, take legal action to recover payment of duties, agricultural levies and debts due in the context of the Common Agricultural Policy, together with related costs and interest. In the United Kingdom, therefore, customs etc., debts due in any other Member State are recoverable by action taken by Customs and Excise against any debtor within the jurisdiction. There are safeguards to ensure that the defendant has had an opportunity to contest liability, and to prevent the recovery machinery being used if he can show that he has not. This directive also applies to value added tax and is discussed further in Chapter 11. It is further implemented by Directive 77/794. (35)

Payment of duty

4.54 It is necessary to ascertain the point in time at which duties are chargeable in order to deal with such questions as tariff rates, reliefs, valuation and the like. At the same time, the opportunity exists to clarify the identity of the person or persons liable to make payment. These two topics are now covered respectively by Regulations 2144/87 (36) and 1031/88 (37), which deal with duties and levies both on import and—where applicable—on export.

(32)   See e.g. the recital to Regulation 1999/85, note (26) above.
(33)   OJ 1981 L 144/1 as last amended by Reg. 945/87 OJ 1987 L 90/3.
(34)   OJ 1976 L 73/18, as last amended by Dir 79/1071 OJ 1979 L 331/10.
(35)   OJ 1977 L 333/11, as last amended by Dir 86/489 OJ 1986 L 283/23.
(36)   OJ 1987 L 201/15, as last amended by Reg 4108/88 OJ 1988 L 361/2.
(37)   OJ 1988 L102/5.

4.55 Exceptions are made for cases of *force majeure*, authorised destruction of goods and goods re-exported from the Community. The customs debt is of course primarily discharged by payment of the duty, but may also be discharged in a number of other circumstances detailed in the legislation but notably by limitation, cancellation of an entry by Customs or by remission. Confiscation of the goods also operates to extinguish duty liability, but criminal penalties related to duty payable on forfeited goods are unaffected, and there is a saving regarding national provisions on seizure and forfeiture of goods.

4.56 Detailed rules apply to specific situations such as inward processing and certain preferential trade regimes, and there is a saving for national rules which impose liability on other persons than those listed in the Community legislation. In general, the combined effect of the regulations in relation to duty points on importation and liable persons may be summarised in the following table.

Circumstances in which duty is payable	Person liable for payment
(a) The acceptance of an entry where the goods are put into free circulation	The person in whose name the entry is made and any principal
(b) The physical entry of goods into the customs territory of the Community in violation of customs procedure	The persons bringing the goods into the territory and any person acquiring them or associated with the offence
(c) The time at which goods under customs control are removed therefrom	The person removing the goods from control and any person acquiring them or associated with the offence
(d) The time at which a condition to which goods are subject is breached, or they are admitted to a customs regime subject to conditions which they did not satisfy	The person liable to carry out the conditions or to satisfy them initially
(e) The point at which goods are used for a purpose other than that for which an end-use relief has been given, or at which they are put into free circulation without satisfying a condition subject to which such relief was given	The person responsible for compliance with the end-use obligations or conditions
(f) The moment at which goods are destroyed with a repayment or remission of duty if the waste or scrap remaining from them is retained within the Community	The person in whose name the goods are entered and any principal

4.57 The post-clearance recovery of duties is governed by Regulation 1697/79 (38). Duties not paid at the normal time (or not fully paid) may be recovered from the person liable for their payment at any time within three years from the date of the original duty assessment or, if none, the date of the duty point. This time limit does not apply if the initial non-recovery was due to action liable to penalty, in which case national time limits apply. Various provisions safeguard the debtor: no recovery may take place if the underpayment was due to incorrect information given by the administration, or was made under provisions later quashed or annulled by a court; likewise, a mistake by the administration which could not reasonably have been detected by the person liable to pay duty, acting in good faith and in compliance with the law, will prevent recovery action in cases specified in subordinate regulations.

4.58 *Case 161/88, Binder v. Hauptzollamt Bad Reichenall* (39) demonstrated, however, the limitations of these provisions. In that case, the official German Customs manual showed the duty on certain goods at 10.4% on the basis of a Commission proposal to reduce the duty to that level; the proposal, however, was not adopted by the Council, and the duty remained at 13%. The importer, who had imported goods in reliance on the information contained in the manual and had been charged duty at 10.4%, claimed to be entitled to the benefit of the regulation. The Court held that, since the correct position had been apparent from the Official Journal, the full duty must be recovered.

4.59 Under Regulation 1854/89 (40) rules are established governing the assessment of duty and the time limits within which it must be done. Following determination of the duty, the amount payable must be communicated to the person liable to pay, unless the amount is the same as that shown in the import entry, in which case the release of the goods may be taken to be the requisite communication. If security is given, there may be composite assessments to duty where goods are allowed to be removed from charge over a period not exceeding 31 days, the assessments being made within five days thereafter. Otherwise, duty may not normally be assessed later than two days after the release of the goods from customs charge, or the happening of events which crystallise a liability. Subject to any rights of appeal, payment is then due within a maximum of ten days (or less in the case of composite assessments, if the result would be to give the importer longer than he would be entitled to under deferment).

(38) OJ 1979 L 197/1, as last amended by Reg 918/83 OJ 1983 L 105/1.
(39) (Not yet reported).
(40) OJ 1989 L 186/1. See now also 4046/89 OJ 1989 L 388/24 on security to be given for payment of customs debts.

4.60 Deferred payment of duty, interest free, for up to 30 days from the date the duty is assessed is also provided for in Regulation 1854/89 (40). Deferment may be given by reference to all the amounts assessed over a period not exceeding 31 days, or by reference to composite assessments in respect of clearances during a similar period—in which case the deferment period is reduced by half the number of days in the assessment periods—or by reference to individual assessments. Any delay in assessment beyond the permitted time limit is deducted from the deferment period. Any further period of credit may only be granted on commercial terms. Member States must require bonds or guarantees for the duty thus deferred. The means of payment acceptable are for Member States to determine.

4.61 Lastly, a variety of circumstances, laid down in Regulation 1430/ 79 (41), may entitle the importer to remission or repayment of duty subject to the time limits indicated, and subject to conditions to prevent abuse. Applications for relief are decided upon in the Member State where duty was assessed, even if the goods have since passed elsewhere in the Community. The cases include: error in assessment (three years); entry in error for free circulation instead of for a customs regime (three months); and goods rejected by an importer because of failure to comply with the requirements of the contract under which they were imported, or which were damaged in transport to the customs post where they were entered or while in customs charge (12 months).

4.62 Remission etc., is also given for goods which are dispatched in error, unsuitable for use by reason of a mistake in the order for them, are discovered after release not to comply with the legal requirements relating to their use (or where such requirements are changed after release), delivered later than a strict contractual time limit, or given to charities where the charity sends them overseas or could have imported them itself with relief from duty—(three months). It is generally necessary for the goods either to be re-exported, destroyed under customs control or, exceptionally, to be warehoused, placed in a free zone, or in certain cases given to charity.

Customs control

4.63 Provisions about customs control are frequently found in Community legislation dealing with individual customs regimes or reliefs and, in so far as not superseded by such legislation, in national provisions

(41)   OJ 1979 L 175/1, as last amended by Reg. 3799/86 OJ 1986 L 352/19.

such as the United Kingdom legislation referred to below. Some Community instruments also lay down general rules in this sphere, notably Directive 79/695 (42) on the procedures for the release of goods into free circulation, Regulation 3632/85 (43) on the conditions under which persons may be permitted to make a customs entry and Directive 81/177 (44) on customs procedures on the export of goods.

4.64 Regulation 4151/88 (24) deals in further detail with the procedures to be adopted by importers and Customs on the arrival of goods in the Community customs territory. It governs the movement of goods into Customs charge, their handling, the making of entries or customs declarations and the point at which goods under the external Community transit procedure (see Chapter 3) become subject to the normal customs regime. Liability for compliance with the obligations prescribed is placed on any person who assumes responsibility for the carriage of the goods after they have entered the customs territory of the Community (unless they are simply crossing that territory without having a destination within it), or any person who holds goods after they have been unloaded. Customs authorities are given full powers of control over the movement of goods before clearance, including powers of destruction.

United Kingdom legislation

4.65 As has been seen, much of Community customs law is now in the form of directly applicable regulations, requiring little or no supplementary national legislation. In general, the administrative and procedural provisions will be found in the Customs and Excise Management Act 1979, as amended, and in regulations and orders made thereunder. Two features of the national legislation must be noted in particular.

4.66 The first concerns valuation disputes. Under section 127 of the 1979 Act these are referred to the arbitration of a referee appointed by the Lord Chancellor. A reference to him may be sought by the importer within three months of payment of the duty demanded and, in the event of an overpayment being found to have occurred, the excess is repayable with interest. Secondly, the recovery action which may be taken on behalf of another Member State under Directive 76/308 (34), is provided for in the United Kingdom by section 11 of the Finance Act 1977. By this provision, a Community customs or agricultural debt is recoverable

(42) OJ 1979 L 205/19, as last amended by Dir. 81/853 OJ 1981 L 319/1.
(43) OJ 1985 L 350/1.
(44) OJ 1981 L 83/40, as implemented by Dir. 82/347 OJ 1982 L 156/1.

as a debt due to the Crown, and the proceedings available for the purpose are detailed in that section.

4.67 The general law on the direct applicabilty of Community regulations is sufficient to ensure that no implementing legislation is needed in the United Kingdom for the charging of Community customs duties. Section 5 of the European Communities Act 1972, nonetheless, specifically authorises the charge of such duties and treats them as duties due to the Crown. Section 6, similarly, treats agricultural levies as Community customs duties, and provides for the Commissioners of Customs and Excise to collect them on behalf of the Intervention Board for Agricultural Produce.

CHAPTER 5

Trade with Non-Community Countries

5.01 The Treaty envisages the Community being a party to foreign trade agreements and conventions, entering negotiations and forming association agreements with third countries. Article 210 provides that the Community shall have legal personality. This gave the Community the capacity to establish links with third countries in varying areas of activity which form the subject-matter of the Treaty and enabled the Community to enjoy the capacity to establish contractual links with non-Member States over the whole field of objectives defined in Part I of the Treaty (*Case 22/70, Commission v. Council (AERTA)*) (1). Another important step was the decision of the Court of Justice, *Cases 21–24/72, NV International Fruit Company and others v. Produktschap* (2) that the GATT rules bind the Community, because the Member States were originally parties to GATT and the commercial policy powers of the Member States were taken over by the Community.

5.02 Article 113 of the Treaty provides that the common commercial policy shall be based on uniform principles, particularly in regard to changes in tariff rates, the conclusion of tariff and trade agreements, the achievement of uniformity in measures of liberalisation, export policy and measures to protect trade such as those to be taken in case of dumping or subsidies. Where agreements with third countries need to be negotiated, the Commission must make recommendations to the Council which authorise the Commission to open the necessary negotiations. The Community has adopted measures under Article 113 in connection with the administration of the Common Customs Tariff in the field of valuation of goods or rules of origin of goods. It has adopted means of protection against unfair trade practices by third countries. Regulation 2176/84 (3) provides for an anti-dumping duty on any product which causes injury to a Community industry if it is dumped. Regulation 2641/84 (4) provides remedies against improper commercial practices. Pursuant to Article 113 the Community has entered into a large number of agreements. The Community is now a party to all GATT agreements

(1) [1971] ECR 263; [1971] CMLR 335.
(2) [1972] ECR 1219; [1975] CMLR 11.
(3) OJ 1984 L 201/1.
(4) OJ 1984 L 252/1.

(including the original one by virtue of the decision in *NV International Fruit Company*). (2)

5.03 An important set of agreements is with the EFTA countries which have not joined the Community (Austria, Finland, Iceland, Norway, Sweden and Portugal). In the case of the agreements between the EEC and Austria (5), Iceland (6), Norway (7), Sweden (8) and Switzerland (9), the primary reason for the agreements was to consolidate and to extend, upon the enlargement of the Community in 1972, the economic relations between the Community and the EFTA states (see the preambles to the agreements), whilst the agreement with Finland (10) expresses a desire to contribute appropriate solutions to the economic problems facing Finland as a result of the enlargement (see preamble). The aim of all the agreements is the harmonious development of economic relations leading to an improvement in living and employment conditions in both the EEC and its treaty partner, fair conditions of competition between the contracting parties, and liberalisation of world trade. The main instrument in achieving this is the creation of a free trade zone between the parties to each agreement through the removal of tariff barriers in relation to certain industrial products originating in either the Community or the contracting state. Rules governing the free movement of goods constitute an important part of the agreements. Arrangements for the dismantling of customs duties prohibit the introduction of any new customs duties or of charges having the equivalent effect to customs duties and charges and equivalent measures on exports between the parties, and lay down timetables for the progressive abolition of existing duties (now completed). (See Articles 9–12).

5.04 To determine whether or not products are covered by the provisions of the main agreements, Protocol 3 to all the agreements sets out the detailed rules for determining their origin. The rules of origin have been amended several times since the original agreements were signed. Modifications and derogations were codified in 1984, replacing and repealing the original Protocol 3 by an exchange of letters, now in OJ 1984 L 323. Further adjustments appear in OJ 1986 L 134 and L 47. The last agreement dealing with Protocol 3 concerning the definition of the concept of "originating product" and methods of administrative cooperation was concluded in 1988. (OJ 1988 L 149/75). Article 13 prohibits

(5)   OJ 1972 L 300/2.
(6)   OJ 1972 L 301/2.
(7)   OJ 1973 L 171/2.
(8)   OJ 1972 L 300/97.
(9)   OJ 1972 L 300/189.
(10)   OJ 1973 L 328/2.

the introduction of quantitative restrictions on imports or measures having equivalent effect between the Community and the EFTA state with provision for the abolition of existing ones. The agreements do not apply to agricultural products, but the contracting parties have granted each other a number of agricultural and fishery concessions, particularly in the case of Iceland, one half of whose exports to the Community were fisheries. Internal fiscal measures which may directly or indirectly discriminate between products of one party and like products orginating in the territory of the other are proscribed (Article 18), as are restrictions on payments relating to trade in goods and on commercial credit in which an EEC/EFTA resident participated (Article 19). Derogations from the free movement of goods provisions, if permitted, must not amount to "means of arbitrary discrimination or a disguised restriction on trade".

5.05   The agreements contain a number of safequard clauses concerned with security interests or defence. There are also safequard provisions relating to competition, dumping or serious deterioration in a regional economy, to be invoked in accordance with the procedure prescribed in Article 27. The agreements establish a Joint Committee responsible for the administration of the agreement, to be convened at least once a year. All the agreements contain a "denunciation clause". With the exception of the Finnish one, the agreements can be terminated on twelve months' notice, while the agreement with Finland provides for termination three months after notification has been given. Additional protocols to the agreements were concluded on the accession of Spain and Portugal (11). As we have seen, the agreements contain rules approximating to those of the Treaty concerning the free movement of goods and free competition. However the interpretation of the terms of the agreements does not always have to follow the rules of the EEC Treaty, since their basis is not the Treaty itself with its principles and objectives: *Case 270/80, Polydor Ltd v. Harlequin Record Shops Ltd* (12), dealing with import restrictions based on domestic copyright laws.

5.06   Agreements with the less developed countries are numerous, often granting preferential tariff treatment and often dealing with individual products (e.g. textiles). *Commodity agreements* relate to coffee, cocoa, jute, rubber, tin and wheat. They are intended to stabilise prices and supplies. The Multi-Fibre Arrangement is designed to prevent the decline of traditional textile industries by stabilising imports and has been implemented by bilateral agreements.

(11)   OJ 1986 L 321 & L 337.
(12)   [1982] ECR 329; [1982] 1 CMLR 677.

5.06.1 There are only limited agreements with state trading countries. The agreement with Yugoslavia contains aid features akin to agreements with Maghreb countries under Article 238 (13). New trade arrangements were introduced in 1987 by an additional protocol to the co-operation agreement (Decision 87/605) (14). A second protocol on financial co-operation was agreed in 1987 and implemented by Decision 1987/604 (14). Past agreements with Roumania, Hungary and Poland were limited in their scope and nature, and since then bilateral trade and co-operation agreements have been signed between the Community and Hungary, Czechoslovakia and Poland. The Agreement on Trade and Commercial Economic Co-operation with the USSR, signed on 18 December 1989, covers a wide area of co-operation, but apparently does not affect the level of customs duties. Joint Committees have been set up to discuss and co-ordinate future developments.

5.07 Article 238 of the EEC Treaty forms the basis for a vital part of the commercial policy of the EEC by providing authority for the Community to enter into *association agreements* with a third country or a group of third countries. These agreements now replace many provisions originally included in Part Four of the Treaty dealing with special relations which the original Member States had with former colonial territories either dependent or newly independent. The Community itself is a customs union with a common commercial policy towards third countries and the concept of association involves the extension of customs union to the Associated State. Association does not transfer sovereign powers to common institutions, but the principle of association extending the customs union to the Associated States avoids the contravention of the General Agreement on Tariffs and Trade. Article 238 provides that the Community may conclude with a third state, a union of states or an international organisation agreements establishing an association involving reciprocal rights and obligations, common action and special procedures. These agreements are to be concluded by the Council acting unanimously after having received the assent of the European Parliament, which must achieve an absolute majority of all its members. The long-term objective of association agreements is the raising of living standards and economic levels of the associated parties, the system of "reciprocal rights and obligations" being aimed at promoting the political and social development of the third state rather than creating strict equality of obligations between the contracting parties (*Case 87/75, Bresciani*). (15)

5.08 Article 238 also states that association is to involve its partners in common action and special procedures, and so association agreements

(13) OJ 1983 L 41/1 et seq.
(14) OJ 1987 L 389/65, 73.
(15) [1976] ECR 129; [1976] 2 CMLR 62.

establish an institutional framework along the lines of the Community model itself. A Council of Ministers, parliamentary bodies composed of parliamentary delegates and adjudicative institutions (an arbitration tribunal or the European Court of Justice) are responsible for the management and development of the association. As part of Community law association agreements take precedence over conflicting provisions of domestic law (*Case 17/81, Pabst*) (16). The Community is competent to enter into any association agreement whose subject-matter falls within the scope of the Treaty, although Article 238 envisages agreements falling outside this scope by referring to a procedure laid down in Article 236. Where the division of competence between Member States on the one hand and the Community on the other is not clearly demarcated, the Member States and the Community have concluded what are known as *mixed agreements*, agreements to which Member States and the Community are signatories, so that they are valid in relation to one group if not the other. In order to safeguard national competence, yet still to produce a common Community position, the Member States have entered into *internal implementation agreements*, e.g. Internal Implementation Agreement 86/127 (17) in relation to the Third Lomé Convention which provides for the common position to be supported by the representatives of the Community in the Council of Ministers under the Convention. The establishment of the European Development Fund called for an internal agreement where financial assistance agreed upon is borne by the Member States. The Community is competent to agree upon financial assistance in its own right if it forms part of the Community budget. In *Case 1/76, Stillegungsfonds* (18) the Court held that mixed agreements were only authorised so long as they did not infringe the allocation of competence between the Community and the Member States and Member States' participation was necessary for the realisation of the agreement. The Court will only apply those provisions of mixed agreements which fall within the Community's competence.

5.09 Article 238 has been used to conclude a number of association agreements which fall into three general categories. Agreements with Greece, Turkey and Malta contemplated eventual membership of the EEC. (The association agreement with Greece lapsed on 1 January 1981 when Greece became a full member of the EEC.) The same also applies to Cyprus. The second group of agreements is with countries in the Mediterranean, as part of a unified and global approach by the Community. The Community has concluded co-operation agreements with

(16)   [1982] ECR 1331; [1983] 3 CMLR 11.
(17)   OJ 1986 L 86/221.
(18)   [1977] ECR 741; [1977] 2 CMLR 279.

Maghreb countries (Algeria, Morocco and Tunisia) and Mashrek countries (Egypt, Lebanon, Jordan and Syria). These agreements are strictly speaking association agreements entered into under Article 238 although known as co-operation agreements. Similar provisions exist in the protocols supplementing a trade agreement with Israel, the Protocols being based on Article 238. A third group of agreements is represented by the Conventions between the Community and a number of African, Caribbean and Pacific (ACP) states (see paras 5.16–21). Article 131 envisaged these agreements in their original form. The association agreements represent in most cases several agreements, permanent or interim, which reflect changes in the economic climate. Agreements may also take the form of an exchange of letters in the field of trade in specific groups of products.

5.10 The association agreement with Turkey, which was entered into in 1963 (19). contemplated three stages for achieving a customs union and the harmonisation of measures in various fields. During the first stage, traditional preferential duties were applied by the Community to specified Turkish exports. The Community also provided loans through the European Investment Bank. During the second stage, which began in 1973, reciprocal trade concessions covered industrial and agricultural products. Regulation 562/81 (20), amended by Regulation 3825/81 (21), provided for the reduction or elimination of customs duties on agricultural products imported by the Community. The third stage has not yet been reached as originally contemplated for a variety of reasons of a political and economic nature. The original agreement was supplemented by Agreement 88/227. (22)

5.11 The association agreement with Malta provides for two stages of five years with the object of attaining a customs union. The agreement provides for a reduction of duties in the industrial sector of 70% by the Community and 35% by Malta, and in the agricultural sector by 35% by Malta only. The original agreement was implemented by Regulation 492/71 (23). It was extended as to the validity of arrangements by Regulation 3670/81 (24) and in respect of trade arrangements by Regulation 3508/80 (25) and Regulation 3681/85 (26). Financial and technical

(19)   OJ 1964 217 3687.
(20)   OJ 1988 L 53/91.
(21)   OJ 1981 L 65/1.
(22)   OJ 1981 L 388/3.
(23)   OJ 1971 L 61/2.
(24)   OJ 1981 L 367/2.
(25)   OJ 1980 L 367/86.
(26)   OJ 1985 L 351/87.

cooperation was further dealt with by a protocol in 1986 (Decision 87/177). (27)

5.12 The agreements, known as *co-operation agreements*, with the three Maghreb countries, Algeria, Morocco and Tunisia, are similar. They replace agreements based on Article 113 and are based on Article 238, and came into effect on 1 November 1978. Regulation 2212/78 (28) implements the agreement with Tunisia, Regulation 2211/78 (29) that with Morocco and Regulation 2210/78 (30) that with Algeria. These agreements are supplemented by various protocols, particularly on financial and technical cooperation, the latest being implemented by Decision 88/34 (31) in the case of Tunisia, Decision 88/30 (32) in the case of Algeria and Decisions 88/452 (33) and 88/453 (34) in the case of Morocco. The trade provisions of each agreement allow for free access to the Community from the respective country except for certain agricultural products listed in Annex II of the EEC Treaty. These products can receive access in certain circumstances but subject to restrictions. There are also provisions relating to social security and family allowances of workers from Maghreb countries working in the Community but the agreements do not guarantee freer access to the Community. Attached to the agreements are financial protocols granting development aid.

5.13 There are similar agreements with the Mashrek countries. Co-operation agreements which were based on Article 238 were concluded with Egypt, Jordan, Lebanon and Syria. They were implemented by Regulation 2213/78 (35) with Egypt, Regulation 2214/78 (36) with Lebanon, Regulation 2215/78 (37) with Jordan and Regulation 2216/78 (38) with Syria. Additional protocols to these co-operation agreements were implemented by Decision 88/31 (39) in the case of Egypt, Decision 88/33 (40) in the case of Lebanon, Decision 88/32 (41) in the case of Jordan and Decision 88/598 (42) in the case of Syria. These agreements

(27)   OJ 1987 L 71/29.
(28)   OJ 1978 L 265/1.
(29)   OJ 1978 L 264/1.
(30)   OJ 1978 L 263/7.
(31)   OJ 1988 L 22/33, 34.
(32)   OJ 1988 L 22/1, 2.
(33)   OJ 1988 L 452/17, 18.
(34)   OJ 1988 L 452/32, 33.
(35)   OJ 1978 L 266/1.
(36)   OJ 1978 L 267/1.
(37)   OJ 1978 L 268/1.
(38)   OJ 1978 L 269/1.
(39)   OJ 1988 L 22/9.
(40)   OJ 1988 L 22/25.
(41)   OJ 1988 L 22/17.
(42)   OJ 1988 L 327/57.

resemble the agreements with Maghreb countries as to trade arrangements and machinery, although there are no provisions relating to social security. Maghreb and Mashrek agreements also focus on economic and social development cooperation, diversification of the economic structure and promotion of investment. Regulation 3973/86 (43) deals with the application of the protocols on financial and technical cooperation concluded between the Community and Maghreb and Mashrek countries, Malta and Cyprus.

5.14 Israel is another Mediterranean country where agreements under Article 238 provide for a Co-operation Council (Additional Protocol) and development aid in form of regular European Investment Bank loans (Financial Protocol). These protocols are implemented by Regulation 2217/78 (44) and they form a supplement to a trade agreement with Israel concluded in 1975 under Article 113 and providing for free trade (Regulation 1274/75) (45). These instruments taken together represent an association agreement as usually effected. The Third Protocol of 18 December 1984, entered into under Article 113, provided for the abolition of customs duties by 1 January 1989 (Regulation 3565/84) (46). The definition of "originating products" was further dealt with in Regulation 4163/87 (47) in the light of the co-operation agreement. Important protocols were concluded in 1988: the Fourth Additional Protocol to the agreement between the Community and Israel, implemented by Decision 88/596 (48) and a Protocol relating to financial co-operation, implemented by Decision 88/597 (49). The agreement of 1975 was interpreted by the Court of Justice in *Case 174/84, Bulk Oil (Zug) AG v. Sun International Ltd* (50), where a prohibition of export of oil from a Member State (in this case the United Kingdom) to Israel was held to be outside the terms of the Agreement.

5.15 The association of Cyprus with the Community is now governed by Decision 87/607 of 21 December 1987 (51) laying down the conditions and procedures for the implementation of the second stages of the original agreement. Decision 87/608 (52) deals with the conclusion of the protocol to the association agreement consequent upon the accession of

(43)   OJ 1986 L 370/5.
(44)   OJ 1988 L 270/1.
(45)   OJ 1975 L 136/1.
(46)   OJ 1984 L 332/1.
(47)   OJ 1987 L 397/1.
(48)   OJ 1988 L 327/35.
(49)   OJ 1988 L 327/51.
(50)   [1986] ECR 599.
(51)   OJ 1987 L 393/1.
(52)   OJ 1987 L 393/36.

Spain and Portugal. The provisions of the original agreement were laid
down in a protocol, implemented by Regulation 1247/73, (53) which
introduced a mutual reduction of import duties by 35 per cent over five
years, but this has been overtaken by the second stages mentioned
above.

African, Caribbean and Pacific Countries

5.16 An association between the Community and dependent territories
outside Europe was originally provided for by Articles 131–136 of the
Treaty. After these territories (mainly Francophone) obtained independence, they joined in a formal agreement which is represented by the
Yaoundé Convention of 1964, replaced by the Second Yaoundé Convention of 1969. Other (Anglophone) African countries (Kenya, Uganda
and Tanzania) sought a comparable agreement, resulting in the Arusha
Convention of 1968, renewed in 1969. The second Arusha Agreement of
1969 was essentially limited to trade matters (the second Yaoundé
Convention had provided for Community assistance as well) and was
based on Article 238. After the accession of the UK in 1972 independent
Commonwealth countries took up the option of joining a comprehensive
agreement replacing the Yaoundé Convention. The parties to the
Yaoundé Convention with Mauritius and the Arusha Agreement, independent Commonwealth countries and African countries unconnected
with the Member States, collectively known as African, Caribbean and
Pacific (ACP) countries, all joined, after long negotiations, a comprehensive convention signed at Lomé on 28 February 1975. The extent and
nature of the Convention is best illustrated by the two lists annexed at
the end of this chapter.

5.17 The Lomé Convention continues the principles of free trade and
development assistance. It does not refer to "association" but in fact it
is such an agreement. Regulation 199/76 (54), which is the legal instrument of the Community in concluding the Convention, refers to Article
238. The Lomé Convention covers trade and commercial co-operation,
stabilisation of export revenues, financial and technical co-operation and
industrial co-operation. The provisions of trade arrangements are non-
reciprocal and exports from ACP states are admitted to the Community
free of import duties and quantitative restrictions. A small proportion of
agricultural exports is subject to certain restrictions. An important part
of the Convention is a system for the stabilisation of export earnings
(Stabex) with a separate protocol on sugar. Under the Stabex system

(53)   OJ 1973 L 133/87.
(54)   OJ 1976 L 25/1.

payments are made to ACP economies to compensate for falls in export earnings which normally would have come from the market, but which have been prevented by production or other economic difficulties. The Sugar Protocol is contractual in nature, involving a commitment on the part of the Community to purchase annually at a guaranteed price agreed quantities of cane sugar from ACP producer countries, and a reciprocal commitment on the part of the ACP countries to supply the Community with those quantities. The Protocol was concluded for an indefinite period and although it has been annexed to successive Conventions, it exists independently. There is a clause providing for termination at the end of five years, subject to two years' notice.

5.18 The Second Lomé Convention, signed at Lomé on 31 October 1979, extends the stabilisation system (Stabex) to agricultural products and to a limited degree to some minerals (Sysmin) and increases the allocation to the European Development Fund, which distributes aid under the Convention. Sysmin is a system of aid designed to help those ACP countries whose economies depend on mining products, its principal objective being to maintain production capacity at viable levels.

5.19 The Third Lomé Convention, signed at Lomé on 8 December 1984, entered into force for five years on 1 March 1985. It was implemented by Decision 86/125 (55) amended by Regulation 1825/87 (56). Objects and principles of the Convention aim at creating a model for relations between developed and developing countries. Most notable of the principles is Article 4 which stresses the concept of self-development, social and cultural values, ideas of human potential and capacity, recognition of the role of women and respect for the desires of the individual. The Community, however, was unsuccessful in its efforts to incorporate into the Convention legally binding obligations regarding human rights in spite of the reference in the preamble. Agricultural and rural development (Articles 26–49) is now given top priority, as the ACP states have found themselves increasingly reliant on food imports. Control of the effects of drought and desertification is stressed as well as the need to raise living standards of rural population. Successful rural development calls for development of storage facilities and processing of agricultural products as well as of market conditions. Exchange of information and procedures is covered and the Technical Centre for Agricultural and Rural Co-operation is to provide the ACP states with information, research facilities, education and advice (Article 37). The

(55) OJ 1986 L 86/1.
(56) OJ 1987 L 173/6.

Convention (Lomé III) attaches considerable weight to fisheries (Articles 50–59). Set in the context of the UN Sea Convention, Lomé III deals with two aspects of co-operation: encouraging development and exploitation of ACP fisheries resources, and fishery agreements between the ACP countries and the Community, of which there is a series of bilateral ones. Social and cultural co-operation constitutes an important aspect of Lomé development policy, and training is considered part of the enhancement of the value of human resources. The fields of co-operation include rehabilitation of existing industrial capacity and the promotion of small and medium-sized businesses, development of mining and energy, transport and communications, trade and services, with emphasis on the development of a coherent trade policy, on tourism and on establishing export credit and insurance houses in ACP countries. Articles 129–147 deal with trade co-operation. The Convention improves access for ACP agricultural products by facilitating procedures for dealing with requests for preferential access to the Community (Article 130); introduces a "prior consultation" clause (Article 140) before safeguard measures under Article 139 are adopted or extended; and simplifies and relaxes the rules of origin (Article 138 and Protocol 1), enabling ACP products with a slightly higher "non-ACP" content to enjoy the consequent freedom from customs duties and charges of equivalent effect and, in many cases, from quantitative restrictions.

5.20 Annexed to the Convention are two protocols dealing with exports of bananas (no 4) and rum (no 5) from the ACP states to the Community. The protocol on bananas maintains access to the markets and the advantages acquired by each ACP state which exports bananas to the Community and provides for joint effort to enable the ACP states to establish themselves in new markets in the Community. The protocol on rum allows for duty-free import into the Community subject to an annual quota. Lomé III increases its funding of Stabex, requiring for the first time a degree of ACP accountability to the Community for the use to which they put the Stabex transfers. It also increases funding to Sysmin and introduces some procedural alterations. In the field of financial co-operation the Convention provides for very favourable terms for loans to the ACP countries (Article 196) and lays down methods of financing, particularly of risk capital and co-financing (Articles 196–200).

5.21 The Convention also marks a shift in emphasis away from public sector investment towards private funding as the motive force behind ACP development (Articles 240–247). Articles 255–264 list the least developed, landlocked and island ACP states which are eligible for more favourable arrangements. (They are listed in the Annex to this chapter.) Articles 265–281 deal with the institutional arrangements. The Convention is managed by a Council of Ministers (consisting of members of the Council of the EEC, a member of the Commission and a minister of each ACP state), the Committee of Ambassadors and the Joint Assembly (a body consisting of the consultative assembly and the joint committee of earlier conventions). Under Article 291 the contracting parties must enter into negotiations 18 months before the expiry of the Convention.

5.21.1 The Fourth Lomé Convention, signed on 15 December 1989, covers the same area as the Third Convention and deals with the same subjects.

South-East Asian Nations

5.22 The Community has a cooperation agreement with the Association of South-East Asian Nations (Indonesia, Malaysia, The Philippines, Singapore, Thailand) signed in 1980. The Community and SEAN grant each other most favoured nation status, and they have agreed to study means of fostering investment, technological co-operation and other similar measures. This agreement is based on Articles 113 and 235 of the EEC Treaty (Regulation 1440/80) (57) and it was extended to Brunei in 1985. (58)

North America

5.23 The agreements with North American countries are comparatively limited in number and scope. There are agreements negotiated under Articles XXVIII and XXIV of GATT with the United States on olive oil residues (OJ 1967 L 292/46), on certain types of manufactured tobacco and on petroleum products (OJ 1967 L 131/15) going back to 1967. There are arrangements in the form of an exchange of letters with the United States concerning trade in certain steel products (OJ 1985 L 9/2, L 355/2). More important is an agreement concerning fisheries off the coast of United States, amended and extended in 1989. (OJ 1984 L 272/13, OJ 1989 L 63/23). (Also see Chapter 7.)

5.24 Canada equally has agreements negotiated under the GATT Articles (OJ 1967 L 292/46, OJ 1968 L 97/15, OJ 1980 L 111/18) and further agreements for commercial and economic co-operation with the European Community and the European Coal and Steel Community (OJ 1976 L 260/228). There are specific agreements covering trade in certain

(57) OJ 1980 L 144/2.
(58) OJ 1985 L 81/2.

products, and their nature is best illustrated by the subject of the agreements, such as those covering alcoholic beverages (Decision 89/189) (59), women's and girls' footwear (Decision 86/123) (60), and boneless manufacturing beef (Decision 86/101) (61). There is an agreement covering fisheries (Decision 81/1053) (62) and a Joint EC-Canada Committee dealing with economic co-operation. In the field of atomic energy Canada and the European Community are involved in co-operation in several sectors.

Conclusion

5.25 Looking at the whole of the Community legislation in force, one can say that there are some agreements with most of the sovereign countries in the world, some agreements being more limited than others, but all the same enabling the Community to develop closer trade links, should the opportunity arise. Another example of action following political developments is the co-operation agreement between the European Community and the Co-operation Council of the Arab States of the Gulf, implemented by Decision 89/147. (63)

ANNEX

List of the 66 ACP States

Africa

Angola	Gambia	Nigeria
Benin	Ghana	Rwanda
Botswana	Guinea	Sao Tomé & Principe
Burkina Faso	Guinea-Bissau	Senegal
Burundi	Ivory Coast	Seychelles
Cameroon	Kenya	Sierra Leone
Cape Verde	Lesotho	Somalia
Central African Republic	Liberia	Sudan
Chad	Madagascar	Swaziland
Comoros	Malawi	Tanzania
Congo	Mali	Togo
Djibouti	Mauritania	Uganda
Equatorial Guinea	Mauritius	Zaire
Ethiopia	Mozambique	Zambia
Gabon	Niger	Zimbabwe

(59) OJ 1989 L 71/41.
(60) OJ 1986 L 100/26.
(61) OJ 1986 L 87/33.
(62) OJ 1981 L 379/53.
(63) OJ 1989 L 54/1.

Caribbean

Antigua & Barbuda	Grenada	St. Vincent & Grenadines
Bahamas	Guyana	Suriname
Barbados	Jamaica	Trinidad & Tobago
Belize	St. Christopher & Nevis	
Dominica	St. Lucia	

Pacific

Fiji	Solomon Islands	Vanuatu
Kiribati	Tonga	Western Samoa
Papua New Guinea	Tuvalu	

The least-developed, landlocked and island ACP states

Title V of Part Three of the Convention specifies which ACP States are regarded as the least-developed, landlocked and island ACP States (see below). These countries are eligible for more favourable arrangements in the following areas of the Convention:

(a) agricultural and food co-operation
(b) industrial development
(c) transport and communication
(d) development of trade and services
(e) regional co-operation
(f) general trade arrangements
(g) Stabex and Sysmin
(h) financial and technical co-operation
(i) investment
(j) rules of origin

The least-developed ACP States (Art. 257)

Antigua and Barbuda	Grenada	Sao Tomé and Principe
Belize	Guinea	Seychelles
Benin	Guinea-Bissau	Sierre Leone
Botswana	Kiribati	Solomon Islands
Burkina Faso	Lesotho	Somalia
Burundi	Malawi	Sudan
Cape Verde	Mali	Swaziland
Central African Republic	Mauritania	Tanzania
Chad	Mozambique	Togo
Comoros	Niger	Tonga
Djibouti	Rwanda	Tuvalu
Dominica	Saint Christopher and Nevis	Uganda
Equatorial Guinea		Vanuatu
Ethiopia	Saint Lucia	Western Samoa
Gambia	Saint Vincent and the Grenadines	

Landlocked ACP States (Art. 260)

Botswana	Lesotho	Swaziland
Burkina Faso	Malawi	Uganda
Burundi	Mali	Zambia
Central African Republic	Niger	Zimbabwe
Chad	Rwanda	

Island ACP States (Art. 263)

Antigua and Barbuda	Jamaica	Sao Tomé and Principe
Bahamas	Kiribati	Seychelles
Barbados	Madagascar	Solomon Islands
Cape Verde	Mauritius	Tongo
Comoros	Papua New Guinea	Trinidad and Tobago
Dominica	Saint Christopher and	Tuvalu
Fiji	Nevis	Vanuatu
Grenada	Saint Vincent and the	Western Samoa
	Grenadines	

CHAPTER 6

Agriculture

I. GENERAL

The scope of the common agricultural policy

6.01   The "adoption of a common policy in the sphere of agriculture" is an activity which the Community was obliged to pursue by Article 3(d) of the Treaty, and by virtue of Article 38 the common market extends to "agriculture and trade in agricultural products".

6.02   The extension of the common market to agriculture means that conceptually there is, throughout the Common Market, only one market for agricultural products instead of twelve national markets. Thus when, in the context of sugar quotas, an Italian producer alleged that Italian producers should not be obliged to assist in financing surpluses for which other producers were responsible, the Court replied that "Such a view is incompatible with the very principle of a common market, in which the undertakings of the Member States responsible for any surplus production cannot be identified": *Case 250/84, Eridania v Cassa Conguaglio Zucchero* (1). Great progress has been made towards achieving a single market in agricultural products, but the concept has, of course, proved difficult to translate fully into practice, and even where there is a common organisation of the market in a product, the "single market" can be divided. Thus, for instance, differences of 30% have been recorded in the selling prices of sheepmeat between the United Kingdom and other Member States, which arise because the common organisation in sheepmeat and goatmeat provides for two different support systems. However, strenuous efforts are being made to complete the achievement of a single market by 1992 and an example of this is the new regulation concerning the common organisation in sheepmeat and goatmeat, which provides for a transition to a single support system in this difficult sector. (2)

Definition of "agricultural products"

6.03   The word "agriculture" is not defined in the Treaty, but the term "agricultural products" is defined in Article 38(1) as "the products of

(1)   [1986] ECR 117.
(2)   Council Regulation 3013/89 OJ 1989 L289/1.

the soil, of stock-farming and of fisheries and products of first-stage processing directly related to these products". A list of such products was provided in Annex II of the Treaty, and others were added to this list by Council Regulation 7a of 18 December 1959 under the authority of Article 38(3) of the Treaty. Any product which does not appear in these lists is not an "agricultural product" for the purposes of Article 38 and the provisions of the Treaty concerned with agriculture (Articles 39 to 46) do not apply to it.

6.04 The Treaty does not define the products described in Annex II, which are often described in fairly general terms. It does not, for instance, state that the expression "animal products not elsewhere specified or included" does not include wool, as has been held by the Court. However, the Annex uses certain headings and descriptions of the 1950 Customs Co-operation Council Nomenclature (the "Brussels Nomenclature"), on which the Common Customs Tariff (the "CCT") was based before January 1988. (Similarly, regulations setting up common organisations before January 1988, when the Combined Nomenclature came into use (see paragraph 4.06), specified products by reference to the Brussels Nomenclature.) Therefore where there is doubt about a product described in Annex II (or a pre-1988 regulation which used the headings and descriptions of the Brussels Nomenclature), one can, in the absence of any Community provisions resolving the doubt, turn to the following aids:

(a) the Explanatory Notes to the Brussels Convention: *Case 61/80, Co-operatieve Stremsel- en Kleurselfabriek v. Commission* (3); and

(b) the established interpretations and methods of interpretation relating to the CCT before it was based on the new Combined Nomenclature: *Case 77/83, CILFIT v Italian Ministry of Health.* (4)

6.05 The expression "products of first-stage processing directly related to these products" was discussed in *Case 185/73, Hauptzollamt Bielefeld v. König* (5). Here, in holding that the dilution of alcohol after its distillation did not prevent the resulting product from falling within the expression, the Court stated that the concept of direct relationship implies "a clear economic interdependence between basic products and the processed products, irrespective of the number of processing operations involved". The Court added, however, that where "processed products have undergone a productive process, the cost of which is such

(3) [1981] ECR 851, [1982] 1 CMLR 240.
(4) [1983] ECR 1257.
(5) [1974] ECR 607.

that the price of the basic agricultural raw materials becomes a completely marginal cost", they are excluded from the definition.

Objectives of the common agricultural policy

6.06   Article 38(4) of the Treaty states that "the operation and development of the common market for agricultural products must be accompanied by the establishment of a common agricultural policy among the Member States". Thus there must be an agricultural policy common to all Member States rather than merely a co-ordination of national agricultural policies. The objectives of the common agricultural policy are set out in Article 39(1) of the Treaty as follows:

> "(a) to increase agricultural productivity by promoting technical progress and by ensuring the rational development of agricultural production and the optimum utilisation of the factors of production, in particular labour;
> (b) thus to ensure a fair standard of living for the agricultural community, in particular by increasing the individual earnings of persons engaged in agriculture;
> (c) to stabilise markets;
> (d) to assure the availability of supplies;
> (e) to ensure that supplies reach consumers at reasonable prices."

In working out the common agricultural policy, account must also be taken of:

> "(a) the particular nature of agricultural activity, which results from the social structure of agriculture and from structural and natural disparities between the various agricultural regions;
> (b) the need to effect the appropriate adjustments by degrees;
> (c) the fact that in the Member States agriculture constitutes a sector closely linked with the economy as a whole."

Since these objectives are for the protection of competing interests, that of agricultural producers as well as that of consumers, they must sometimes conflict. When a choice has to be made between these objectives or factors, it is for the Community institutions to decide on which to give priority, taking account, where necessary, of the principle of Community preference in favour of the farmers: *Case 5/67, W. Beus GmbH & Co. v. Hauptzollamt München* (6). However, the European Court has also recently made it clear that "efforts to achieve objectives of the common agricultural policy, in particular under common organisations of the markets, cannot disregard requirements relating to the public interest such as the protection of consumers or the protection of the health and life of humans and animals, requirements which the

(6)   [1968] ECR 83, [1968] CMLR 131.

Community institutions must take into account in exercising their powers": *Case 68/86, Re Agricultural Hormones: UK v. Council.* (7)

Development of the common agricultural policy

6.07 In 1960 the Council drew up guidelines for working out and implementing the common agricultural policy, based on proposals of the Commission submitted under Article 43 of the Treaty. These guidelines stressed the importance of the free movement of agricultural products, a joint agricultural and commercial policy, a common price level for agricultural products and the co-ordination of structural reform: Council Resolution of 20 December 1960. (8)

6.08 The general guidelines having been drawn up by virtue of Article 43, Member States were then to "develop the common agricultural policy by degrees during the transitional period" (ending on 31 December 1969) and to "bring it into force by the end of that period at the latest". In the case of most products, this was in fact done. Basic regulations for common market organisations in certain products were adopted from 1962 on, and in 1964 the first common price was agreed (for cereals), with the first common organisation based on a single price system following in 1967. The next year the customs union was introduced, replacing national duties for common duties in respect of all agricultural products by 1st January 1970. The common agricultural policy was applied to the UK between 1973 and 1978 by virtue of Article 9 of the Act of Accession.

Legal powers

6.09 Legislation in the agricultural sector is generally made under, or implements legislation made under, Articles 42 and 43 of the Treaty and, until recently, where national legislation was to be harmonised, under Article 100 of the Treaty (see paragraph 6.53 below). Article 103, which empowers the Council to decide upon measures of conjunctural policy, was used as a matter of emergency when monetary compensatory amounts were introduced (because under this Article the European Parliament does not have to be consulted), and this was held by the European Court to be a lawful use of that Article.

(7) [1988] 2 CMLR 543.
(8) EC Bulletin 1/61, p. 83.

6.10   Article 43(2) of the Treaty provides that:

> "The Council shall, on a proposal from the Commission and after consulting the Assembly, acting unanimously during the first two stages and by a qualified majority thereafter, make regulations, issue directives, or take decision, without prejudice to any recommendations it may also make."

Article 42 makes provision for the Council to determine to what extent the Treaty rules on competition shall apply to the production of and trade in agricultural products and Article 43(3) empowers the Council, subject to certain conditions, to replace national market organisations by common organisations.

6.11   The Council which adopts Community agricultural legislation usually consists of Ministers of Agriculture, whose meetings are prepared by a Special Committee for Agriculture made up of senior civil servants dealing with agriculture in their own states.

1. Procedure of the Council

6.12   Pursuant to Article 43(2) of the Treaty, the Council can now act by qualified majority (the reference to the "first two stages" during which voting had to be unanimous is a reference to the first two stages of the original transitional period). In practice, until the 1980s, unanimity was the rule, and this was reinforced by the Luxembourg Compromise of January 1966 when France gave its view that "where very important interests are at stake the discussion must be continued until unanimous agreement is reached". Nowadays, this rule is no longer absolute: during the 1980s the Council pressed through legislation without achieving unanimity on a few occasions, and in July 1987 Article 100a of the Treaty entered into force, allowing the Council to adopt measures for the approximation of laws by a qualified majority for the purpose of establishing the internal market by 31 December 1992 (Article 18 of the Single European Act).

6.13   The basic regulations concerning the common agricultural policy must be made strictly in accordance with the procedure laid down in Article 43. Thus, for instance, the obligation placed upon the Council to consult Parliament before making laws has been held to include an obligation to wait for the opinion of that body before acting: *Case 138/79, Roquette v Council and Commission* (9).

(9)   [1980] ECR 3333.

6.14 The Council is not, however, required to follow the full procedure laid down in Article 43 every time it legislates on the details concerning the common agricultural policy. For instance, in *Case 19/88, Kingdom of Spain v. Council* (10), in deciding that the Council had acted lawfully in fixing a milk quota by Council Regulation 1343/86 without consulting the European Parliament, the Court stated that "it is sufficient for the purposes of (Article 43) that the basic elements of the matter to be dealt with have been adopted in accordance with the procedure in question; however, the provisions implementing the basic regulations may be adopted by the Council according to a procedure different from that laid down in Article 43". The Council must, however, always observe the essential elements of the basic regulations upon which the Parliament was consulted: *Case 46/86, Romkes* (11).

2. Procedure of the Commission

6.15 The procedure of the Commission when exercising implementing powers is laid down by Council Decision 87/373 (12), made under Article 145 of the Treaty as amended by Article 10 of the Single European Act. There are three basic procedures. The first requires the Commission to obtain the opinion of the appropriate committee, composed of the representatives of the Member States and chaired by the representative of the Commission, and to take the "utmost account of the opinion delivered by the committee". The second is essentially the management committee procedure which was already well established before 1987 (see the next paragraph), and the third places an obligation upon the Commission to obtain the consent of the appropriate committee before it can act. These basic procedures are not absolutely watertight and the Decision does not affect the procedures for the exercise of the powers conferred on the Commission in acts which predate its entry into force.

3. Management committee procedure

6.16 When delegating legislative power to the Commission, the Council often requires the Commission to consult the appropriate "management committee". A management committee is set up for each group of products covered by a common organisation, and is made up of representatives of the Member States with a chairman who is a non-voting

(10) (Not yet reported).
(11) [1988] 3 CMLR 524.
(12) OJ 1987 L 197/33.

representative of the Commission. The procedure has two main advantages. Firstly it enables the Member States to know what is going on concerning the implementation of the agricultural policy and to empower them to bring a matter before the Council if they disagree with what the Commission is doing. Secondly, matters on which Member States agree can be dealt with without the necessity for a formal Council decision. The votes of the representatives of the Member States are weighted in accordance with the qualified majority procedure laid down in Article 148(2) of the Treaty as amended by the various Acts of Accession.

6.17 Under the management committee procedure the Commission submits its implementing measures to the committee, whose chairman sets a time limit during which the committee must deliver its opinion on the proposal. The measures take immediate effect, but if the management committee disagrees with them the Commission refers them to the Council and may postpone their application, normally for up to one month (although under Council Decision 87/373 (13) the Council may prescribe a period of up to three months). During this time the Council, by qualified majority, may substitute a measure which may be inconsistent with the views of both the Commission and the committee. If the Commission makes no decision within the time limit then the Commission's measures remain in force. In fact, it is very rare for the Council to reverse a Commission measure.

II. COMMON ORGANISATIONS

The European market organisation

6.18 Article 40(2) of the Treaty provided that in order to attain the objectives set out in Article 39 a common organisation of agricultural markets was to be established. Such common organisation was to take one of the following forms, depending on the product concerned:

(a) common rules on competition;

(b) compulsory co-ordination of the various national market organisations;

(c) a European market organisation.

In fact the European market organisation has been the form chosen for common organisations and nearly all products are now covered by such

(13)   OJ 1987 L 197/33.

an organisation (14). There are some exceptions, however. Thus, potatoes are excluded from the ambit of the common organisation for fresh fruit and vegetables, and there are no common organisations for alcohol, honey, wood or wool. A European market organisation is "based on the concept of the open market to which every producer has access and which is regulated solely by the instruments provided for by these organisations": (*Case 83/78, Pigs Marketing Board v. Redmond* (15)), and involves the abolition of barriers to intra-Community trade, the establishment of a common system of border regulations for imports and exports, and the application of common rules on competition.

Procedure in relation to common organisations

6.19	The procedure the Council adopts in relation to common organisations is to lay down the main principles but to delegate the laying

(14)	Common organisations have been set up in respect of:
	Cereals: Council Regulation 2727/75 (OJ 1975 L 281/1) as last amended by Reg. 2860/89 OJ 1989 L274/41.
	Pigmeat: Council Regulation 2759/75 (OJ 1975 L 282/1) as last amended by Reg. 1249/89 OJ 1989 L 129/12.
	Eggs: Council Regulation 2771/75 (OJ 1975 L 282/49) as last amended by Reg. 1235/89 OJ 1989 L 128/29.
	Poultry: Council Regulation 2777/75 (OJ 1975 L 282/77) as last amended by Reg. 1235/89 OJ 1989 L 128/29.
	Fresh fruit and vegetables: Council Regulation 1035/72 (OJ L 118/1) as last amended by Reg. 1119/89 OJ 1989 L 118/12.
	Wine: Council Regulation 822/87 (OJ 1987 L 084/1) as last amended by Reg. 1236/89 OJ 1989 L 128/31.
	Milk products: Council Regulation 804/68 (OJ L 148/13) as last amended by Reg. 763/89 OJ 1989 L 84/1.
	Beef and veal: Council Regulation 805/68 (OJ L 148/24) as last amended by Reg. 571/89 OJ 1989 L61/43.
	Rice: Council Regulation 1418/76 (OJ 1976 L 166/1) as last amended by Reg. 1806/89 OJ 1989 L 177/1.
	Oils and fats: Council Regulation 136/66 (OJ 1966 L 172/3025) as last amended by Reg. 2902/89 OJ 1989 L 280/2.
	Sugar: Council Regulation 1785/81 (OJ L 177/4) as last amended by Reg. 1069/89 OJ 1989 L 114/89.
	Flowers and live plants: Council Regulation 234/68 (OJ L 055/1) as last amended by Reg. 3991/87 OJ 1987 L 377/19.
	Dried fodder: Council Regulation 1117/78 (OJ 1978 L 142/1) as last amended by Reg. 3996/87 OJ 1987 L 377/35.
	Products processed from fruit and vegetables: Council Regulation 426/86 (OJ 1986 L 049/1) as last amended by Reg. 1125/89 OJ 1989 L 118/29.
	Raw tobacco: Council Regulation 727/70 (OJ 1970 L 094/1) as last amended by Reg. 1251/89 OJ 1989 L 129/16.
	Flax and hemp: Council Regulation 1038/70 (OJ 1970 L 146/1) as last amended by Reg. 3995/87 OJ 1987 L 377/34.
	Hops: Council Regulation 1696/71 (OJ 1971 L 175/1) as last amended by Reg. 3998/87 OJ 1987 L 377/40.
	Seeds: Council Regulation 2358/71 (OJ 1971 L 246/1) as last amended by Reg. 3997/87 OJ 1987 L 377/37.
	Sheepmeat and goatmeat: Council Regulation 3013/89 OJ 1989 L 289/1.
	Certain other agricultural products: Council Regulation 827/68 (OJ 1968 L 151/16) as last amended by Reg. 789/89 OJ 1989 L 85/3.
(15)	[1978] ECR 2347, [1979] 1 CMLR 177.

down of the details to the Commission, which has power under Article 155 of the Treaty to "exercise the powers conferred on it by the Council for the implementation of the rules laid down by the latter" (see further paragraph 6.15). Thus, for instance, the Council reserves to itself decisions relating to agricultural prices, but a myriad of more minor matters are regulated by the Commission. Implementing powers given to the Commission by the Council in this context are given a wide interpretation. It was held in *Cases 279-280/84 and 285-286/84, Firma Walter Rau Lebensmittel Werke and others v. EEC* (16) that, since only the Commission is in a position to keep track of agricultural market trends and to act quickly when necessary, the Council may confer on it wide powers of discretion and action in that sphere, and when it does so the limits of those powers must be determined in the light of the essential aims of the market organisation.

General rules relating to common organisations

1. Exclusion of discrimination
6.20 Article 40(3) of the Treaty states that the common organisation shall exclude any discrimination between producers or consumers within the Community. As pointed out in *Case 5/73, Balkan-Import-Export GmbH v. Hauptzollamt Berlin-Packhof* (17), this provision is part and parcel of the Community principle of equality of treatment. It was held in *Cases 279–280/84 and 285–286/84, Firma Walter Rau Lebensmittel Werke and others v. EEC* (18) that agricultural products "which compete with each other and are partial substitutes for each other are covered by the rule in Article 40(3) regarding discrimination." But this does not prevent comparable situations being treated differently if such a difference in treatment is justified. The Court went on to decide that there is such objective justification where:

(a) the common organisation of the market in one product (here, milk, including butter) is conceived in a very special context compared to that of the other competing product (here, vegetable fats, including margarine),

(b) the place occupied by the two competing products is entirely different, and

(c) one product but not the other is subject to a structural imbalance which requires special measures.

In the event the Court held that the introduction of the Christmas butter scheme by Commission Regulation 2956/84, whereby intervention butter

(16) [1988] 2 CMLR 704.
(17) [1973] ECR 1091.
(18) [1988] 2 CMLR 704.

was sold over Christmas at reduced prices, thereby undercutting the price of margarine, was within the powers of the Commission as delegated to it by Council Regulation 804/68.

2. Exclusion of national rules

6.21 Where there is a common organisation of an agricultural market the Member States are obliged to abstain from all measures which would derogate from it: *Case 177/78, Pigs and Bacon Commission v. McCarren & Co. Ltd* (19). This doctrine applies in respect of all unilateral measures, even those which would help to achieve the common policy: *Case 274/87, Commission of the European Communities v. Federal Republic of Germany* (20). However, Member States "remain competent to make such measures as they consider appropriate to improve structures in (a) sector, so long as they observe the mechanisms and principles governing the common organisation of the market:" *Case 148/85, Procureur de la République v. Forest (Sangoy).* (21)

General arrangements

6.22 A common organisation may "include all measures required to attain the objectives set out in Article 39" of the Treaty, "in particular regulation of prices, aids for the production and marketing of the various products, storage and carry over arrangements and common machinery for stabilising imports and exports": Article 40(3) of the Treaty. The organisations vary considerably from one product to another. In the case of some products, such as cereals and milk, there is a price and trading system, while other products, such as various meats and eggs, only receive external protection, and a scheme for quality standards is imposed in the fresh fruit and vegetable sector. In addition, a variety of rules applies to certain sectors, for instance on the maintenance of minimum stocks to prevent shortages (in the sugar sector) and the provision of aids for the formation of producer's organisation (e.g. in the fisheries sector). Measures often taken include the following.

1. A price policy

6.23 Article 40(3) of the Treaty states that "any common price policy shall be based on common criteria and uniform methods of calculation". Member States are precluded from adopting unilateral measures which conflict with such a policy: *Case 31/74, Galli* (22). A typical price structure makes use of the following concepts:

(19) [1979] ECR 2161, [1979] CMLR 389(18).
(20) (Not yet reported).
(21) [1988] CMLR 577.
(22) [1975] ECR 47, [1975] CMLR 211.

6.24 (a) *Target or guide prices.* These are the prices set by the Council which it is hoped producers will achieve during the marketing season for which they are fixed. They do not bind anyone and are intended merely to help producers to plan the year ahead with some indication of likely prices, although in the case of some products, such as oil seeds, there is a production subsidy equivalent to the difference between the target and intervention prices: Council Regulation 136/66 (23). Member States may not make laws (*Case 31/74, Galli* (24)) or adopt practices (*Case 60/75, Russo* (25)) which could prevent producers from having the opportunity of obtaining a price approximating to the target price.

6.25 (b) *Intervention prices.* These, in principle, are the prices at which the intervention agencies (in the UK, the Intervention Board for Agricultural Produce) purchase all Community-produced commodities offered to them. They are fixed (by the Council on a proposal by the Commission after consulting the Parliament) below the target price of the relevant product. Nowadays, however, the full intervention price is not always paid: see further para. 6.37.

2. A trading system
The typical trading system includes threshold prices, levies and refunds, and import and export licences.

6.26 (a) *Threshold prices.* These are entry prices for certain imports into the Community from third countries and are used to calculate levies. They are fixed by the Council acting by qualified majority (in practice, unanimously) on a proposal from the Commission at a level which makes the selling price of the products concerned the same as the target price for those products. In this way Community farmers are protected from cheap subsidised imports from third countries. In the pigmeat, egg and poultry sectors a "sluice-gate" price takes the place of the threshold price.

6.27 (b) *Levies.* Levies are amounts charged on imports or exports of agricultural products to compensate for the difference between world prices and Community prices. They are "primarily intended to protect and stabilise the Community market, in particular by preventing price fluctuations on the world market affecting prices within the Community": *Case 113/75, Frecassetti v. Italian Finance Administration.* (26)

(23)   OJ 1966 L 172/3025 as last amended by Reg. 1225/89 OJ 1989 L 128/15.
(24)   [1975] ECR 47, [1975] 1 CMLR 211.
(25)   [1976] ECR 45.
(26)   [1976] ECR 983.

Import levies are fixed daily by Commission regulations at a rate which ensures that the price in the Community of products imported into the Community is the same as, or higher than, the price of Community products. They are collected in the UK by HM Customs and Excise and the procedures are set out in Customs Notices. However, levies are not customs duties and they have a very different purpose, with the result that different rules apply to them. Thus, for instance, changes in prices on the world market (and therefore in levies) after the date of acceptance by Customs of an import declaration are not reflected in the rate of levies *(Case 113/75, Frecassetti v. Italian Finance Administration)* (27), whereas there is a Customs rule that where the rate of customs duty goes down after goods have been declared for customs purposes before being finally cleared and released from Customs the goods qualify for a lower rate of duty. Export levies have been introduced in respect of some agricultural products whose prices are higher on the world market than on the Community market. They are collected in the UK by the Intervention Board for Agricultural Produce (section 6(4) of the European Communities Act 1972). Commission Regulation 120/89 (28) lays down common, detailed rules for the application of export levies and charges on agricultural products.

6.28 (c) *Export refunds*. These are payments made to exporters of agricultural products to compensate in whole or in part for the difference between the Community prices of agricultural products exported and the generally higher world prices. They are fixed for each product periodically in accordance with the management committee procedure and are the same throughout the Community, although they may vary according to the destination of the exports. Where goods are trans-shipped within the Community they are regarded, for the purpose of the payment of export refunds, as goods exported from the first European Community port in which the customs export formalities are carried out: *Case 337/85, Commission v. Ireland.* (29)

6.29 The common detailed rules for the application of the system of export refunds are laid down in Commission Regulation 3665/87 (30), and rules relating to the advance payment of export refunds are laid

---

(27) *ibid.*
(28) OJ 1989 L 16/19.
(29) [1987] ECR 4237.
(30) OJ 1987 L 351/1 as last amended by Reg. 3993/88 OJ 1988 L 354/22.

Council Regulation 565/80 (31). To ensure uniform presentation of the lists of agricultural products on which refunds are granted an agricultural product nomenclature for export refunds has been drawn up (Commission Regulation 3846/87 (32)) which correlates to the Combined Nomenclature (see paragraph 4.06). In the United Kingdom, the Intervention Board for Agricultural Produce is the authority responsible for the payment of export refunds.

1. Advance fixing of levies and refunds
6.30 In order to enable importers and exporters to know what rate of levy or refund will be applicable to goods at the time when trading contracts are made, levies and refunds may be fixed in advance. The rate of levy or refund is then that applicable on the day of the application for an advance fixing certificate, adjusted according to the threshold price which will be in force in the month of importation, with a premium added to take account of future trends in world prices. A levy fixed in advance should do no more than compensate for the difference between the prices ruling outside and those ruling within the Community: *Case 6/77, Schouten v. Hoofproduktschap voor Akkerbouwprodukten* (33). However, in the case of refunds this rule does not seem to have been strictly applied, and a trader who has obtained an advance fixing certificate is only entitled to the amount of refund fixed in advance, even if the refund which he would have obtained at the time of export had he not had the refund fixed in advance is higher. The issue of an advance fixing certificate imposes an obligation on the trader to import or export the stated quantity during the period of the validity of the licence, plus or minus a small percentage, and the rules relating to deposits in relation to such certificates are the same as those in relation to import and export licences which are spelt out below. Common detailed rules relating to advance fixing certificates are laid down in Commission Regulation 3719/88. (34)

2. Import and export licences
6.31 Generally speaking agricultural products may not be imported into or exported from the Community without an import or export licence. In the United Kingdom licences are issued by the Intervention Board for Agricultural Produce. Common detailed rules for the application of the system of import and export licences are contained in

(31) OJ 1980 L 62/5 as last amended by Reg. 2026/83 OJ 1983 L 199/12.
       See also Commission Regulation 1475/80 amending various common agricultural policy regulations following the consolidation of advance payment provisions.
(32) OJ 1987 L 366/1 as last amended by Reg. 88/90 OJ 1990 L 11/23. The full version of the agricultural product nomenclature for export refunds applicable from 1 January 1990 was established by Commission Regulation 3445/89 OJ 1989 L 336/1, which replaced the Annex to Regulation 3846/87.
(33) [1977] ECR 1291.
(34) OJ 1988 L 331/1, as last amended by Reg. 1903/89 OJ 1989 L 184/22.

Commission Regulation 3719/88 (35), and rules applying to particular products are laid down in the rules on the common organisation of the product concerned.

6.32 Certain general exceptions to the requirement for licences are spelt out in Commission Regulation 3719/88. Thus licences are not required for operations which do not in the strict sense constitute imports or exports. For instance, licences are not required in respect of products:

(a) which are not placed in free circulation within the Community;

(b) in respect of which export is effected under a customs procedure which allows import free of customs duties, charges having equivalent effect or levies, or under special arrangements which allow export free of export duties;

(c) which are placed in free circulation under provisions governing the treatment of returned goods;

(d) for re-export in respect of which the exporter provides proof of a favourable decision for the repayment or remission of import duties.

Nor are they required, in cases in which advance fixing of a levy or a refund is not requested, for the purpose of operations:

(a) for the victualling within the Community of seagoing vessels or aircraft, to international organisations established within the Community, or to armed forces stationed within the territory of, but not subject to the flag of, a Member State;

(b) of a non-commerical nature; and

(c) relating to products in small quantities.

6.33 One of the main aims of the system of licences is to provide statistics to enable the Community to assess market developments and thus to manage the market more effectively. The system also goes some way towards ensuring that the rules concerning the common organisations are uniformly applied. A licence therefore consitutes an obligation as well as an authorisation to carry out the transaction to which it relates (Article 8 of Commission Regulation 3719/88), and a transaction is regarded as having been carried out when customs formalities have been completed, subject to the product being actually put into free circulation (Article 29 of that Regulation). A 5% variation on the quantity stated in a licence is generally permitted (and the special rules applying to particular products sometimes allow a wider variation, for instance 7% in the case of cereals and rice: Commission Regulation

(35) *ibid.*

891/89) (36). Generally, the issue of a licence is conditional upon the lodging of a deposit guaranteeing that the transaction will be carried out during the period of validity of the licence. Where it is not, the deposit will be forfeited, in whole or in part (Commission Regulation 2082/87) (37). Some or all of a deposit will also be forfeited where proof of the completion of customs formalities has not been furnished within a specified period of the expiry of a licence (Commission Regulation 3913/86). Common detailed rules for the application of the system of securities for agricultural products are set out in Commission Regulation 2220/85. (38)

6.34 Article 36 of Regulation 3719/88 expressly excludes forfeiture of the deposit in cases of force majeure. Force majeure is not limited to absolute impossibility but must be understood in the sense of "unusual circumstances, outside the control of the importer or exporter, the consequences of which, in spite of the exercise of all due care, could not have been avoided except at the cost of excessive sacrifice" (*Case 158/73, Kampffmeyer v. Einführ- und Vorratsstelle für Getreide und Futtermittel* (39), where it was held that the loss of a licence or certificate may constitute a case of force majeure). The false assurance of a national customs official that the period of validity of a licence could be extended does not in itself constitute force majeure: *Case 125/83, Corman.* (40)

3. Quality standards
6.35 An example of a scheme of quality standards is that laid down in the fresh fruit and vegetable sector. Here the preamble to the main regulation concerned, Council Regulation 1035/72 (41), states that the scheme is intended to keep products of unsatisfactory quality off the market and to guide production to meet consumers' requirements. The scheme is exhaustive: there are Community procedures for adopting the standards in question and when such norms have been adopted the products to which they apply may not be displayed or offered for sale, sold, delivered or marketed in any other manner unless they conform to the standards, subject to exceptions spelt out in Regulation 1035/72.

4. The safeguard clause
6.36 When the market for a product undergoes, or is threatened by, serious disturbances as a result of imports or exports of the product,

(36)   OJ 1989 L 94/13.
(37)   OJ 1987 L 195/11.
(38)   OJ 1985 L 205/5 as last amended by Reg. 1181/87 OJ 1987 L 113/31.
(39)   [1974] ECR 101.
(40)   [1985] ECR 3039.
(41)   OJ 1972 L 118/1 as last amended by Reg. 1119/89 OJ 1989 L 118/12.

certain actions may be taken by the Commission, and in certain urgent cases, by a Member State in trade with third countries pending the Commission's decision. The measures taken by the Commission may be referred to the Council by a Member State. Depending on the products concerned, the measures that may be taken are total or partial suspension or the predetermination of levies or refunds, total or partial suspension of the issue of import or export certificates; total or partial refusal of pending applications for predetermination and licences; the suspension of imports or exports; or the levy of duties on exports.

5. Intervention buying

6.37 Intervention buying is, in principle, the buying of agricultural products on behalf of the Community at guaranteed minimum ("intervention") prices. The system of intervention buying is a major feature of several of the common market organisations and constitutes one of the main supports for the farmer. Although originally designed as a safety net, it rapidly became seen as a guarantee of an unlimited market for production, and this gave rise to problems of overproduction (see para. 6.39). The intervention price is the price which will be paid to a farmer for his product if he cannot sell it on the market at a higher price. Subject to the changes in the rules as instanced in paragraph 6.40(c) below, once an offer has been made and has come to the knowledge of an intervention agency that agency has a binding obligation to buy the quantity offered: *Case 49/71, Hagen v Einführ- und Vorratsstelle für Getreide* (42).

6.38 Products bought-in by an intervention agency under intervention arrangements have to be stored, and their movement and subsequent disposal are controlled. (In the case of fresh fruit and vegetables, which cannot be stored, producers may withdraw their produce from the market at a withdrawal price, and receive financial compensation from intervention agencies. Most of the produce withdrawn is then destroyed). Agricultural products which have been bought-in should normally be stored in the territory of the Member State within the jurisdiction of which they fall, although, with prior authorisation, they may be stored outside the territory of that Member State: Article 1 of Council Regulation 1055/77 (43). Common detailed rules for the application of this Regulation on the storage and movement of products bought in by an intervention agency have been laid down by the Commission in Regulation 1722/77 (44), and common detailed rules for controlling and verifying the use and/or destination of agricultural

(42) Case 49/71, [1972] ECR 23, [1973] CMLR 35.
(43) OJ 1977 L 128/1.
(44) OJ 1977 L 189/36 as last amended by Reg. 3826/85 OJ 1985 L 371/1.

products which have been removed from intervention stock have been laid down by the Commission in Regulation 569/88. (45)

6. Other means of intervention

6.39 Various other means of intervening in the market for agricultural products are adopted by the Council as it considers appropriate. These include the grant of production aids in several sectors, such as the olive oil sector, to contribute to the establishment of a fair income to producers, production refunds to encourage the use of certain products for manufacturing purposes, such as those granted in the cereals sector to encourage the use of certain cereal products instead of non-cereal products for manufacturing starch, storage aids, non-marketing of milk premiums, and many others. All these interventions are financed by FEOGA (see para. 6.62) and general rules for this financing are laid down in Council Regulation 1883/78 (46). A list of measures which comply with the concept of intervention for financing purposes appears in the Annex to Commission Regulation 380/88. (47)

The problem of over-production

6.40 The guaranteed market offered by the intervention system has been a major factor in creating the surplus production that there has been of many agricultural products. This surplus is very expensive for the Community, which has to pay to buy it in and then store and dispose of it. A policy, in parts very successful, has therefore been adopted to reduce both the level of surplus production and the level of surplus stocks, as follows:

(a) A restrictive pricing policy has been adopted.

(b) Farmers have been exposed more to the realities of the market place through greater co-responsibility for surpluses in some products, such as milk and cereals. Thus, for instance, a co-responsibility levy is payable by producers in respect of cereals produced in the Community and placed on the market or sold to an intervention agency. A recent refinement is the introduction of an additional co-responsibility levy until and including the 1991/92 marketing year which is repayable in full when cereal production throughout the Community is equal to or less than the maximum guaranteed quantity (see below) and in part when production is less that 3% more than the maximum guaranteed quantity.

(45)   OJ 1988 L 55/13 as last amended by Reg. 3060/89 OJ 1989 L 293/29.
(46)   OJ 1978 L 216/1 as last amended by Reg. 787/89 OJ 1989 L 85/1.
(47)   OJ 1988 L 38/10 as last amended by Reg. 961/89 OJ 1989 L 102/33, which replaced the Annex to Reg. 380/88.

(c) Intervention mechanisms have been changed from being, in effect, an unlimited guarantee to being a safety net. Among the changes are the following new measures:

   (i) in respect of some products, intervention agencies are obliged to buy-in only during a particular period of the year ("the intervention period"), and/or up to a certain quantity, and then sometimes only if the average Community price is lower than the intervention price;

 (ii) buying-in is no longer always at the full intervention price: it may, for instance, be at 94% of the intervention price;

(iii) in respect of many products intervention volumes or thresholds have been specified, beyond which financial liability is transferred to producers by, for instance, reducing the basic and buying-in prices for the following marketing year or imposing a system of levies on overproduction. Examples of such systems are the milk co-responsibility levy introduced by Council Regulation 1079/77 OJ 1977 L 131/6 and the milk quota system's "additional levy" introduced by Council Regulation 856/84 OJ 1984 L 90/10.

(d) New outlets for agricultural production have been sought. Thus, for instance, regulations regarding the use of sugar and starch by the chemical industry have been adopted and the viability of making ethanol from agricultural products for use as an alternative octane enhancer in petrol has been examined.

(e) Structural reforms have been aimed at reducing the production of surplus products (see para. 6.83).

Products not subject to common market organisations

6.41 Agricultural products in respect of which a common market organisation has not been established are subject to the general rules of the Treaty (but see paras. 6.43 et seq regarding competition rules).

(a) The provisions with regard to the removal of customs duties and quantitive restrictions (Articles 14 and 33 of the Treaty) apply to them (*Case 288/83, Commission v Ireland* (48), where the European Court decided that the imposition of a licence requirement on the importation of potatoes produced outside the Community into Ireland was unlawful). This is so whether or not the products are covered by a national organisation of the market, which may not derogate from such rules: *Case 48/74, Charmasson v Minister for Economic Affairs* (49). The application of this rule is absolute, to the extent that Member States are denied the right even to take protective measures where the Community

(48) [1985] ECR 1761, [1985] 3 CMLR 152.
(49) [1974] ECR 1383, [1975] 2 CMLR 208.

has not yet exercised its own powers: *Case 804/79, Commission v United Kingdom* (50); and

(b) state trading monopolies must be eliminated (Article 37 of the Treaty).

6.42 In addition to the above, certain provisions have been made in respect of specific products which are not subject to a common market organisation. Thus, for instance, the common rules on import and export licences apply in respect of isoglucose and agricultural products in the form of goods not covered by Annex II of the Treaty, special measures have been laid down to encourage silkworm rearing and the production of cotton, with provision in both cases for aids and the recognition of producer groups, and special measures involving guide prices, minimum prices and threshold prices have been laid down for peas and field beans. Other rules include provision in respect of glucose and lactose, ethyl alcohol, and sweet and new potatoes.

III. RULES RELATING TO COMPETITION

6.43 The competition rules of the Treaty do not automatically apply to the production of and trade in agricultural products. By virtue of Article 42 of the Treaty they apply "only to the extent determined by the Council within the framework of Article 43(2) and (3)" (the common agricultural policy) ". . . account being taken of the objectives set out in Article 39". The Council may, in particular, authorise the granting of aid:

"(a) for the protection of enterprises handicapped by structural or natural conditions;
(b) within the framework of economic development programmes."

6.44 The Council has determined the extent to which the competition rules apply in Council Regulation 26/62 (51) and in various regulations establishing common organisations of the market. The broad effect of these determinations is as follows.

Rules applying to undertakings (Articles 85–90 of the Treaty)

6.45 Articles 85 to 90 of the Treaty apply to the production of or trade in agricultural goods by virtue of Article 1 or Council Regulation 26/62 (52), subject to the derogations relating to Article 85(1) set out in Article 2(1) of that Regulation.

(50) [1981] ECR 1045, [1982] 1 CMLR 543.
(51) OJ 1962 p. 993 amended by Reg. 49/62 OJ 1982 P 53/1571.
(52) *ibid.*

6.46 According to Article 2(1) of Council Regulation 26/62, Article 85(1) of the Treaty shall not apply to such of the agreements, decisions, and practices as:

(a) "form an integral part of a national market organisation" (53), or

(b) are necessary for the attainment of the objectives set out in Article 39 of the Treaty.

and the second sentence of that Article goes on to state that in particular, Article 85(1) of the Treaty:

> "shall not apply to agreements, decisions, and practices of farmers, farmers' associations, or associations of such associations belonging to a single Member State which concern the production or sale of agricultural products or the use of joint facilities for the storage, treatment, or processing of agricultural products, and under which there is no obligation to charge identical prices, unless the Commission finds that competition is thereby excluded or that the objectives or Article 39 of the Treaty are jeopardised".

The Commission has sole power, subject to review by the European Court, to determine which agreements, decisions and practices fulfil these conditions. Where its determination is in the negative, the agreement etc. will be void under Article 85(2) of the Treaty.

6.47 These derogations are not as useful as they may appear, for the following reasons:

(a) That spelt out in (a) above is now of little significance, since most national market organisations have been replaced by common organisations.

(b) In the case of that spelt out in (b) above, it has proved to be somewhat difficult to establish that an agreement etc. is "necessary for the attainment of the objectives" of the common agricultural policy unless the common organisation for the product concerned has expressly contemplated or impliedly permitted such an agreement: *Preserved Mushrooms* (54). Moreover, it appears that to come within this exception an agreement must be necessary for the attainment of all, and not merely some, of the objectives of Article 39 of the Treaty: *Case 71/74, Frubo v. Commission* (55).

(c) The second sentence of Article 2(1) gives examples of the type of agreement which could fall within the first sentence and is not a separate exception in its own right: *the Meldoc Case.* (56)

---

(53) For a definition of a national market organisation, see *Charmasson*, Case 48/74, [1974] ECR 1383, [1975] 2 CMLR 208.
(54) OJ 1975 L 29/26, [1975] CMLR D83 (47).
(55) [1975] ECR 563, [1975] 2 CMLR 123.
(56) Decision 86/595 OJ 1986 L 348/50.

State aids (Articles 92–94 of the Treaty)

6.48 In the case of products in respect of which there is no common organisation, the substantive rules on state aids do not apply. However, where there is a common organisation, firstly state aids may not interfere with the operation of that common organisation: *Case 177/78, Pigs and Bacon Commission v. McCarren* (57), and secondly, the regulations setting up common organisations very often specifically provide for Articles 92–94 of the Treaty to be applied "save as otherwise provided in this regulation." The Treaty provisions on state aids do not have direct effect, and this is so even when those provisions have been incorporated into regulations which themselves have direct effect: *Case 78/76, Steinike und Weinlig v. Germany* (58).

6.49 Apart from the substantive rules on state aids, Article 4 of Regulation 26/62 provides that the provisions of Article 93(1) and the first sentence of Article 93(3) of the Treaty shall apply to aids granted for the production of or trade in the products listed in Annex II to the Treaty. Article 93(1) places an obligation on the Commission to "keep under constant review all systems of aid existing in the Member States and to propose to them any appropriate measures required by the progressive development or by the functioning of the common market", and the first sentence of Article 93(3) states that the "Commission shall be informed, in sufficient time to enable it to submit its comments, of any plans to grant or alter aid". However, the real substance of this Article, which provides that the Member States shall not put their proposed measures into effect until the Commission has reached a final decision on the aid, has not been applied in relation to agricultural products.

Countervailing charges

6.50 Where there is no common organisation the rules on state aids do not apply, but the free movement of goods rules do. An example of the unfairness to which this situation can give rise was the inability of France legally to prevent or restrict the import of lamb which had benefited from the UK system of deficiency payments. Article 46 of the Treaty therefore provides that:

---

(57) [1979] ECR 2161, [1979] 3 CMLR 389.
(58) [1977] ECR 595, [1977] 2 CMLR 688.

"Where in a Member State a product is subject to a national market organisation or to internal rules having equivalent effect which affect the competitive position of similar production in another Member State, a countervailing charge shall be applied by Member States to imports of this product coming from the Member State where such organisation or rules exist, unless that State applies a countervailing charge on export."

6.51 The effect of this provision is to enable the Commission to adopt immediate safeguards where competition is distorted by Member States' national support measures encouraging low-priced exports. In each case "it is for the Commission to ensure that the duration and the amount of the charge remain within the limits circumscribed by the need to re-establish equilibrium": *Case 337/82, St Nikolaus Brennerei v. Hauptzollamt Krefeld* (59). In deciding upon the appropriate safeguards, the Commission does not have to "set up a highly complex system of data gathering and calculation" which would delay the adoption of those safeguards: *Case 181/85, Re Countervailing Charge on French Ethyl Alcohol: France v. Commission* (60). In this case it was held that the Commission had not exceeded its discretion or made an error in law in adopting a method for calculating the charge based on a single export price, even though there were in fact different export prices for different grades of alcohol.

IV. HARMONISATION OF LEGISLATION

6.52 The rules of Member States relating to frontier health inspections are not affected by the regulation of market organisations by the Community. Insofar as these rules differ between Member States they can constitute a barrier to trade, and various measures have therefore been taken to harmonise there rules. Added impetus has been given to the process of harmonisation of agricultural legislation by the adoption of the Single European Act, in particular Article 8a thereof, which provides that the "internal market shall comprise an area without internal frontiers in which the free movement of goods . . . is ensured in accordance with the provisions of this Treaty".

Legal powers

6.53 Until recently agricultural harmonisation measures were usually taken under both Article 100 of the Treaty (the specific power to harmonise legislation) and Article 43 at the same time. Article 100 provides that:

(59) Case 337/82, [1984] ECR 1051, [1985] 3 CMLR 83.
(60) Case 181/85, [1988] 2 CMLR 225.

"The Council shall, acting unanimously on a proposal from the Commission, issue directives for the approximation of such provisions laid down by law, regulation or administrative action in Member States as directly affect the establishment or functioning of the common market. The Assembly and the Economic and Social Committee shall be consulted in the cases of directives whose implementation would, in one or more Member States, involve the amendment of legislation."

There is, however, a difference in voting procedure under Article 43 (where a qualified vote is sufficient) and under Article 100 (where normally (61) a unanimous vote is necessary). This difference in voting procedure did not really matter when the Council always in fact sought unanimity under Article 43, but now that this is no longer necessarily the case it can be of great importance. Thus, in *Case 68/86, United Kingdom v. Council* (62) the UK sought the annulment of Directive 85/649, which prohibited the administration to farm animals of certain hormonal substances, on the ground that it should have been adopted under Article 100 and not Article 43 alone, thus requiring a unanimous vote. However, the Court refused to annul the Directive on that ground, holding that "Article 43 is the appropriate legal basis for any legislation concerning the production and marketing of agricultural products listed in Annex II to the Treaty which contributes to the achievement of one or more of the objectives of the Common Agricultural Policy". Now, therefore, where appropriate, harmonisation measures in the agricultural field are taken under Article 43 alone.

1. Harmonisation of veterinary laws
6.54 The objectives of harmonisation measures taken so far in the veterinary field have been to protect human and animal health and animal well-being, to control epizootic diseases, and to eliminate obstacles to intra-Community trade in livestock and livestock products. Most of the directives in this field concern the public health requirements of the Member States in relation to trade between each other. By and large these directives allow certain animals and meats to be exported from one Member State to another for the purposes of breeding, production or slaughter only if accompanied by a veterinary certificate issued by the exporting Member State certifying that the animals or meats comply with the health requirement of the relevant directive. The health requirements generally relate to standards of vaccination, inspections and freedom from certain specified diseases. As to verification, the ultimate

(61) Now, in the case of measures for the approximation of laws adopted by the Council for the purpose of establishing the internal market by 31 December 1992, a qualified vote is sufficient by virtue of Article 100a of the Treaty, introduced by Article 18 of the Single European Act.
(62) [1988] 2 CMLR 543.

objective of the Community is that the same health checks on animals and products should be applied whether they are intended for the home market or for intra-Community trade, with checks being made at the place of production and destination rather than at the internal frontiers of the Community (62a). In the meantime, checks and controls at frontiers are simplified as much as possible, and the Court takes a fairly restrictive view of those frontier controls which are permitted: *Case 186/88, Commission v. Germany* (62b).

6.55 In particular, measures have been taken:

(a) in respect of intra-Community trade, concerning animal health problems of cattle and pigs: Council Directive 64/432; (63)

(b) laying down animal health requirements applicable to intra-Community trade in, and imports from third countries of, deep-frozen bovine semen: Council Directive 88/407; (64)

(c) in respect of the pure-bred breeding of cattle: Council Directive 77/504; (65) and of sheep and goats: Council Directive 89/361 (66); and to oblige Member States to accept pure-bred cattle for breeding purposes: Council Directive 87/328 (67),

(d) in respect of zootechnical standards applicable to breeding pigs: Council Directive 88/661; (68)

(e) relating to health problems affecting intra-Community trade in fresh meat from domestic animals: Council Directives 64/433 (69) and 72/461; (70)

(f) relating to health problems affecting trade in fresh poultrymeat: Council Directive 71/118; (71)

(g) relating to health problems affecting intra-Community trade in meat products: Council Directive 77/99 (72); and to animal health problems affecting that trade: Council Directive 80/215; (73)

(62a) With this in view the Council has made a directive reinforcing co-operation between the authorities responsible for applying veterinary and zootechnical rules in each Member State: Directive 89/608 OJ 1989 L 351/34.
(62b) (Not yet reported).
(63) OJ 1964, p. 1977 (S Edn. 1963–64, p. 164) as last amended by Directive 88/406 OJ 1988 L 194/1.
(64) OJ 1988 L 194/10.
(65) OJ 1977 L 206/8 as last amended by Directive 85/3768 OJ 1985 L 362/8.
(66) OJ 1989 L 153/30.
(67) OJ 1987 L 156/54.
(68) OJ 1988 L 382/36.
(69) OJ 1964, p. 2012 (S Edn. 1963–4, p. 185) as last amended by Directive 88/657 OJ 1988 L 382/3.
(70) OJ 1972 L302/24 (S Edn. 1972 (31 Dec) (3), p. 3) as last amended by Directive 87/489 OJ 1987 L 280/28.
(71) OJ 1971 L55/23 (S Edn. 1971 (I), p. 106) as last amended by Directive 88/457 OJ 1988 L 382/3.
(72) OJ 1977 L 23/85 as last amended by Directive 89/227 OJ 1989 L 93/25.
(73) OJ 1980 L 47/4 as last amended by Directive 88/660 OJ 1988 L 380/35.

(h) relating to health and animal problems affecting intra-Community trade in heat-treated milk: Council Directive 85/397; (74)

(i) to control certain animal diseases, in particular for the eradication of brucellosis, tuberculosis and leucosis in cattle: Council Directive 77/391 (75) and Council Decision 87/58 (76); the control of foot-and-mouth disease: Council Directive 85/511 (77); and the control and eradication of swine fever in pigs: Council Directives 80/217 (78) and 80/1095; (79)

(j) to deal with problems concerning the health and veterinary inspection of cattle and pigs and of fresh meat imported from third countries. The Council is authorised, on a proposal from the Commission, to designate third countries or parts of them from which Member States may authorise imports: Council Directive 72/462; (80)

(k) laying down the health rules applying to meat intended for the domestic market: Council Directive 88/409 (81); and to the production of, and trade in, minced and small-chopped meat and meat preparations: Council Directive 88/657; (82)

(l) to prohibit the use in livestock farming of certain substances having a hormonal action: Council Directive 88/146; (83)

(m) laying down hygiene and health requirements concerning the production and placing on the market of egg products for direct human consumption or for the manufacture of foodstuffs; (84)

(n) to lay down minimum standards for the production of laying hens kept in battery cages: Council Directive 88/166 (85); and to approximate laws regarding the protection of animals used for experimental and scientific purposes: Council Directive 86/609; (86)

(o) to protect animals during international transport: Council Directive 77/489; (87) and relating to the stunning of animals before slaughter: Council Directive 74/577; (88)

(74) OJ 1985 L 226/13, as last amended by Directive 89/165 OJ 1989 L 61/57.
(75) OJ 1977 L 145/44 as last amended by Directive 85/3768 OJ 1985 L 362/8.
(76) OJ 1987 L 024/51.
(77) OJ 1985 L 315/11 (implemented by Directive 88/397 OJ 1988 L 189/25).
(78) OJ 1980 L 47/11 as last amended by Directive 87/486 OJ 1987 L 280/21.
(79) OJ 1980 L 325/1 as last amended by Directive 87/487 OJ 1987 L 280/24.
(80) OJ 1972 L 302/28 (S Edn. 1972 (31 Dec) (3), p. 7 as last amended by Directive 89/227 OJ 1989 L 93/25.
(81) OJ 1988 L 194/28.
(82) OJ 1988 L 382/3.
(83) OJ 1988 L 70/16, and see Council Directive 88/299 OJ 1988 L 128/36 on trade in animals treated with certain hormonal substances and their meat.
(84) OJ 1989 L 212/87.
(85) OJ 1988 L 74/83.
(86) OJ 1986 L 358/1.
(87) OJ 1977 L 200/10.
(88) OJ 1974 L 316/10.

(p) laying down conditions governing animal health controls on intra-Community trade in, and import from third countries of embryos of domestic cattle: Council Directive 89/556. (88a)

2. Harmonisation of legislation on animal feeds

6.56 Measures have been taken to harmonise control of the composition and marketing of animal feeds. These have necessitated the introduction of Community methods of sampling and analysis and the Commission has been authorised, in consultation with a Standing Committee for Feedingstuffs set up under Article 3 of Council Directive 70/373 (89) as amended by Council Regulation 3768/85 (90), to issue directives laying down Community rules establishing uniform methods for sampling and analysing animal feedingstuffs: Council Directive 70/373. To date the Commission has exercised this power about ten times.

6.57 To control the composition of animal feeds measures have been taken:

(a) to control the addition of additives (substances added to feedingstuffs to enhance their nutritional value): Council Directive 70/524 (91). The Directive lists the authorised substances and specifies the quantities which are permitted as additives and lays down that feedingstuffs which contain additives may only be marketed if the additives are specified on the packaging or by means of a label giving prescribed particulars;

(b) to fix maximum permitted levels for certain identified undesirable substances and products in feedingstuffs: Council Directive 74/63 (92). "Undesirable substances" are substances either found naturally in feedingstuffs or their constituents, or present as residues from processing which, if present in excessive quantities, can endanger animal or human health;

(c) to control the use as, or as constituents of, animal feedingstuffs of certain products used in animal nutrition: Council Directive 82/471 (93). This Directive requires Member States to prescribe that feedingstuffs belonging to certain product groups or containing certain products may only be marketed if they comply with the requirements of the Directive.

These rules do not apply to products intended for export to third countries, and amendments to the lists of additives, substances and

---

(88a) OJ 1989 L 302/1.
(89) OJ 1970 L 170/2 (S Edn. (II), p. 535 as last amended by Directive 85/3768 OJ 1985 L 362/8.
(90) OJ 1985 L 362/8.
(91) OJ 1970 L 270/1 (S Edn. 1970 (III), p. 840 as last amended by Directive 89/23 OJ 1989 L 11/34.
(92) OJ 1974 L 38/31 as last amended by Directive 87/419 OJ 1987 L 304/38.
(93) OJ 1982 L 213/8 as last amended by Directive 89/520 OJ 1989 L 270/13.

products may be made by the Commission in the light of scientific or technical developments. Guidelines for the assessment of certain products (94) and additives (95) used in animal nutrition have been fixed.

6.58 To control the marketing of animal feeds harmonised rules have been laid down on the marketing of straight feedingstuffs: Council Directive 77/101 (96); and compound feedingstuffs: Council Directive 79/373 (97). The Directives regulate the presentation, packaging and labelling of feedingstuffs. Generally, feedingstuffs may only be marketed if they are wholesome, unadulterated, of merchantable quality and do not represent a danger to animal or human health, and are not presented or marketed in a manner which is likely to mislead.

3. Harmonisation of plant health laws
6.59 Rules for the protection of plants from diseases and for the progressive eradication of diseases have been harmonised. At the same time measures have been taken to protect human and animal health by fixing maximum levels for pesticide residues. The aim of the Community regarding verification in this area is that checks will be restricted to places of production, supervised by a Community inspectorate, with compliance ensured by an official stamp, and Council Directive 89/439 (98), providing for certain checks to be carried out by experts under the authority of the Commission, is a step in this direction. The following are some of the measures which have been taken.

(a) Council Regulation 77/93 (99) lays down protective measures against the introduction into Member States of harmful organisms of plants or plant products. Plants, plant products, their packaging and vehicles in which they are transported must all be officially examined before entering the territory of a Member State to ensure that they are not contaminated by a prohibited organism and that other requirements of the Regulation have been met in respect of them. Once plants or plant products have been issued with a phytosanitary certificate on the basis of the official examination they may not be prohibited or restricted from entry into another Member State on plant health grounds unless a Member State considers that it is in imminent danger of the introduction or spread of harmful organisms. In such a case that Member State may take temporary protective measures, which may then be amended or

(94) Council Directive 83/228 OJ 1983 L 126/23.
(95) Council Directive 87/153 OJ 1987 L 64/19.
(96) OJ 1977 L32/1 as last amended by Directive 87/234 OJ 1987 L 102/31.
(97) OJ 1979 L86/30 as last amended by Directive 87/235 OJ 1987 L 102/34.
(98) OJ 1989 L 212/106.
(99) OJ 1977 L 26/20 as last amended by Directive 89/439 OJ 1989 L 212/106.

rescinded by the Commission in consultation with the Standing Committee on Plant Health set up by Council Decision 76/894. (100)

(b) Directives have been issued which lay down minimum measures to be taken by the Member States to control certain diseases: potato wart disease, potato cyst eelworm, San Jose scale, carnation leaf-rollers and potato ring rot. (101)

(c) Maximum levels for pesticide residues in and on fruit and vegetables: Council Directive 76/895; (102) cereals: Council Directive 86/362; (103) and foodstuffs of animal origin: Council Directive 86/363. (104)

(d) The placing on the market and use of plant protection products containing certain active substances have been prohibited by Council Directive 79/117. (105)

4. Harmonisation of restrictions on the marketing of seeds and propagating material

6.60 Directives on the marketing of seeds of beet (Council Directive 66/400) (106), fodder plants (Council Directive 66/401 (107) and Commission Directive 86/109) (108), cereals (Council Directive 66/402) (109), seed potatoes (Council Directive 66/403) (110), oil-bearing and fibrous plants (Council Directive 69/208) (111) and vegetable seed (Council Directive 70/458) (112) restrict the marketing of seeds and young plants to those of which the identity, varietal purity and value for cultivation and use has been officially verified in accordance with minimum conditions specified in the directives. Member States may impose additional or more stringent requirements for the certification of seed in their own territory. Subject to certain exemptions, seed which satisfies the prescribed criteria must not be subject to any other marketing restrictions. Directives incorporating similar provisions have been

(100)   OJ 1976 L 340/25.
(101)   Council Directives 69/464 (OJ 1969 L 323/1), 69/465 (OJ 1969 L 323/3), 69/466 (OJ 1969 L 323/5), 69/647 (OJ 1969 L 352/41) and 80/665 (OJ 1980 L 180/30) respectively.
(102)   OJ 1976 L 340/26 as last amended by Directive 89/186 OJ 1989 L 66/36.
(103)   OJ 1986 L 221/37 as last amended by Directive 88/298 OJ 1988 L 126/53.
(104)   OJ 1986 L 221/43.
(105)   OJ 1979 L 33/36 as last amended by Directive 87/477 OJ 1987 L 273/40.
(106)   OJ 1966, p. 2290 (S Edn. 1965–66, p. 124) as last amended by Directive 88/380 OJ 1988 L 187/31.
(107)   OJ 1966, p. 2298 (S Edn. 1965–66, p. 132) (82) as last amended by Directive 89/389 OJ 1989 L 100/36.
(108)   OJ 1986 L 93/21.
(109)   OJ 1966, p. 2309 (S Edn. 1965–66, p. 143) as last amended by Directive 89/2 OJ 1989 L 5/31.
(110)   OJ 1966 p. 2320 (S Edn. 1965–66, p. 154) as last amended by Directive 89/366 OJ 1989 L 159/59.
(111)   OJ 1969 L 169/3 (S Edn. 1969 (II), p. 315) as last amended by Directive 89/245 OJ 1989 L 99/30.
(112)   OJ 1970 L225/7 (S Edn. 1970 (III), p. 674) as last amended by Directive 88/380 OJ 1988 L 187/31.

issued in respect of the marketing of forest reproductive material (as regards genetic and external quality) (Council Directives 66/404 (113) and 71/161) (114) and vine reproductive material (Council Directive 68/193) (115). The UK is exempt from Directive 68/193 by virtue of Commission Decision 75/287. (116)

6.61 Council Directive 70/457 (117) provides for a common catalogue of varieties of agricultural plant species. This catalogue is based on the national catalogues of the Member States. Directive 70/457 establishes criteria for inclusion in the common catalogue of those varieties of beet, fodder plant, cereal, potato and oil and fibre plants the marketing of the seeds of which is subject to the directives specified above.

V. FINANCIAL MECHANISMS

European Agricultural Guidance and Guarantee Fund

6.62 Article 40(4) of the Treaty provides that:

> "In order to enable the common organisation referred to in paragraph 2 to attain its objectives, one or more agricultural guidance and guarantee funds may be set up".

In the event, there is only one fund, called the European Agricultural Guidance and Guarantee Fund, for all the common market organisations together. This fund, sometimes referred to as EAGGF but better known by the French initials FEOGA, was set up by the Council of Ministers in Regulation 25/62 of 4 April 1962. (118) It is not an autonomous agency or institution of the Community but forms part of the Community budget (Council Regulation 729/70, (119)) and in line with the philosophy that the financial consequences of measures taken by the Community concerning price and trade systems and structural reforms should be borne by the Community's own resources, revenue from import levies goes into the Community budget (Article 2 of Decision 70/243 (120)), while FEOGA finances export refunds, intervention and structural reforms.

---

(113) OJ 1966, p. 2326 (S Edn. 1965–66, p. 161) as last amended by Directive 88/332/ OJ 1988 L 151/82.
(114) OJ 1971 L87/14 (S Edn. 1971 (I), p. 222) as last amended by Directive 85/3768 OJ 1985 L 362/8.
(115) OJ 1968 L93/15 (S Edn. 1968 (I), p. 93) as last amended by Directive 88/332 OJ 1988 L 151/82.
(116) OJ 1975 L 122/15.
(117) OJ 1970 L 225/1 as last amended by Directive 89/380 OJ 1988 L 187/31.
(118) OJ 1962 p. 991 as last amended by Reg. 741/67 OJ 1967 P 252/2.
(119) OJ 1970 194/13 as last amended by Reg. 2048/88 OJ 1988 L185/1.
(120) OJ 1970 L94/19.

6.63 Under Council Regulation 17/64 (121) the Fund was split into two sections: the Guarantee Section, which finances the common marketing and price policy, and the Guidance Section, which finances Community structural reforms.

6.64 The general administration of FEOGA is the responsibility of the Commission (Article 10 of Council Regulation 729/70). At the national level the Commission relies on the national authorities. Under Council Decision 70/243 (122) the national authorities collect monies due under the common agricultural policy on behalf of the Community and make payments due under Community rules. Cash advances are made to Member States in accordance with periodical estimates of expenditure by virtue of Regulation 729/70. The question inevitably arises, what happens if Community money runs out? It was held in *Case 99/74, Grands Moulins des Antilles v. Commission* (123) that if FEOGA refuses, or is unable, to reimburse payments, the Member States are nevertheless still liable to make payments under Community rules, and in 1987, when it appeared that the Community budget might become exhausted, Council Regulation 3183/87 (124) required the Member States to continue to make payments when the guarantee allocation for 1987 had been used up on the basis that the Member States must bear the costs of the policies to which they have agreed.

Control of FEOGA money
6.65 Article 4(2) of Council Regulation 729/70 as amended by Regulation 2048/88 (125) obliges Member States to ensure that the credits made available to them are used without delay and solely for authorised purposes. It also requires Member States to take the measures, in the form of administrative and judicial procedures, necessary to enable them:

(a) to satisfy themselves that transactions financed by the fund are actually carried out and executed correctly,

(b) to prevent and deal with irregularities, and

(c) to recover sums lost as a result of irregularities or negligence.

6.66 Member States can only recover from FEOGA money which has been spent in accordance with correctly interpreted Community legislation (correct interpretation being settled, if necessary, by the European Court). Thus, for instance, financing by FEOGA of expenditure by the Netherlands on export refunds for mackerel caught in excess of the

(121) OJ 1964 p. 586 (94).
(122) OJ 1970 L 94/19.
(123) [1975] ECR 1531.
(124) OJ 1987 L304/1.
(125) OJ 1988 L185/1.

national quota allowed by Community conservation measures was refused in *Case 262/87, Kingdom of the Netherlands v. Commission* (126). Moreover, where Member States adopt national practices which are incompatible with Community law it is not only the resulting net increase in expenditure which is disallowed but the whole of monies wrongfully paid, disregarding any resulting decreases in expenditure which would, but for the illegality, have been recoverable from FEOGA: *Case 347/85, Re United Kingdom Dual Milk Pricing* (127). The only exceptions to this rule are that expenditure falling within a reasonable exercise of a discretion may be recoverable, and that where an incorrect application of Community law is attributable to a Community institution, the Community ought to bear the financial consequences of it: *Case 11/76* (128), *Case 18/76* (129), *and Cases 15 and 16/76.* (130)

6.67 A scrutiny system has been set up to minimise irregularities in management and use of the resources of FEOGA involving the inspection of accounts and documents relating to transactions financed by it which are in the possession of national agencies (Council Regulation 729/70) (131) or the beneficiaries of Community aid (Council Regulation 4045/89) (132). In addition, a system for mutual assistance and for information exchange between Member States and the Commission concerning irregularities and the recovery of sums wrongly paid has been organised: Council Regulation 283/72) (133). The increasing number of cases of fraud and irregularities notified to the Commission by Member States under Articles 3 and 5 of this Regulation has been giving concern, and in July 1988 a Commission anti-fraud unit was established to combat this problem.

Common prices

6.68 A basic tenet of the CAP is that prices of agricultural products should be the same throughout the Community, and Article 40(3) of the Treaty provides that "Any common price policy shall be based on common criteria and uniform methods of calculation." Thus the common price policy is based on the fixing of a single price, which is measured now in ECUs.

(126) (Not yet reported).
(127) [1988] 2 CMLR 487.
(128) [1979] ECR 245.
(129) [1979] ECR 343.
(130) [1979] ECR 321.
(131) OJ 1970 L 94/13 as last amended by Reg. 2048/88 OJ 1988 L 185/1.
(132) OJ 1989 L 388/18.
(133) OJ 1972 36/1 (S Edn. 1972 (I), p. 90).

The ECU

6.69 The ECU as a unit of account was introduced as the basis of the new European monetary system by Council Regulation 3180/78 (134) and Council Regulation 3181/78 (135). It is a "basket" currency unit whose value is equal to fixed amounts of the currencies of each Member State. The daily value of the ECU in terms of Member States' currencies is published in the "C" series of the Official Journal. For the purpose of agricultural prices, it is converted into national currencies at the "green rate."

The "green rate"

6.70 Most Member States did not want the level of agricultural price support in their territory to change immediately every time their currency appreciated or depreciated against the old unit of account or, later, the ECU. Therefore a special agricultural conversion rate (the "green" rate), rather than the official market conversion rate, is used for converting agricultural prices expressed in ECU into national prices. By this means farm and food prices are protected from the immediate effect of exchange rate fluctuations. They are normally fixed annually as part of the price fixing decisions, usually at the central rate for the national currency vis-a-vis the ECU, by the Council acting under Article 2(3) of Council Regulation 1676/85 (136). The rates currently applicable are fixed under Council Regulation 1678/85 (137). Detailed rules on the conversion rates to be applied have been made in Commission Regulation 3152/85 (138). The same Member State may have different rates for different products, with the consequence that some products in some countries have greater protection from exchange rate fluctuations than others. This has increasingly been so since the changes in the calculation of MCAs introduced in 1984 (see para. 6.75): for instance in March 1988 France had six green rates and the United Kingdom five.

6.71 The European Court has held that the partitioning of the market caused by the adoption of "green" rates does not contravene the prohibition on discrimination in the Treaty: *Case 138/78, Stolting v. Hauptzollamt Hamburg-Jonas* (139). In so holding the Court stated that:

> "The application of these exchange rates may possibly involve advantages or disadvantages which may appear as discriminatory, but it none the less remains true that in general such application serves to remedy monetary situations which, in the absence of (those rates) would result in much more serious, obvious and general discrimination."

(134) OJ 1978 L 379/1 as last amended by Reg. 2626/84 OJ 1984 L 247/1.
(135) OJ 1978 L 379/2 as last amended by Reg. 3066/85 OJ 1985 L 290/95.
(136) OJ 1985 L 164/1 as last amended by Reg. 1636/87 OJ 1987 L 153/1.
(137) OJ 1985 L 164/11 as last amended by Reg. 63/90 OJ 1990 L 8/43.
(138) OJ 1985 L 310/1 as last amended by Reg. 2300/89 OJ 1989 L 220/8.
(139) [1979] ECR 713, [1979] 3CMLR 588.

6.72   The protection afforded by the "green" rate is supposed to be only temporary, so the Council is constantly having to adjust it to reduce the difference between that and the market rate. In the meantime, the difference is covered by trade in monetary compensatory amounts. This is necessitated by the fact that rates of exchange, having been allowed to float, change more rapidly than the Community "single prices", and this plays havoc with the single price system. Thus, for instance, an intervention price for a commodity in a state whose exchange rate did not alter between the fixing of the prices and a particular transaction would remain stable in terms of its own currency, but if that commodity was sold into intervention in a state whose exchange rate had risen, a higher intervention price would be achieved taking into account the rate of conversion back into the first state's currency.

Monetary compensatory amounts
6.73   Under the pre-1984 system, the purpose of MCAs was, more or less, to fill the "real monetary gap" between the green rate and the market rate. Real monetary gaps are calculated for each Member State and, if differentiated, for each market (see para. 6.70), according to whether or not the Member State participates in the Exchange Rate Mechanism and observes the narrow fluctuation. The Exchange Rate Mechanism is a mechanism by which Member States agree to maintain the market rates for their currencies within an agreed range on either side of their bilateral central rates. The agreed range in respect of Belgium, Denmark, Germany, France, Ireland, Luxembourg and the Netherlands is plus or minus 2.25% and that for Italy was 6% (139a). Greece and the United Kingdom do not participate in the Exchange Rate Mechanism. For those Member States which observe the narrow fluctuation band the ECU central rate is used as a proxy for the market rate so that the monetary gap, and therefore the MCAs, are "fixed", changing only if the green or central rates change. For the other Member States, including Italy, the ECU central rate cannot be used as a proxy for the market rate and the MCAs are reviewed weekly and are therefore "variable". The rules on MCAs were consolidated in Council Regulation 1677/85 (140), and the Commission has laid down detailed rules for the calculation of MCAs in Commission Regulation 3153/85 (141) and for the administrative application of MCAs in Commission Regulation 3154/85 (142). MCAs are fixed by the Commission (see Regulation 1876/89) (143) and advance

---

(139a) After a currency re-alignment on 5 January 1990 effective 8 January Italy agreed to observe the narrow fluctuation of plus or minus 2.25%.
(140)   OJ 1985 L 164/6 as last amended by Reg. 3578/88 OJ 1988 L 312/16.
(141)   OJ 1985 L 310/4 as last amended by Reg. 2301/89 OJ 1989 L 220/9.
(142)   OJ 1985 L 310/9 as last amended by Reg. 1546/89 OJ 1989 L 151/24.

fixing of MCAs is available where import or export licences have been issued and the appropriate refunds or levies have been fixed in advance: Commission Regulation 3155/85 (144).

6.74 The fluctuations in exchange rates and the consequent imposition of MCAs necessarily constitute a partitioning of the market, and they also necessitate border controls to verify that transactions in respect of which MCAs are levied or paid actually take place. In the interest of regaining unity of the market, the Community has undertaken the gradual abolition, or "dismantlement", of MCAs. However, experience has shown that dismantlement is difficult to achieve because Member States still do not want exchange rates to take immediate effect on agricultural prices in their territory. This is particularly so in the case of positive MCAs, which are those applied by Member States with strong currencies, like Germany and the Netherlands, whose agricultural prices in national currency are above the common price level and who therefore apply MCAs as a levy on imports and a subsidy on exports, because the dismantlement of MCAs in their case would bring about lower prices when expressed in national currencies, and therefore lower incomes for their farmers. It was in their interest that in 1979 a "gentlemen's agreement" was reached by a majority of Council Members to the effect that any reduction in MCAs would not be allowed to lead to a reduction in prices expressed in national currencies.

6.75 In 1984, in an attempt to move towards dismantlement of positive MCAs, what has been called the "switchover mechanism" was introduced by Council Regulation 1677/85 (145), at first on a provisional basis, but now extended. The switchover mechanism involves "switching" positive MCAs into negative ones and avoiding the creation of new positive MCAs in future for the fixed rate currencies. The switch is achieved by multiplying each central rate (using a notional central rate for the floating currencies) by a correcting factor, thus creating a whole new notional set of exchange values, called the "green ECU". The monetary gap, to be covered by MCAs, is then calculated as the percentage difference between the green rate and the green ECU instead of between the green rate and the real ECU. In effect, the ECU is revalued for agricultural purposes, to keep up with the strongest currency (Germany), resulting in an increase in the real level of agricultural prices. According to the Special Report No 1/89 of the Court of Auditors on the agrimonetary system dated 30 March 1989 (146), the

(144) OJ 1985 L 310/22 as last amended by Reg. 1678/89 OJ 1989 L 164/12.
(145) OJ 1985 L 164/6 as last amended by Reg. 3578/88 OJ 1988 L 312/16.
(146) OJ 1989 C 128/1.

cumulative effect of these revaluations was that the level of common prices had been raised in this way by 13.7% since April 1984, so that the green ECU (the real price level) was then 13.7% higher than the real ECU. The importance of this is that "dismantlement" since 1984 has only meant dismantling the monetary gaps between the green rates and the new national set of exchange rates achieved by the correcting factor, instead of between the green rates and the market rates. Thus, when "dismantlement" has been achieved, if it is, there will still be a gap between the green rates and real exchange rates. This is a problem which is likely to be insoluble in the absence of monetary union.

6.76 In 1987 automatic arrangements for dismantling new negative MCAs were adopted: Council Regulation 1889/87 (147). These arrangements applied to both "natural" negative MCAs (the "natural" part of an MCA being that part which results from changes in the exchange rate of a Member State's currency) and "artificial" negative MCAs (the "artificial" part of an MCA being that part which results from the operation of the switchover), but in different ways. The arrangements were supplemented in 1988 by decisions to dismantle the remaining negative MCAs of the Member States observing the narrow fluctuation band in four stages up to 1992, and Commission Regulation 3578/88 (148) lays down detailed rules for this. A commitment was made in respect of the other Member States, although no details were fixed.

6.77 As in the parallel case of the "green rate" (see para. 6.72 above), the European Court does not regard the system of MCAs as illegal even though they consitute a partitioning of the market, because without the system there would be more danger to the unity of the common market than there is with them: *Case 9/73, Schluter v. Hauptzollamt Lorrach* (149). In fact it could be said that it is the Member States who have partitioned the market by allowing their exchange rates to float, possibly in contravention of Article 105 of the Treaty, which obliges Member States to "coordinate their economic policies": *Cases 80 and 81/77, Ramel v. Receveur des Douanes.* (150)

6.78 Certain consequences follow from the fact that the objective of MCAs is only to protect the single market. Firstly, they should only be applied where application of the monetary measures in question would lead to disturbances in trade in the relevant agricultural products. The

(147) OJ 1987 L 182/1.
(148) OJ 1988 L 312/16 as last amended by Reg. 3063/89 OJ 1989 L 293/34.
(149) [1973] ECR 1135.
(150) [1978] ECR 927.

Commission has a wide discretion in assessing the risk of disturbance, and in reviewing the legality of the exercise of such discretion the Court must confine itself to examining whether it contained a manifest error or constituted a misuse of power or whether the authority did not clearly exceed the bounds of its discretion: *Case 55/75, Balkan v. Hauptzollamt Berlin-Packhof* (151). Secondly, where MCAs are payable on import into a Member State, they are only attracted if the goods actually enter the market of the Member State of import: *Case 254/85, Irish Grain Board* (152). Thirdly, MCAs which are applied to trade with non-member countries must not, unlike levies or customs duties, consitute a protective component at the external frontiers of the Community, and will be unlawful if they do: *Case 236/84, Malt GmbH v. HTZ Düsseldorf* (153). In order that that part of a Community price which represents levy is not subjected to conversion at the "green rate" as well as a positive MCA, thus over-compensating for differences in exchange rates, in trade with third countries MCAs are subject to a special coefficient. The rules regarding accession compensatory amounts are also subject to this special co-efficient: Commission Regulation 3153/85 (154) Article 6.

Accession compensation

6.79 When a new state joins the Community it is necessary to compensate for the differences between the price levels of agricultural products in that state and those in the other Member States until the prices are co-ordinated. This is the function of accession compensatory amounts (ACAs). They take the place of levies and refunds in trade between the new Member State and the rest of the Community, and they are added to or subtracted from levies and refunds in trade with non-Member States (see e.g. Article 55 of the 1972 Act of Accession, Article 51 of the Greek Act of Accession, and Articles 72 and 240 of the Spanish and Portuguese Act of Accession). Commission Regulation 86/548 (155) lays down detailed rules for the application of ACAs.

VI. STRUCTURAL AND GUIDANCE MEASURES

6.80 One of the objectives of the common agricultural policy is:

"to increase agricultural productivity by promoting technical progress and by ensuring the rational development of agricultural production and the optimum utilisation of the factors of production, in particular labour" (Article 39(1)(a) of the Treaty)"

(151) [1976] ECR 19.
(152) [1987] 1 CMLR 727.
(153) [1986] ECR 1923.
(154) OJ 1985 L 310/4 as last amended by Reg. 2301/89 OJ 1989 L 220/9.
(155) OJ 1986 L 55/52 as last amended by Reg. 3494/88 OJ 1988 L 306/24.

and Article 39(2) goes on to provide that in working out the common agricultural policy account shall be taken of:

> "(a) the particular nature of agricultural activity, which results from the social structure of agriculture and from structural and natural disparities between the various agricultural regions."

6.81 When the EEC was first formed, its farming was characterised by large numbers of small, inefficient farms and it was recognised from the start that structural reforms were necessary if the objectives of the common agricultural policy were to be achieved. When FEOGA was split into two sections by Council Regulation 17/64 (156) structural measures were added to the guidance section, and every five years the Council fixes the total amount of money which may be charged to the Guidance Section during the next five years (Council Regulation 870/85 (157).

The Mansholt Plan

6.82 In 1968 the Commission put forward its "Memorandum on the Reform of Agriculture in the EEC" (the "Mansholt Plan") with the aim of creating larger, more efficient farms, and as a result three Directives (158–160) were enacted in 1972 on the modernisation of farms, encouraging the cessation of farming by small and inefficient farms and improving occupational skills by workers in agriculture. For future applications for grants and aids these Directives were effectively replaced by Council Regulation 797/85. (161)

Measures taken

6.83 The following structural measures have been taken to increase or reduce production: (161a)

(a) Member States are obliged to introduce an aid scheme to encourage the *set-aside of arable land*. Under a "set-aside" scheme, a producer who sets aside at least 20 per cent of his arable land for at least five years is granted aid, the rate varying according to the use of the set-aside land and whether or not the land is situated in a less-favoured area or not

(156) OJ 1964 p. 117.
(157) OJ 1985 L 95/1.
(158) Council Directive 72/159 OJ 1972 L 96/1 as last amended by Reg. 3768/85 OJ 1985 L 362/8.
(159) Council Directive 72/160 OJ 1972 L 96/9 as last amended by Reg. 797/85 OJ 1985 L 93/1.
(160) Council Directive 72/161 OJ 1972 L 96/15 as last amended by Reg. 797/85 OJ 1985 L 93/1.
(161) OJ 1985 L 93/1 as last amended by Reg. 1191/89 OJ 1989 L 123/1.
(161a) Shortly before going to press, some of the provisions described below were amended "with a view to expediting the adjustment of agricultural production structures": see Council Regulation 3808/89 OJ 1989 L 371/1.

(162). Commission Regulation 1272/88 lays down detailed rules for applying the set-aside scheme. (163)

(b) Member States are to introduce an aid scheme to promote *extensification for surplus products* (162). This provision, together with that described in (c) below, was given for the purpose of adjusting the various production sectors to market requirements, in particular reducing production where there is a surplus. "Extensification" means reducing the output of the product concerned by at least 20 per cent for a period of at least five years without other production capacity being increased, and surplus products are those for which there are consistently, at Community level, no normal unsubsidised outlets, and these are listed in Annex I to Commission Regulation 4115/88, which regulation lays down detailed rules for applying this aid scheme. (164)

(c) Member States are to introduce an aid scheme to encourage the *conversion of production towards non-surplus products*. (162)

(d) Provision is made for Member States to introduce a system of *investment aid to farmers* who practise farming as their main occupation, possess adequate occupational skill and competence, who submit an "improvement plan" for materially improving their holding, and who undertake to keep simplified accounts, and provided that the labour income per man-work unit is less than a reference income to be fixed by Member States at a level not exceeding the average gross wage of non-agricultural workers in the relevant region. The aid may take the form of capital grants or the equivalent thereof in interest-rate subsidies, or deferred repayments or a combination of these, but it may not cover expenditure incurred in buying land, or pigs, poultry or calves for slaughter. Special provision is made for young farmers under 40. (Articles 2–8 of Regulation 797/85).

(e) Member States may introduce a scheme to encourage the *introduction of accounting* on agricultural holdings. Farmers whose main occupation is farming may qualify for aid spread over at least the first four years during which accounts are kept on the understanding that accounts will be kept for at least four years (Article 9 of Regulation 797/85).

(f) Member States may grant a *"launching aid"* to various groups and agricultural associations with the object of encouraging mutual aid, joint use of agricultural equipment and the provision of farm management services (Articles 10, 11 and 12 of Regulation 797/85).

(g) Specific measures have been taken to *assist mountain and hill farming* and farming in certain less-favoured areas. Farmers in less-

---

(162) Council Regulation 797/85, as amended in particular by Reg. 1760/87, OJ 1987 L 167/1 and Commission Regulation 1094/88 OJ 1988 L 106/28.
(163) OJ 1988 L 121/36.
(164) OJ 1988 L 361/13.

favoured areas (which are defined in Directive 75/268) (165) may be paid an annual compensatory allowance to assist farming activities. The farmer, who must have at least three hectares of usable agricultural area, must undertake to pursue a farming activity for at least five years from the first payment. Where a less-favoured area is suitable for the development of a tourist or craft industry, an investment aid may be provided for this purpose together with aid for investment in an agricultural activity (Articles 13–17 of Regulation 797/85).

(h) Provision has been made for measures to be taken to encourage *early retirement from farming*. Member States may grant an annual allowance to farmers who practise farming as their main occupation, who are over 55, and who permanently cease all farming activities. Agricultural production on a recipient's land (or 2/3 of the land if it is leased) must be halted for the period from cessation of farming until he reaches normal retiring age (which is to be at least five years, including, if necessary, a period beyond usual retiring age), or the agricultural area of the holding must be used to enlarge that of one or more other agricultural holdings, the farmer of which undertakes not to increase production of surplus products on the total area of his holding after enlargement (Council Regulation 1096/88). (166)

(i) The Council may decide on specific measures to encourage agriculture as a whole in *regions suffering structural or infra-structural handicaps* (Article 18 of Regulation 797/85).

(j) Specific aid schemes may be introduced for areas, to be determined by Member States, which are "particularly sensitive" from the point of view of *protection of the environment* or preservation of the landscape and the countryside. The aid consists of an annual premium per hectare granted to farmers in such areas who undertake, under a specific programme for the area concerned, to introduce or maintain, for at least five years, farming practices compatible with the requirements of the protection of the environment and of natural resources or with the requirements of the maintenance of the landscape and of the countryside (Council Regulation 1760/87). (167)

(k) The Commission may grant aid of, in principle, 25% of the cost of a project aimed at *improving the conditions under which agricultural products are processed and marketed*. The intention is that the aid

(165) OJ 1975 L 128/1 as last amended by Reg. 797/85 OJ 1985 L 93/1.
(166) OJ 1988 L 110/1.
(167) OJ 1987 L 167/1 as last amended by Reg. 1094/88 OJ 1988 L 106/28.

should guarantee to producers of basic agricultural products an adequate and lasting share in the resulting economic benefits. A project must generally form part of a programme drawn up by a Member State and approved by the Commission and must fulfil certain conditions and criteria set out in Article 11 of Council Regulation 355/77 (168). These criteria relate to such matters as the development of new outlets, the easing of the burden on intervention mechanisms and the use of by-products, particularly by recycling waste.

(l) The development of certain *producer groups* and associations of groups of producers in areas (not including the United Kingdom) where they were needed was promoted by the Council in its Regulation 1360/78 (169) by the provision of aid for such groups and associations for the first five years following their recognition. In order to qualify for aid, groups and associations must lay down common rules for production and for placing goods on the market. Detailed rules of application concerning the economic activity of producer groups and associations thereof are laid down in Commission Regulation 2083/80. (170)

Collection of data concerning agricultural holdings

6.84 In order that the structural policy can be based on meaningful statistics the Council has set up a Community-wide network for the collection of accountancy data on the incomes and business operation of agricultural holdings: Council Regulation 79/65 (171). Annual surveys of selected agricultural holdings are carried out under Commission Decision 78/463 (172) which established a Community typology for agricultural holdings. In addition, in line with a United Nations Food and Agriculture Organisation recommendation for a world census of agriculture, to be conducted some time around 1990, Member States must carry out surveys on the structure of agricultural holdings on their territories: Council Regulation 571/88 (173). Surveys are also carried out on the earnings of permanent and seasonal workers employed in agriculture: Council Directive 82/606. (174)

---

(168) OJ 1977 L 51/1 as last amended by Reg. 4256/88 OJ 1988 L 374/25 and extended in operation to 30 April 1995 by Regulation 1932/84 OJ 1984 L 180/1.
(169) OJ 1978 L 166/1 as last amended by Reg. 3875/88 OJ 1988 L 346/3 and extended in operation to 31 December 1991 by Reg. 1760/87 OJ 1987 L 167/1.
(170) OJ 1980 L 203/5 as last amended by Reg. 2238/89 OJ 1989 L 215/12.
(171) OJ 1965, p. 1859 (S Edn. 1965–66, p. 70) as last amended by Reg. 3644/85 OJ 1985 L 348/4.
(172) OJ 1978 L 148/1 as last amended by Reg. 542/84 OJ 1984 L 293/22.
(173) OJ 1988 L 56/1 as last amended by Reg. 807/89 OJ 1989 L 86/1.
(174) OJ 1982 L 257/22 as last amended by Reg. 562/88 OJ 1988 L 309/33.

VII. INTRODUCTION OF EC AGRICULTURAL LAW INTO THE UK

The Intervention Board

6.85 Section 6(1) of the European Communities Act 1972 established the Intervention Board for Agricultural Produce (IBAP) as follows:

> "There shall be a Board in charge of a government department, which shall be appointed by and responsible to the Ministers [i.e. MAFF and the Secretaries of State respectively concerned with agriculture in Scotland and Northern Ireland, acting jointly] and shall be by the name of the Intervention Board for Agricultural Produce a body corporate . . . ; and the Board (in addition to any other functions that may be entrusted to it) shall be charged, subject to the direction and control of the Ministers, with such functions as they may from time to time determine in connection with the carrying out of the obligations of the United Kingdom under the common agricultural policy of the Economic Community."

By virtue of section 6(2) of that Act, provision was made for the consitution and membership of the Board before Accession under the Intervention Board for Agricultural Produce Order 1972. (175)

6.86 The Board has, *inter alia*, the following functions:

(a) those which the Ministers (see para. 6.88) determine in connection with the obligations of the UK under the common agricultural policy (section 6(1) above);

(b) those "other functions" that may be entrusted to it (section 6(1) above), including functions concerning the implementation of the common agricultural policy under section 2(2) of the European Communities Act 1972 which do not involve "obligations" of the UK;

(c) that of receiving and recovering agricultural levies charged on goods exported from the UK or shipped as stores (section 6(4) of the 1972 Act) (import levies being the responsibility of the Commissioners of Customs and Excise under section 6(5)).

6.87 The 1972 Order enabled the Board, with the approval of the Ministers, to arrange for the performance of any of its functions by another statutory body concerned with agriculture or agricultural produce. By virtue of this power functions have been delegated to the Home Grown Cereals Authority in respect of cereals and to the Meat and Livestock Commission in respect of livestock and livestock products (The Intervention Functions (Delegation) Regulations 1972) (176), to

(175) SI 1972/1578.
(176) SI 1972/1679.

the Hops Marketing Board in respect of hops under the Intervention Functions (Hops) Regulations 1979 (177) and to the Milk Marketing Boards under the Intervention Functions (Delegation) (Milk) Regulations 1982 (178) and the Dairy Produce Quotas Regulation 1986 (179).

Section 2(2) of the European Communities Act 1972

6.88   The Secretary of State for Scotland and the Minister of Agriculture, Food and Fisheries have been designated as the "designated Minister or department" who may make regulations with regard to the implementation of the common agricultural policy: The European Communities (Designation) Order 1972 (180).

Schedules 3 and 4 of the European Communities Act 1972

6.89   These schedules themselves implemented some provisions of Community law concerning, for instance, plant and animal health.

Section 6(5) of the European Communities Act 1972

6.90   This provision stipulates that import levies are to be levied, collected and paid as if they were Community customs duties and they are therefore collected by the Commissioners of Customs and Excise. Since it is the national agencies who collect levies, it is for the Member States themselves to take the necessary criminal or civil proceedings to enforce or recover them: *Cases 178–180/73, Belgium and Luxembourg v. Mertens and others* (181). Vice-versa, a trader who thinks he has been wrongfully charged levies must proceed against the national authorities and not against the Community (*Case 96/71, Haegeman v. Commission*) (182), and a trader who thinks money is due to him under Community legislation must act against the national authorities: *Case 99/74, Grands Moulins des Antilles v. Commission* (183).

(177)   SI 1979/433.
(178)   SI 1982/1502.
(179)   SI 1986/470.
(180)   SI 1972/1811.
(181)   [1974] ECR 33, [1974] CMLR 523.
(182)   [1972] ECR 1005, [1973] CMLR 365.
(183)   [1975] ECR 1531.

CHAPTER 7

Fisheries

Basis

7.01 Article 38 of the Treaty defines agricultural products to include the products of fisheries and the products of first stage processing therefrom. Accordingly, the common fisheries policy (CFP) emerged from the common agricultural policy, of which in principle it remains part: *Case 141/78, France v. United Kingdom*; (1) although in practice it now stands on its own as the organisation of a common market in fishery products. Since 1983, the CFP has provided for the limiting of fish catches, price support and quality control, conservation measures and third country agreements.

7.02 From the very earliest stages of Community development, however, it was established that the basic principle of non-discrimination found throughout Community law must be applied to fishing within the waters over which Member States enjoyed sovereignty or exercised jurisdiction. Thus, Regulation 101/76 (2), replacing even earlier legislation, established that there was to be no discrimination in regard to access to the fishing waters of each Member State by vessels flying the flag of any other Member State. A Council Resolution of 6 November 1976 urged Member States to extend their overall fishing zones along North Atlantic and North Sea coasts to 200 nautical miles from 1st January 1977, and Resolution 507/81 (3) offered detailed guidance on its application. The principles of Community law apply in the zones thus extended, or in any less extensive zone actually claimed by a Member State.

7.03 Regulation 170/83 (4), however, allows limitations to this general rule. First, an exclusive fishing zone for each state up to a maximum of twelve nautical miles is permitted. Second, previously existing arrangements between Member States allowing rights to each others' fishermen in reserved waters may be continued. Thirdly, there are special restrictions relating to fishing by larger vessels in the Orkney/Shetlands 'box'.

(1)   [1979] ECR 2923; [1980] 1 CMLR 6.
(2)   OJ 1976 L 20/19.
(3)   OJ 1981 C 105/1.
(4)   OJ 1983 L 24/1.

Equal access to Spanish and Portuguese waters will not be established before 2002. (5)

7.04 Lastly, Article 227(5)(c) of the Treaty provides that the Treaty applies to the Channel Islands and the Isle of Man to the extent necessary for the implementation of the arrangements concerning them included in the 1972 Act of Accession of the United Kingdom, Ireland and Denmark (6). Protocol 3 of that Act makes provision accordingly. The general effect is to require the islands to apply Community rules to the extent necessary for their enforcement, but to exclude them from the scope of the Common Fisheries Policy as such: see *Case 32/79, Commission v. United Kingdom.* (7)

Total allowable catches and quotas

7.05 The regulation of fishing activity to ensure conservation of resources is now a matter within the Community's competence rather than that of the Member States: *Case 804/79, Commission v. United Kingdom* (8). Regulation 170/83 (4) provides the framework within which overall limits for the quantity of fish which may be taken are laid down by subsequent detailed regulations. These are normally made by reference to particular fish types, and are usually issued on an annual basis. The total allowable catch, or TAC as it is known, is calculated globally in the first instance, by reference to species and areas and then (generally) allocated among Member States. Regulation 4047/89 (9) fixes the TACs for 1990, and Regulation 4055/89 (10) makes provision for the Regulatory Area defined in the Northwest Atlantic Fisheries Organisation (NAFO) Convention—see para. 7.17.

7.06 The implementing regulations are made in the light of advice from the Scientific and Technical Committee for Fisheries, based on research on the capacity of the fishing grounds. Because the greater part of the Community waters is subject to common access, over-fishing by fishermen from state B can lead to state A's fishermen being prejudiced by being unable themselves to use up their own quotas; or under-use of a quota by state A can lead to part of the TAC being unused even if states B, C and D exhaust their own quotas entirely. This problem is dealt with by means of quota exchanges between states under Regulation 170/83,

(5)   OJ 1985 L 302.
(6)   OJ 1972 L 73.
(7)   [1980] ECR 2403; (1981) 1 CMLR 219.
(8)   [1981] ECR 1045; [1982] 1 CMLR 543.
(9)   OJ 1989 L 389/1.
(10) OJ 1989 L 389/67.

(4) and by a further procedure for adjustments between them laid down in Regulation 493/87. (11)

7.07 Regulation 170/83 (4) imposes on Member States the duty of determining the detailed rules for the utilisation of the quotas allocated to them, for example to discourage the tendency for all the quotas to be used up as soon as possible, with the attendant flooding of the market early in the season and shortages later on. In *Case 207/84, De Boer v. Produktschap voor Vis en Visprodukten* (12), the Court held that Member States might in this context limit the taking of part of their quotas to vessels of a certain size.

7.08 Where the figures indicate that a national quota has been used up, the Member State must issue a provisional prohibition order to stop further fishing; the Commission subsequently makes a definitive order after checking that there are no unused quotas from the same TAC in other Member States. If a Member State is prevented, by the adoption of conservation measures, from utilising its full TAC, measures may be adopted to compensate its fishing interests for the prejudice suffered.

7.09 A claim by a Member State to be entitled to prevent the practice known as "quota-hopping", where vessels of state A register to fly the flag of state B in order to gain access to the latter's national quota, was referred to the Court by the House of Lords in *R. v. Secretary of State for Transport, ex parte Factortame and others* (13). But in *Case 223/86, Pesca Valentia v. Ministry of Fisheries and Forests* (14) the Court upheld the right of a Member State to require that a specified minimum proportion of the crews of vessels flying the flag of that state and fishing in Community waters should be Community nationals. In *Case C3/87, R. v. Ministry of Agriculture exp. Agegate Ltd* and *Case C216/87, R. v. Ministry of Agriculture exp. Jaderow Ltd* (14a) the Court held that Member States could insist on a real economic link with the state whose flag a vessel is flying and therefore stipulate that the vessel should operate out of national ports, but not that it should land its catch, nor that a proportion of its crew should reside, in the state in question; and one state could also require the crew to contribute to its social security system.

7.10 Regulations 3440/84 (15), 1866/86 (16) and 3094/86 (17) are

(11) OJ 1987 L 50/13.
(12) [1985] ECR 3210; [1987] 2 CMLR 515.
(13) *Case 221/89*, (Not yet reported).
(14) [1988] 1 CMLR 888.
(14a) (Not yet reported).
(15) OJ 1984 L 318/23.
(16) OJ 1986 L 162/1, as last amended by Reg. 887/89 OJ 1989 L 94/1.
(17) OJ 1986 L 288/1, as last amended by Reg. 4057/89 OJ 1989 L 389/78.

among those laying down detailed technical measures which, in addition to the system of TACs, are designed to promote conservation of fish stocks. These measures include minimum mesh sizes, restrictions on the type of fishing gear and vessels which may be used, specification of the minimum size of fish of certain types which may be taken and the designation of closed areas and closed seasons.

Enforcement measures

7.11 Although enforcement measures are, as usual, primarily a matter for the Member States, specific Community provisions exist and Regulation 2241/87 (18) consolidates the Community legislation on controls. This legislation covers the recording of information about catches by means of logbooks kept by skippers, landing records and the inspection and control of fishery vessels. It also lays down the conditions in which nets which may not be used lawfully must be stored meanwhile. Member States are required to report the statistics thus established to the Commission.

7.12 The Commission has power to monitor enforcement by means of inspectors who accompany national officials, but who do not deal direct with the fishermen. Detailed rules about recording catches are contained in Regulation 2807/83 (19). Regulation 2930/86 (20) defines terminology relating to fishing vessels for the purposes of all Community legislation concerning fisheries, and gives a common meaning to terms such as "length", "breadth", "tonnage" and "engine power". The inspection of vessels is provided for by Regulation 1382/87 (21), and the marking and recording of vessels by Regulation 1381/87. (22)

7.13 Regulation 3251/87 (23) makes provision in the context of NAFO for the designation of Community inspectors (assigned by Member States) and their functioning in conjunction with the inspectors of other contracting parties to the Convention, and the conditions under which inspections take place are also prescribed. The registration of vessels remains a function of the Member States, but Regulation 163/89 (24) provides for details of all vessels registered or removed from the registers to be reported to the Commission monthly. This gives the Commission an overall view of the Community fishing fleet, and the individual items

(18)   OJ 1987 L 207/1.
(19)   OJ 1983 L 276/1, as last amended by Reg. 473/89 OJ 1989 L 53/34.
(20)   OJ 1986 L 274/1.
(21)   OJ 1987 L 132/11.
(22)   OJ 1987 L 132/9.
(23)   OJ 1987 L 314/1, as last amended by Reg. 1956/88 OJ 1988 L 175/1.
(24)   OJ 1989 L 20/5.

of information thus centrally held may only be divulged to the Member State from whose register they are drawn.

Structural policy

7.14 This refers to the measures taken to update and improve the economic and material features of the fishing industry. The central instruments by reference to which this is done are the Multiannual Guidance Programmes (MGP) which the Member States adopt, submit for approval to the Commission, and then are responsible for implementing. Yearly reports on these programmes are made to the Commission, together with proposals as necessary for adjustments during a programme's validity. The various types of grant outlined below must all be approved in the context of the MGP. The principal legislation is contained in Regulation 4028/86 (25), though there is much implementing and subsidiary legislation based on this regulation.

7.15 The regulation provides for a series of grants, funded jointly by the Member States and the Commission, to be available within the parameters referred to above, for the following purposes:

(a) the purchase or construction of individual fishing vessels, with a bias towards owner-operated vessels replacing ones more than fifteen years old;

(b) the modernisation of fishing fleets as a whole;

(c) the development of fish-farming installations and structural works in coastal waters;

(d) exploratory operations to establish the viability of long-term exploitation of fishery resources by Community vessels in Community waters or elsewhere;

(e) joint venture projects relating to the catching, marketing and processing of fish and the use of the technology relevant to it;

(f) temporary or permanent withdrawal of certain vessels from fishing activity;

(g) the improvement of port facilities, and obtaining new outlets and markets for surplus or underfished species.

External relations

7.16 The counterpart of the CFP is necessarily a common external policy with regard to trade with non-Community countries. The Common Customs Tariff applies to third country imports, and Regulation 3796/81 (26) prohibits Member States from applying any charge equiva-

(25) OJ 1986 L 376/7, as last amended by Reg. 2321/88 OJ 1988 L 202/18.
(26) OJ 1981 L 379/1; last amended by Reg. 1495/89 OJ 1989 L 148/1 and Reg. 4042/89 OJ 1989 L 388/1.

lent to a customs duty or any quantative restriction to such trade. The Court has held that the corollary of internal Community competence in the area of fisheries is that the Community is now solely empowered to deal with third countries or international organisations: *Cases 3, 4 & 6/76, Kramer* (27). The Community has accordingly made agreements with a very wide range of individual countries allowing for fishing rights to be exercised in their waters by Community fishermen i.e. by vessels flying the flag of a Member State, or in Community waters by vessels flying the flag of the third country.

7.17   Likewise, the Community has entered as a contracting party into several conventions, such as the Northwest Atlantic Fisheries Convention in 1978 (28) (the NAFO Convention) and the Northeast Atlantic Fisheries Convention in 1981 (29) (the NEAFC Convention). Article 234 of the Treaty expressly preserves the operation of international agreements entered into before the Treaty itself, and a similar provision is contained in Article 5 of the 1972 Act of Accession of the United Kingdom, Ireland and Denmark. (6) This means that, to the extent that Member States' bilateral agreements have not been superseded by Community-wide treaties, they remain binding. The same appears from the Court's judgement in *Case 181/80, Arbelaiz-Emazabel* (30) to be the case in relation to agreements entered into after the date of the Treaty (or the Accession), but before the Community actually assumed internal competence in the area.

7.18   When setting the TAC of fish which migrate to or from Community waters, the Community will attempt to do so in agreement with the third countries affected by the migrations. A large number of bilateral agreements between the Community and third countries now exists regulating the conduct of fishing and mutual rights. An example is the bilateral European Community–United States agreement (31). Regulation 2622/79 (32) applies, so far as Community vessels are concerned, certain conservation measures relating to net mesh sizes and by-catch allowances agreed under the NAFO Convention. Regulations 1956/88 and 2868/88 (33) lay down detailed rules for the joint international inspection scheme.

Regulation of the internal market

7.19   As in the case of the Common Agricultural Policy, the CFP aims

(27)   [1976] ECR 1279; [1976] 2 CMLR 440.
(28)   OJ 1978 L 378/2.
(29)   OJ 1981 L 227/22.
(30)   [1981] ECR 2961.
(31)   OJ 1984 L 272/3, as last amended by Agreement 307/89 OJ 1989 L 63/23.
(32)   OJ 1979 L 303/1.
(33)   OJ 1988 L 175/1 & L 257/20.

to create an organised and controlled market in fish and fish products. The object of doing this, in contrast to the rules designed to ensure free markets in industrial products and in services, is to stimulate productivity by stabilising the market, ensuring a fair standard of living for those engaged in it, and to provide for continuity of supplies and reasonable prices for consumers. This is done primarily by regulating price levels for a defined range of products: fresh, dried, salted, frozen, chilled and smoked fish, crustaceans or molluscs, and certain other fish-related products. The principal legislation is contained in Regulation 3796/81. (26)

7.20 By reference to fish species, the Council sets a guide price at the start of each year, and this is done taking account of market conditions, supply availability and the objectives of the CFP generally. There is then established a Community withdrawal price by fish types. These prices are always below the guide price, but may be adjusted for specified ports in order to compensate for any distortion likely to result from a port's remoteness from the main centres of consumption. When actual market prices fall to the withdrawal price or Community selling price, the goods are taken off the market by intervention buying. Special provision is made in respect of certain species where required by market conditions.

7.21 Regulation 105/76 (34) provides for the recognition by Member States of producers' organisations, who open their membership to all Community producers within their area, according to detailed criteria laid down in subsequent regulations. In general, they must provide for their members to market their produce through them, and adopt measures designed to improve product quality. They may receive aid within prescribed limits from the Member States, but may not occupy a dominant position in the common market unless necessary in pursuance of Treaty objectives.

7.22 The producer organisations are empowered to operate the withdrawal system and to buy in produce when prices fall below the withdrawal price, and they receive the financial support necessary for that purpose and, in certain cases, for the purpose of storing produce bought in. The intervention arrangements are structured to encourage producers to gear supply to actual demand by reducing progressively the level of payments for withdrawals, so that the more production exceeds demand, the less the producer is compensated for his output.

7.23 In order to be eligible for financial compensation in this way, or

(34) OJ 1976 L 20/39, as last amended by Reg. 3940/87 OJ 1987 L 373/6.

to be marketed within the Community, produce must conform to Community standards relating to quality, size, weight, packing and labelling which are prescribed in supplemental regulations. Thus, common marketing standards are laid down by Regulation 103/76 (35) for fresh or chilled fish. These provisions are in general applicable equally to Community caught fish and that caught by vessels flying the flag of a third country.

7.24   In dealing with imports to the Community of fish or fish products, the same principles are applied as in the case of other goods where there is a common market organisation. A reference price is established for each type of fish product on the Community market, and duties are imposed if it is considered necessary to bring their value up to the relevant Community level in order to prevent disturbance to the internal market. Conversely, export refunds are available to enable the export of products to the world market (or to a particular third country market) where the price is lower than the Community price, and the export of the product in question is considered to be important to the Community economy. General rules for the grant of export refunds, and the criteria by reference to which the amounts are fixed, are the subject of Regulation 110/76. (36)

(35)   OJ 1976 L 20/29, as last amended by Reg. 33/89 OJ 1989 L 5/18.
(36)   OJ 1976 L 20/48.

CHAPTER 8

Free Movement of Workers and Social Security

8.01 Title III of the EEC Treaty under the heading of "Free movement of persons, services and capital" covers in Chapter 1 free movement of workers, in Chapter 2 the right of establishment, the right of business enterprises to move across national frontiers and in Chapter 3 the right to provide services across national frontiers. Chapter 4 deals with the right to move capital between the Member States.

8.02 Article 48 of the Treaty is concerned with the free movement of workers. It specifies the rights which are involved in such free movement and provides that the freedom of movement shall entail the abolition of any discrimination based on nationality between workers of Member States as regards employment, renumeration and other conditions of work and employment; it entails the right, subject to limitations justified on grounds of public policy, public security or public health (a) to accept offers of employment actually made; (b) to move freely within the territory of Member States for this purpose; (c) to stay in a Member State for the purpose of employment in accordance with the provisions governing the employment of nationals of that State; (d) to remain in the territory of a Member State after having been employed in that State. Employment in the public service is excluded from the scope of the Article.

8.03 Article 49 of the Treaty provides for the Council to issue directives or make regulations setting out the measures required to bring about freedom of movement for workers as defined in Article 48. It should be noted that the Court of Justice has established the scope of the Article by deciding that the Article has direct effect (*Case 167/73, Commission v. French Republic* (1); *Case 41/74, Van Duyn v. Home Office*). (2)

8.04 The term "worker" covers all persons working under a contract of employment and it covers salaried employees and executives as well as manual workers. The Court of Justice, however, has gone further and in

(1) [1974] ECR 359; [1974] 2 CMLR 216.
(2) [1974] ECR 1337; [1975] 1 CMLR 1.

130

Case 53/81, Levin v. Staatssecretari van Justitie (3) ruled that a person was a worker as long as he performed paid work of some substantial duration; full-time work was not required, but the work had to be more than of a casual nature. The term "worker" is also defined in Regulation 1408/71 (4) in terms of being insured by a social security scheme. The question of who is to be considered as a national of a Member State must normally be determined by national law. As far as the United Kingdom is concerned the term "nationals" refers to individuals who have the right of abode in the United Kingdom and therefore are exempt from United Kingdom immigration control. Restrictions cannot be imposed on the right of a national of any Member State to enter the territory of another Member State, to stay there and to move within it unless his presence or conduct constitutes a genuine and sufficiently serious threat to public policy (*Case 36/75, Rutili v. Ministre de l'Intérieur*, (5) in which case it was held that reasons must be given to enable the worker to assess whether or not the restriction imposed on him is supported by reference to considerations of public policy, and to exercise effectively his right to challenge the restriction if appropriate). However in *Case 175/78, R. v. Saunders* (6) the Court held that a Member State may limit the freedom of movement of one of its own nationals in its own territory (a British court had required a United Kingdom national to reside for three years outside England and Wales as a condition of suspending a sentence for theft).

8.05   The provision of Article 48(4) dealing with employment in the public service is subject to varying interpretation. The Court of Justice in *Case 152/73, Sotgiu v. Deutsche Bundespost* (7) held that the exception provided by the Article applies only to the access to public service occupations and not to the functions performed. In *Case 149/79, Kingdom of Belgium v. Commission* (8) the Court seemed to indicate that it is the functions which are performed which may involve the protection of the public interest. In *Case 225/85, Commission v. Italian Republic* (9) the Court stated that for the exception to apply it must be shown that the persons employed are charged with the exercise of powers conferred by public law or are responsible for safeguarding the general interests of the State. Article 48(2), dealing with the abolition of discrimination based on nationality, is more specific than the general rule on non-discrimination embodied in Article 7 of the Treaty.

(3)   [1982] ECR 1035; [1982] 2 CMLR 454.
(4)   OJ 1971 L 149/2.
(5)   [1975] ECR 1219; [1976] 1 CMLR 140.
(6)   [1979] ECR 1129; [1979] 2 CMLR 216.
(7)   [1974] ECR 153.
(8)   [1980] ECR 3881; [1981] 2 CMLR 413.
(9)   [1987] ECR 2625; [1988] 3 CMLR 635.

8.06 The anti-discrimination rules contained in the provisions mentioned are not validly given effect by a Member State if as a matter of administrative practice such a State simply does not apply existing legislation of a discriminatory nature to nationals of other Member States. The discriminatory rules must be amended to make them formally inapplicable to Community nationals (*Case 167/73, Commission v. French Republic*) (10). The Treaty also prohibits discrimination during the course of employment and the Court of Justice has made it clear that this implies equal treatment over dismissals. A national rule which prohibits dismissal of certain employees (e.g. handicapped persons) without prior authorisation, but which applies to nationals and residents only, must be extended to all Community nationals (*Case 44/72, Marsman v. Rosskamp*) (11). The Court of Justice has reaffirmed the Community national's right to enter another Member State and to reside there in connection with the free movement of workers. The Court ruled that the right to take up residence is conferred by the Treaty and does not depend upon the discretion of national authorities (*Case 48/75, Royer* (12); and *Case 8/77 Sagulo*) (13). In the case of Royer the Court stressed that the right of entry and residence conferred by Community law is equally conferred on members of workers' families.

8.07 Article 48 is administered by legislation made under Article 49. This legislation is represented by a number of Community instruments. Regulation 1612/68 (14) lays down the principles governing the freedom of movement of workers within the Community. It provides that any national of any Member State irrespective of his residence has a right to take up an activity as an employed person and to pursue this activity within the territory of another Member State in accordance with the provisions laid down by law, regulation or administrative action governing the employment of nationals of that State. He must have the right to take up available employment in the territory of another Member State with the same priority as nationals of that State. The right to take employment is extended to the family of the worker. The worker is entitled to all the rights and benefits accorded to national workers in housing matters and his children are entitled to education and vocational training as nationals of the State concerned. This includes grants for higher education. In addition Directive 77/486 (15) provides for special free tuition to facilitate the initial reception of the children in the

(10)   [1974] ECR 359; [1974] 2 CMLR 216.
(11)   [1972] ECR 1243; [1973] CMLR 501.
(12)   [1976] ECR 497; [1976] 2 CMLR 619.
(13)   [1977] ECR 1495; [1977] 2 CMLR 585.
(14)   OJ 1968 L 257/2.
(15)   OJ 1977 L 199/32.

new Member State, including training in the official language. The Regulation provides for equal rights to become members of trade unions but here the workers are excluded from certain workers' tribunals. Directive 68/360 (16) complements the Regulation by requiring the abolition of restrictions on the movement and residence of nationals of the Member States and members of their families to whom the Regulation applies. Passports and identity cards must be issued or renewed by Member States, which must allow entry to their territory simply on production of a valid identity card or passport. No entry visa or equivalent may be demanded except for those members of the worker's family who are not nationals of a Member State. (*Case 157/79, R. v. Stanislaus Pieck*) (17). The Directive lists documents on the production of which a residence permit must be issued by the Member State. Such permit is valid for at least five years and is automatically renewable. Commission Regulation 1251/70 (18) regulates the position of workers who have worked in the territory of another Member State. It deals with their right to remain in the territory of the Member State in which the worker has ceased working.

8.08 Article 48(3) subjects the freedom of movement of workers to exceptions on the grounds of public policy, public security or public health. Directive 64/221 (19) effected the co-ordination of national provisions regulating these exceptions. This Directive was extended by Directive 72/194 (20) to nationals of Member States and members of their families who remain in the territory of a Member State after having been employed in that State. Directive 64/221 provides that grounds of public policy, public security or public health must not be invoked to serve economic ends. Measures taken on the ground of public policy or public security must be based exclusively on the personal conduct of the individual concerned. Previous criminal convictions do not in themselves constitute grounds for taking such measures. The expiry of the identity card or passport used by the person concerned to enter the country does not justify expulsion from the territory and the State which issued the identity card or passport shall allow the holder of such document to re-enter the territory without any formality although the document is no longer valid or the nationality of the holder is in dispute. Article 3 of the Directive was held to be directly applicable in *Case 41/74, Van Duyn v. Home Office* (2). In *Case 30/77, R. v. Boucherau* (21) the court laid down

(16)   OJ 1968 L 257/13.
(17)   [1980] ECR 2171; [1980] 3 CMLR 220.
(18)   OJ 1970 L 142/24.
(19)   OJ 1964 L 56/850.
(20)   OJ 1972 L 121/32.
(21)   [1977] ECR 1999; [1977] 2 CMLR 800.

as test of the application of the public policy exception the existence of a genuine and sufficiently serious threat affecting one of the fundamental interests of society. In that case the Court held that previous convictions do not on their own constitute grounds for imposition of restrictions authorised by Article 48 on the grounds of public policy and public security. The only diseases or disabilities justifying refusal of entry into a territory or refusal to issue a first residence permit under Directive 68/360 (16) are those listed in the Annex to the Directive 64/221 (19), e.g. drug addiction or active tuberculosis.

8.09 Article 50 states that Member States shall, within the framework of a joint programme, encourage the exchange of young workers. The current programme is the Third Joint Programme embodied in Decision 84/636 (22). The Community is in fact going further in the operation of joint programmes in the labour sector by the establishment of a European system for the international clearing of vacancies and applications for employment (the SEDOC system) and since 1982 there has been in operation a mutual information system on employment policies in Europe set up to collect, exploit and disseminate information.

8.10 Social security systems form an intrinsic part of the freedom of movement of workers in the Community. An uneven distribution of rights and benefits throughout the Member States will affect the common market by charges imposed on commerce or industry and thus the ability to compete. Unequal social security systems however are significant obstacles to the free movement of labour, since workers will be reluctant to seek employment in another Member State when that employment involves loss of rights and benefits. Article 51 of the EEC Treaty provides that the Council shall adopt such measures in the field of social security as are necessary to provide freedom of movement for workers; to this end, it must make arrangements to secure for migrant workers and their dependants:

(a) aggregation, for the purpose of acquiring and retaining the right to benefit and of calculating the amount of benefit, of all periods taken into account under the laws of the several countries; and

(b) payment of benefits to persons resident in the territories of Member States.

The Court of Justice has construed Article 51 and its implementing legislation in a large number of cases and the Court's decisions have had great influence on the drafting and implementing of the Community

(22) OJ 1984 L 331/36.

rules relating to social security and led to frequent revision of the appropriate regulations: the interpretations of the Court were incorporated in the new Regulations. In interpreting Article 51 the Court has frequently paid attention to Articles 48 and 49.

8.11   The scope of Article 51 and its implementing Regulations is wide. Regulation 1408/71 (23) states in its Article 4(1) that it shall apply to sickness, maternity benefits, invalidity benefits, old age and survivors' benefits, benefits arising out of workmen's compensation and occupational diseases, death grants, unemployment benefits and family benefits. The Regulation applies only to social security schemes and not to public assistance benefits nor to some types of special legislation. This Regulation is the central provision on social security for families moving within the Community. It has been extended by Regulation 1390/81 (24) to apply to self-employed persons and their families. Thus the Regulation now applies to employed or self-employed persons who are or have been subject to legislation of one or more Member States, and who are Community nationals or stateless persons or refugees residing within the territory of one of the Member States, and to members of their families. The principle underlying all this legislation is that a person residing in the territory of one of the Member States and to whom the legislation applies enjoys the same rights and obligations under the legislation of a Member State as its own nationals. As Article 51 requires, periods of employment and insurance completed in several Member States are to be aggregated for the calculation of benefits. The beneficiary may request the transfer of benefits from one Member State to another. Regulation 1408/71 (23) underwent amendment by Chapter IX of Annex I of the Act of Accession of the United Kingdom, Denmark and Ireland and by Regulation 2001/83 (25) to take account of the social security systems of new Member States. The Regulation is governed in its application by rules contained in Regulation 574/72 (26) which has been amended to allow for changes in the social security systems of Member States and which has been extended to apply to self-employed persons by Regulation 3795/81 (27). Regulation 1209/76 (28) introduced changes to enable workers insured in the United Kingdom who later became disabled in another country to obtain benefits in the United Kingdom. As a result of the accession of Greece some technical changes were made in the legislation and the same followed admission of Spain

(23)   OJ 1971 L 149/2.
(24)   OJ 1981 L 143/1.
(25)   OJ 1983 L 230/6.
(26)   OJ 1972 L 74/1.
(27)   OJ 1981 L 378/1.
(28)   OJ 1976 L 138/1.

and Portugal. Regulation 1305/89 (29) further deals with social security schemes. Regulation 2332/89 (29a) amended Regulation 1408/71 (23) and Regulation 574/72 (26) to take account of changes made by Member States in their social security legislation and introduced some amendments of a technical nature to the implementation procedure. It covers employed persons, self-employed persons and members of their families.

8.12 The Court of Justice gives the Article and regulations made in its pursuance a broad interpretation. Thus the implementing regulations can only increase a worker's rights under national laws and not diminish them: *Case 1/67, Ciechelski v. Caisse Régionale de Sécurité Sociale* (30). On the other hand a worker from another Member State is not entitled to more than national treatment. If social security benefits of nationals are suspended during periods of imprisonment, the same rule may be applied to a worker from another Member State even if the imprisonment occurs in the home State and not in the State liable for benefits. (*Case 1/78, Kenny v. Insurance Officer*) (31). The rules on social security must always be interpreted in such a way that workers moving between Member States are not penalised by doing so. Thus periods of employment treated as periods of insurance in a Member State where the claimant has previously been employed must also be so considered in the other Member State where benefit is claimed. (*Case 126/77, Frangiamore v. Office National de l'Emploi*). (32)

8.13 Each Member State declares the nature of its benefits e.g. unemployment insurance or other measures of social security. This is important as it classifies the benefits for the purposes of Regulation 1408/71. To distinguish social security benefits from welfare benefits the Court of Justice appears to rely on the criterion of whether the entitlement to benefit is one of right or whether it depends on some degree of administrative discretion (*Case 7/75, Mr. & Mrs. F. v. Belgium* (33) concerning special benefits for the handicapped). Persons in employment but not insured as required in the place of their employment as a result of their employer's neglect fall within the ambit of the Regulation (*Case 39/76, Bestuur der Bedrijfvereniging v. Mouthaan*) (34). Benefits accruing under Community law may not be less than those available under

(**29**)   OJ 1989 L 131/1.
(**29a**)   OJ 1989 L 224/1.
(**30**)   [1967] ECR 75; [1967] CMLR 77.
(**31**)   [1978] ECR 1489; [1978] 3 CMLR 651.
(**32**)   [1978] ECR 725; [1978] 3 CMLR 166.
(**33**)   [1975] ECR 679; [1975] 2 CMLR 424.
(**34**)   [1976] ECR 1901.

national laws alone (*Case 112/76, Manzoini v. Fonds National de Retraite*) (35), and this principle was used by the Court to declare Article 46(3) of Regulation 1408/71 invalid when it required a reduction of benefits due to overlap. In interpreting Article 76 of the Regulation the Court held in *Case 24/88, Michel Georges v. ONAFTS* (36) that if the amount of the family allowances actually paid in the Member State of residence was less than that provided for under legislation of another Member State, the worker was entitled to a supplementary allowance equal to the difference between the two amounts, the cost of which is to be borne by the institutions of the other Member State. However the Court held in *Case 313/86, Lenoir v. Caisse d'Allocations Familiales des Alpes-Maritimes* (37) that the terms of Article 77 of the Regulation call for payment by the country of origin of "family allowances" only to the exclusion of other family benefits such as the schooling expenses allowance and single wage allowance provided for by the legislation of the country of origin. Voluntary or contributory insurance has been treated similarly to compulsory insurance in relation to the recognition of insurance periods completed in another Member State. In *Cases 82/86 and 103/86, Laborero and Sabato v. OSSOM* (38) the Court found a voluntary insurance scheme brought the insured person's survivor within the terms of Regulation 1408/71, even if the benefits provided by national rules were based on periods of employment in non-Member States.

8.14 An Administrative Commission on Security for Migrant Workers consisting of one representative of each Member State deals with co-ordination and administration in connection with the implementation of the Community rules on social security and gives (without prejudice to normal recourse to the courts) interpretation of the Community regulations, which are however not legally binding. It also establishes model forms and documents, provides a clearing system for balances of sums due among the various systems and calculates the sums due. Regulation 1408/71 has supplemented this Commission with an Advisory Committee on Social Security for Migrant Workers composed, in addition to two government representatives from each Member State, of two representatives of trade unions and similarly two representatives of employers' organisations. The Committee examines general questions and questions of principle arising under Article 51, formulates opinions for the Administrative Commission and makes proposals for revisions of

(35) [1977] ECR 1647; [1978] 2 CMLR 416.
(36) Not yet reported.
(37) Not yet reported.
(38) [1987] ECR 3401.

the applicable regulations. It is this machinery which resulted in the provision of a degree of free medical care for Community nationals on short visits to other Member States, in addition to provision for migrant workers. The scheme covers dependants whatever their nationality and whether or not they travel alone. The scheme is invoked in the United Kingdom by the issue and production of Form E 111, obtained from the local social security office.

CHAPTER 9
Social Policy

9.01 Title III of the EEC Treaty, under the heading Social Policy, deals with social provisions in its Chapter 1 and the European Social Fund in Chapter 2. The social provisions deal with differing aspects of working conditions in the Community and contain only two specific legislative provisions in Articles 119 and 120, dealing with equal pay for men and women and holidays with pay respectively. The Chapter begins in Article 117 with the belief in the harmonisation of improved working conditions and improved standard of living for workers. Article 118 sets the task for the Commission of promoting closer co-operation between Member States in the social field, particularly in employment, labour law and working conditions, vocational training, social security, prevention of occupational accidents and diseases, occupational hygiene and the right of association and collective bargaining. The Single European Act added an Article 118a which calls for directives to obtain minimum requirements for harmonisation of improved conditions in the area of health and safety of workers.

Sex discrimination and equal pay

9.02 Articles 119 and 120 represent what may be termed labour law provisions which deal in precise terms with two narrowly drawn requirements. Article 119 provides that each Member State shall during the first stage ensure and subsequently maintain the application of the principle that men and women should receive equal pay for equal work. For the purpose of this Article "pay" means the ordinary basic or minimum wage or salary and any other consideration, whether in cash or in kind, which the worker receives, directly or indirectly, in respect of his employment from the employer. Equal pay without discrimination based on sex means: (a) that pay for the same work at piece rate shall be calculated on the basis of the same unit of measurement; (b) that pay for work at time rates shall be the same for the same job. The Article thus requires each Member State to achieve equal pay during the first stage (i.e. by 1 January 1962) and to maintain it thereafter.

9.03 It was not till 1975 that the Council enacted Directive 75/117 (1) on the approximation of laws of the Member States relating to the application of the principle of equal pay for men and women. Accordingly equal pay must be given not only for identical work but for comparable work, work to which equal value is attributed. This concept was considered by the Court of Justice in *Case 129/79, Macarthys Ltd v. Wendy Smith* (2), where the Court ruled that equal pay must be considered in relation to workers performing the same work in succession, the comparison not necessarily involving the same work at the same time. Whether the discrimination is based on sex or other factors is a question of fact for national courts to decide. In *Case 61/81, Commission v. United Kingdom* (3) the Court further stressed that the Directive required equal pay for work of equivalent value, the United Kingdom being at fault in not requiring job classification schemes at all times.

9.04 The interpretation of the provisions of the Directive has been overtaken by the decisions of the Court that Article 119 is of direct effect and self-executing. In *Case 43/75, Defrenne v. Sabena* (4) the Court ruled that Article 119 had become of direct effect at the end of the first stage and that employees could rely on it in proceedings in national courts against private employers. The Court further considered this Article on the basis of its being directly applicable in *Case 69/80, Worringham v. Lloyds Bank Ltd* (5) and *Case 96/80, Jenkins v. Kingsgate (Clothing Productions) Ltd* (6). The latter case suggests that Article 119 might be directly applicable even if the pay differentials were not identical. The former case indicated that fringe benefits are taken into account in defining wages. Considering private pension schemes, the Court decided in *Case 19/81, Burton v. British Railways Board* (7) that early retirement for women did not contravene equal pay provisions since Article 119 is only concerned with remuneration and not access to benefits. The same principle that Article 119 is not concerned with the access to pensions was repeated in *Case 275/81, Koks v. Raad van Arbeid.* (8)

9.05 The Court reiterated in *Case 170/84, Bilka Kaufhaus GmbH v. K. Weber von Hartz* (9) that occupational pension schemes are covered by

(1) OJ 1975 L 45/19.
(2) [1980] ECR 1275; [1980] 2 CMLR 205.
(3) [1982] ECR 2601; [1982] 3 CMLR 284.
(4) [1976] ECR 455; [1976] 2 CMLR 98.
(5) [1981] ECR 767; [1981] 2 CMLR 1.
(6) [1981] ECR 911; [1981] 2 CMLR 24.
(7) [1982] ECR 555; [1982] 2 CMLR 136.
(8) [1982] ECR 3013; [1982] 1 CMLR 626.
(9) [1985] ECR 1607.

Article 119 and where the scheme did not cover part-time workers who were mainly women this amounted to indirect discrimination. Again in *Case 171/88, Ingrid Rinner-Kuhn v. FWW Spezial-Gebäudereinigung GmbH & Co* (10) the Court ruled that the exclusion of part-time employees from the continued payment of wages during illness, where this affects a far greater number of women than men, would be interpreted as being contrary to Article 119, unless it could be shown that it was justified by objective factors unrelated to any discrimination on grounds of sex. However all benefits which have economic value must be considered as pay (*Case 12/81, Garland v. British Rail Engineering*) (11). Thus special travel facilities after retirement for male employees amount to discrimination under Article 119 when these facilities are denied to female employees.

9.06   Where a pay system is characterised by a total lack of transparency, the employer bears the burden of proof of demonstrating that the pay system was not in fact discriminatory. In *Case 109/88, Handels- og Kontorfunktionarernes Forbund I Danmark v. Dansk Arbejdsgiverforening* (11a) the system of individual increments applied to basic pay was operated in such a way that it was impossible for a female worker to identify the reasons for a difference between her pay and that of a male worker. The employer was bound to show how he had applied the incremental criteria and would therefore make his pay scheme transparent.

9.07   The principles enshrined in the Treaty and Article 119 were further given effect in Directive 76/207 (12) on the implementation of the principle of equal treatment for men and women as regards access to employment, vocational training and promotion, and working conditions; in Directive 79/7 (13) on the progressive implementation of the principle of equal treatment for men and women in matters of social security (these two directives being based on Article 235 of the Treaty). The Court considered these two directives in joined *Cases 48/88, 106/88 and 107/88, Acterberg-ye-Riele and others v. Sociale Verzekeringsbank* (14), holding that their purpose (and that of Article 119) was to bring about equal treatment to men and women, not in a general way but solely in their capacity as workers. Directive 86/613 (15) governs the

(10)   Not yet reported.
(11)   [1982] ECR 359; [1982] 1 CMLR 696.
(11a)   Not yet reported.
(12)   OJ 1976 L 39/40.
(13)   OJ 1979 L 6/24.
(14)   Not yet reported.
(15)   OJ 1986 L 359/56.

application of the principle of equal treatment between self-employed men and women and deals with the protection of self-employed women during pregnancy and motherhood. Directive 86/378 (16) governs the implementation of the principle of equal treatment in occupational social security schemes which are defined as schemes not covered by Directive 79/7. (13)

9.08 These directives gave rise to some questions which were to be decided by the Court of Justice. The Court ruled in the case of *Burton*, (7) dealing with a voluntary scheme with differing retirement dates for men and women, that the scheme fell to be considered under Directive 76/207 (12). The fact of differing pensionable age for men and women did not amount to discrimination under the Directive. In *Case 151/84, Roberts v. Tate and Lyle Industries* (17) the Court found that a provision laying down a single age for dismissal with an early retirement pension (where normal retirement for men and women differed) did not consititute discrimination on the ground of sex. In *Case 152/84, Marshall v. Southampton and South West Hampshire Area Health Authority* (18) the Court decided that a Member State could set differing pensionable ages, but this did not entitle an employer to dismiss a woman who reached the normal retiring age for women but not for men. It is significant that the Court ruled that the provisions of the Directive (requiring Member States to prohibit discrimination on the grounds of sex with regard to working conditions and dismissal) were available to an individual in proceedings against the State. The extent to which a Member State is allowed to derogate from the Directive was considered in *Case 222/84, Johnston v. Chief Constable of the Royal Ulster Constabulary* (19). The right of women members of RUC to handle and use firearms could be limited by Article 2(2) of the Directive (12) in the policing arrangements relating to public safety. The requirement for maternity leave does not extend to fathers (*Case 184/83 Ulrich Hoffman v. Barmer Ersatzkasse*) (20).

9.09 In the United Kingdom the principle of equal pay is governed by the Equal Pay Act 1970, as amended, and the Sex Discrimination Act 1975, as amended. However the Equal Pay Act 1970 has been found by the Court of Justice not to satisfy fully the requirements of the equal pay Directive (1) and it ruled that each Member State must endow an

(16) OJ 1986 L 225/40.
(17) [1986] ECR 703; [1986] 1 CMLR 714.
(18) [1986] ECR 723; [1986] 1 CMLR 688.
(19) [1986] ECR 1651; [1986] 3 CMLR 240.
(20) [1984] ECR 3047; [1986] 1 CMLR 242.

authority with the powers to decide whether the work has the same value as other work (*Commission v. United Kingdom*) (3). This led to amendment of the Act by the Equal Pay (Amendment) Regulations 1983. Reference should also be made to the Industrial Tribunals (Rules of Procedure) (Equal Value Amendment) Regulation 1983. Complaints of breach of equal treatment are placed before an industrial tribunal. The Equal Opportunities Commission established under the 1975 Act supervises equal pay and may assist persons to establish their rights.

9.10 Sex discrimination is governed by the Sex Discrimination Act 1975. The legislation providing for an exception for firms employing five persons or fewer and for domestic service was found to be in breach of Community law by the Court of Justice in *Case 165/83, Commission v. United Kingdom* (21) which also found the exception for midwives to be lawful. The Sex Discrimination Act 1986 gave effect to the ruling of the Court in the case of *Marshall* (18). Protection of the employment of women during pregnancy and after giving birth is further afforded in the United Kingdom by the Employment Protection (Consolidation) Act 1978. In the case of *Brown v. Stockton-on-Tees Borough Council* (22) the House of Lords held that pregnancy should not affect reasons for redundancy.

Protection of employment

9.11 This Act also implements Directive 75/129 (23) which deals with arrangements for collective redundancies. Directive 77/187 (24) further safeguards employees' rights in cases of transfer of businesses and is implemented in the United Kingdom by the Transfer of Undertakings (Protection of Employment) Regulations 1981. The Directive was considered in *Case 101/87, P. Bork International A/S v. Foreningen af Arbejdsledere i Denmark* (25), the Court of Justice holding that the Directive applied where the workforce dismissed before the transfer could claim the benefit of the Directive against the transferee. Both the Directive and the United Kingdom Regulations were reviewed by the House of Lords in the case of *Lister and others v. Forth Dry Dock and Engineering Co. and another* (26), where it was held that the Regulations must be read to give effect to the Directive and an employee dismissed shortly before the transfer of a business for a reason connected with the

(21) [1983] ECR 3431; [1984] 1 CMLR 44.
(22) [1988] 2 WLR 935.
(23) OJ 1975 L 48/29.
(24) OJ 1977 L 61/26.
(25) Not yet reported.
(26) Not yet reported.

transfer was deemed to have been a person employed immediately before the transfer and to have been unfairly dismissed (and if the transferor was insolvent the liabilities to the employee were transferred to the transferee). Directive 80/987 (27), amended by Directive 87/164 (28), deals with the protection of employees on the insolvency of the employer.

9.12 Article 120 of the Treaty simply states that Member States shall endeavour to maintain the existing equivalence between paid holiday schemes. The actual impact of the Article appears to be limited since the tendency in all Member States is to increase paid holidays. Articles 121 and 122 of the Treaty indicate the part to be played by the Commission in the harmonisation of social conditions. Under Article 121 the Council may assign to the Commission tasks in connection with the implementation of common measures, particularly as regards social security for migrant workers referred to in Articles 48 to 51. The only implementing act refers to arrangements for the Secretariat for the Administrative Commission for the Social Security of Migrant Workers. Article 122 requires the Commission to include a section on social affairs in its annual report to the European Parliament and does not call for any implementing measures.

The European Social Fund

9.13 Article 3 of the Treaty states that the activities of the Community shall include, as provided in the Treaty: "(i) the creation of a European Social Fund in order to improve employment opportunities for workers and to contribute to the raising of their standard of living". Article 123 establishes the Fund, giving it the task of rendering the employment of workers easier and of increasing their geographical and occupational mobility within the Community. The Fund is to be administered by the Commission assisted by a Committee (Article 124). Article 125 sets out cases where reimbursement may be granted for expenditures by the Member States. They are limited to occupational retraining, resettlement allowances and conversion of enterprises. After the end of the transitional period the Council may under Article 126 cease assistance under Article 125 or entrust to the Fund new tasks within the framework of Article 123.

9.14 A reform of the Fund first took place by Decision 71/66 (29) and secondary legislation following from it. This proved inadequate and so the structure of the Fund was recreated in a simpler form by Decision

(27)   OJ 1980 L 283/23.
(28)   OJ 1987 L 666/11.
(29)   OJ 1971 L 28/15.

83/516 (30). This decision sets out the tasks of the Fund. Regulation 2950/83 (31) deals with its implementation and Decision 83/673 (32) with the management of the Fund. Regulation 3824/85 (33) amends Regulation 2950/83, extending it to self-employed persons. The assistance under Article 125 is no longer granted and Decision 71/66 (29) is repealed. The Fund is now concerned to assist in equipping the workforce with the skills for stable employment and generating employment opportunities, bearing in mind young people and disadvantaged workers, technological changes and regional imbalances. The Commission, following Decision 83/516 (30), also adopted guidelines for the management of the Fund (the latest for 1987 to 1989). Assistance under the Fund is granted to operations carried out by public and private bodies. All applications for assistance are to be submitted through the appropriate national authority, which for the United Kingdom is the Department of Employment. Once the assistance is granted the Commission may carry out checks on the operation under the terms of the Regulation 2950/83. (31)

(30) OJ 1983 L 289/38.
(31) OJ 1983 L 289/1.
(32) OJ 1983 L 377/1.
(33) OJ 1985 L 370/25.

CHAPTER 10

Freedom of Establishment for Professions and Businesses

Freedom of establishment

10.01 The right of establishment, that is the right of business enterprises to move and set up shop across frontiers and the right to conduct non-salaried economic activities, is provided for in Articles 52–58 of the EEC Treaty. These activities are specified in Article 52 of the Treaty, which provides for the abolition by progressive stages of restrictions on the freedom of establishment of nationals of a Member State in the territory of another Member State. The right of establishment covers not only the activities themselves but also activities incidental to the main ones, and covers the setting up of agencies, branches and subsidiaries. The right of establishment includes the right of nationals of other Member States to participate in existing firms or companies on the same conditions as nationals of the host state. This right also comprises the right of entry and residence of nationals of other Member States in the territory of the regulating State in so far as entry and residence are necessary for the performance of economic activity.

10.02 Article 52, which provides for the abolition of restrictions based on nationality, has been held by the Court of Justice to have direct effect; it ruled in *Case 2/74, Reyner v. Kingdom of Belgium* (1) that the requirement of national treatment had become self-executing at the end of the transitional period (1 January 1970), so that it had to be given effect by all national administrative authorities and courts. The same principle applies to new Member States since their respective dates of accession (*Case 11/77, Patrick v. Ministre des Affaires Culturelles*) (2). The Court again emphasised in *Case 221/85, Commission v. Belgium* (3) that Article 52 is intended to ensure that self-employed persons are treated in another Member State in the same way as nationals of that Member State and prohibits any discrimination based on nationality. Article 52 does not limit in any way the obligation of Member States to abolish any national rules which are discriminatory (*Case 159/78,*

(1) [1974] ECR 631; [1974] 2 CMLR 305.
(2) [1977] ECR 1199; [1977] 2 CMLR 523.
(3) [1987] ECR 719; [1988] 1 CMLR 620.

Commission v. Italy) (4). The right of establishment entitles a national of a Member State to pursue his activity in another Member State under the conditions laid down by law for the nationals of that country. The right of establishment applies, in relation to his home State, to a national of a Member State who has been resident in another Member State and subsequently returns to the State of his nationality (*Case 115/78, Knoors v. Secretary of State for Economic Affairs*) (5). The rules on the right of establishment cover not only Community nationals, but also members of their families who want to join them (*Case 48/75, Royer*). (6)

10.03 Article 53 of the Treaty prohibits the introduction of any new restrictions on the right of establishment. In *Case 6/64, Costa v. ENEL* (7) the Court ruled that this provision had direct effect. It also held that the Article was satisfied if no new and more onerous requirements were imposed than those applicable to nationals.

10.04 Article 54 provides for the implementation of the Treaty establishment provisions by means of a General Programme (8) and the enactment of directives. The Article sets out a number of guidelines which the Council and the Commission should follow in enacting the implementing directives. There are guidelines as to time schedules, the right of establishment of migrant workers, acquisition and use of real property, the right to set up agencies, branches and subsidiaries, the abolition of subsidies and standardisation of company law in relation to shareholders' and creditors' protection. The judgments of the Court of Justice in relation to the direct applicability of the Treaty provisions concerned with restrictions on nationality have rendered the number of required directives smaller than it would have been, but the number of enacted directives is still very large, covering a wide range of activities of economic life.

10.05 The directives deal with the right of establishment and the right to supply services (See para. 10.12 below.) Under Directive 64/220 (9), concerned with the removal of restrictions on entry and residence of nationals of the Member States, such persons had to be admitted to any Member State for the purpose of establishment or the provision of services upon presentation of a passport or national identity card. No

(4) [1979] ECR 3247; [1980] 3 CMLR 446.
(5) [1979] ECR 399; [1979] 2 CMLR 357.
(6) [1976] ECR 497; [1976] 2 CMLR 619.
(7) [1964] ECR 585; [1964] CMLR 426.
(8) OJ 1962 2/36.
(9) OJ 1964 O 56/845.

visa might be required and the same applied to relatives of the persons concerned. This Directive is replaced by Directive 73/148 (10) but the changes are minor. Directive 73/148 (10) was the subject of the ruling by the Court of Justice in *Case 81/87, The Queen v. HM Treasury and Commissioners of Inland Revenue ex parte Daily Mail and General Trust PLC* (11) that, properly construed, it confers no right on a company to transfer its central management and control to another Member State.

Freedom to pursue specific occupations

10.06 Business activities are subject of directives in this context: Directive 64/222 (12) and Directive 64/223 (13) deal with activities in wholesale trade, and Directive 68/363 (14) and Directive 68/364 (15) with activities of self-employed persons in retail trade. The coal trade (Directives 70/522 (16) and 70/523) (17) and trade in toxic products (Directives 74/556 (18) and 74/557) (19) are singled out. Self-employed commercial agents are the subject of Directive 86/653 (20). A wide range of directives dealing with particular types of business and profession has now been established. Included among them are:

ARCHITECTS, covered by Directive 85/384 (21)
DENTISTS, covered by Directives 78/686 (22) and 78/687 (23)
DOCTORS, covered by Directives 75/362 (24), 75/363 (25) and 86/457 (26)
NURSES, subject to Directives 77/452 (27) and 77/453 (28); and
VETERINARY SURGEONS, subject to Directives 78/1026 (29) and 78/1027 (30).

(10) OJ 1973 L 172/14.
(11) [1988] 3 CMLR 713.
(12) OJ 1964 O 56/857.
(13) OJ 1964 O 56/863.
(14) OJ 1968 L 260/1.
(15) OJ 1968 L 160/6.
(16) OJ 1970 L 267/14.
(17) OJ 1970 L 267/18.
(18) OJ 1974 L 307/1.
(19) OJ 1974 L 307/5.
(20) OJ 1986 L 382/17.
(21) OJ 1985 L 223/15.
(22) OJ 1978 L 233/1.
(23) OJ 1978 L 233/10.
(24) OJ 1975 L 167/1.
(25) OJ 1975 L 167/14.
(26) OJ 1986 L 267/26.
(27) OJ 1977 L 176/1.
(28) OJ 1977 L 176/8.
(29) OJ 1978 L 362/1.
(30) OJ 1978 L 362/7.

Directive 81/1057 (31) completes the above directives relating to doctors, nurses, dentists and veterinary surgeons. There are directives dealing with midwives (80/154 (32) and 80/155) (33) and pharmacists (85/432 (34) and 85/433). (35)

10.06.1 All these directives deal with mutual recognition of formal qualifications to facilitate the effective exercise of the right of establishment and freedom to provide services as well as dealing with these two freedoms. Other directives deal with freedom of establishment in farming, hairdressing, industry and commerce, transport, the film industry and many other occupations. Personal services in restaurants, cafés, taverns, hotels and rooming houses are subject to Directives 68/367 (36) and 68/368 (37) and Directive 70/451 (38) deals with freedom to provide services by self-employed persons in film production. Goods haulage operation is governed by Directive 74/561 (39) and passenger transport operation by Directive 74/562 (40). Mutual recognition of their qualifications is governed by Directive 77/796 (41). Directive 87/540 (42) deals with the occupation of a carrier of goods by waterway. Insurance brokers and agents are dealt with in Directive 77/92 (43) and hairdressers in Directive 82/489. (44)

Lawyers
10.07 Lawyers are governed by Directive 77/249 (45). This Directive was the subject of *Case 427/85, Commission v. Federal Republic of Germany* (46), where the Federal Republic was found to be in breach of the terms of the Directive by requiring in the circumstances of that case the involvement of a German lawyer in addition to the lawyer from another Member State. The Court also held in *Case 292/86, Claude Gullung v. Conseil de L'Ordre du Barreau de Colmar et al.* (47) that the Directive could not be relied upon by a lawyer who was established in one Member State in order to be permitted to provide legal services in

(31)   OJ 1981 L 385/25.
(32)   OJ 1980 L 33/1.
(33)   OJ 1980 L 33/8.
(34)   OJ 1985 L 253/34.
(35)   OJ 1985 L 253/37.
(36)   OJ 1968 L 260/16.
(37)   OJ 1968 L 260/19.
(38)   OJ 1970 L 218/37.
(39)   OJ 1974 L 308/18.
(40)   OJ 1974 L 308/23.
(41)   OJ 1977 L 334/37.
(42)   OJ 1987 L 322/20.
(43)   OJ 1977 L 26/14.
(44)   OJ 1982 L 218/24.
(45)   OJ 1977 L 78/17.
(46)   [1989] 2 CMLR 677.
(47)   [1988] 2 CMLR 57.

another Member State where he had been barred from access to the profession for reasons relating to dignity, good reputation and integrity. The Court further reiterated the principle (already stated in the *Case 115/78, Knoors*) (5) that the Directive must apply without discrimination to nationals of all Member States who satisfy the conditions for its application. A state cannot deny its application to its own nationals who are established in another Member State of which they are also a national.

10.08 All these provisions must be read together with Article 57 of the Treaty. Article 57 (1) provides that the Council shall issue directives for mutual recognition of diplomas, certificates and other evidence of qualifications. The Court of Justice held in the *Case 71/76 Thieffry v. Conseil de l'Ordre des Avocats* (48) that in the absence of Community directives on mutual recognition of qualifications, if a person wishes to practise his profession in a Member State other than his own, and passes the professional examination in the host state, he must be admitted to do so even if his basic degree is regarded by the state in question as equivalent for academic purposes only. Such a limitation on equivalence cannot justify refusal to admit the applicant to practise and the Member State must apply their law taking into account the requirement of Community law. In this case it was held that completion of Belgian law studies entitled a Belgian student to take the French bar examination. The same principle was applied to a veterinary surgeon with an Italian diploma who wanted to establish himself in France before the enactment of a directive. (*Case 136/78, Ministère Public v. Auer*) (49). The principles enunciated by Articles 52, 54 and 57 were upheld in *Case 107/83, Ordre des Avocats v. Klopp* (50), where the Court ruled that even in the absence of any Directive, Articles 52 *et seq.* prevent the authorities of a Member State from denying, in accordance with national provisions in force, to a national of another Member State the right to enter and to exercise the legal profession solely on the ground that he simultaneously maintains chambers in another Member State.

Other professions
10.09 However the position is clarified with the enactment of Directive 89/48 (51) on a general system for the recognition of higher education diplomas awarded on completion of professional education and training of at least three years' duration. This Directive does not apply to

(48)   [1977] ECR 765; [1977] 2 CMLR 373.
(49)   [1979] ECR 437; [1979] 2 CMLR 373.
(50)   [1984] ECR 2971; [1985] 1 CMLR 99.
(51)   OJ 1989 L 19/16.

professions which are the subject of separate Directives establishing arrangements for the mutual recognition of diplomas by Member States (Article 2). It introduces the concept of regulated professional activity which leads to a diploma or its equivalent; activity also qualifies as such if it is pursued by a member of an association or organisation which awards a diploma and ensures that its members respect the rules of professional conduct which it prescribes. The Annex to the Directive contains a non-exhaustive list of such associations, which in the case of the United Kingdom contains 38 entries, commencing with the Institutes of Chartered Accountants, proceeding through Institutes of Actuaries, Bankers and Energy and the Engineering Council and ending with the British Computer Society. The Directive deals in detail with any adaptation period, aptitude tests and procedures involved in exercising the profession in the host Member State. The Member States have to comply with the Directive by 4 January 1991. The Council further recommended by Recommendation 89/49 (52) that Member States should apply the provisions of the Directive to persons who hold diplomas or other formal qualifications awarded in a third State and are in a position comparable to one of those described in the Directive.

Exercise of official authority

10.10 Parallel to provisions of Article 48(4) in relation to the free movement of workers, Article 55 excludes from the right of establishment activities which are connected with the exercise of official authority. Article 55 should be construed narrowly (*Case 7/68, Commission v. Italy*) (53); it refers to specific activities and not to types of occupation. *Case 2/74, Reyner v. Belgium* (1) dealt with Article 55, stressing that the purpose of the Article is to exclude non-nationals from access to activities which involve the exercise of official authority and which are linked to an activity covered by Article 52. This purpose is served when the exclusion is limited to those activities which, taken in themselves, constitute a direct and specific participation in official authority. The extension of the exception to a whole profession is only permissible if the activities concerned constitute an element which is not separable from the entire professional activity concerned. The Directive dealing with the provision of services by lawyers (77/249 (45)) allows for Article 55 in excluding certain groups with activities exercising public authority who have a monopoly and whose numbers are limited (e.g. notaries in some Member States). In the United Kingdom the Directive excludes from its

(52) OJ 1989 L 19/24.
(53) [1968] ECR 423; [1969] CMLR 1.

provisions by virtue of Article 55 and on the same basis solicitors concerned with conveyancing.

10.11 The general exception of this Article is complemented by the more specific exceptions of Article 56, which on grounds of public policy, public security and public health also permits Member States to derogate from the principle of freedom of establishment. Article 56 reflects similar provisions concerning the free movement of workers (Article 48(3)) and the directives enacted in pursuance of Article 56 reflect these principles. The first directive implementing the Article, Directive 64/221 (54), as extended by Directive 75/35 (55), deals with nationals who are employed, self-employed or rendering a service, and their dependants. In pursuance of Article 56(2) it provides for the co-ordination of national provisions on the derogations of freedom of establishment and freedom to provide services. This Directive and the issues involved are dealt with in greater detail in Chapter 8 on freedom of movement of workers and Article 48(3). The social security legislation extends to self-employed persons and the legislation now covers employed persons and self-employed persons in one instrument (see para 8.11). Directive 75/34 (56) is concerned with the rights of nationals of a Member State to remain in the territory of another Member State after having pursued therein an activity in a self-employed capacity.

Provision of services

10.12 Article 59 provides that restrictions on freedom to provide services within the Community should be abolished in respect of nationals of Member States who are established in a State of the Community other than that of the person for whom the services are intended. The Article also enables the Community to extend the provisions on services to nationals of a third country who provide services and who are established within the Community.

10.13 The non-discriminatory restrictions are not affected. The General Programme for the Abolition of the Restrictions on the Freedom to Provide Services (57) indicates that this involves abolition of regulations which, though applicable regardless of nationality, in fact restrict predominantly the furnishing of services by foreign nationals. Restrictions on the transfer of funds to pay for services are also to be

(54)   OJ 1964 56/850.
(55)   OJ 1975 L 14/14.
(56)   OJ 1975 L 14/10.
(57)   OJ 1962 2/32.

eliminated. *Case 36/74, Walrave & Koch v. Union Cycliste* (58) would imply that in certain circumstances discrimination by a private individual may be covered. This case and *Case 33/74, Van Binsbergen v. Bestuur van de Bedrijfsvereniging* (59) indicate that Article 59, after the end of the transitional period in 1970, now has direct effect.

10.14 Article 60 defines services as "services" within the meaning of the Treaty where they are normally provided for renumeration, in so far as they are not governed by the provisions relating to freedom of movement for goods, capital and persons. "Services" include activities of an industrial or commercial character, and activities of craftsmen and of the professions. The article states that a person providing a service may, in order to do so, temporarily pursue his activity in the State where the service is provided under the same conditions as are imposed by that State on its own nationals. Article 62 prevents Member States from introducing any new restrictions on the freedom to provide services and it has direct effect. Article 63, calling for a general programme, has been implemented by the General Programme (57). It has also been implemented by the actions of the Community in the field of the right of establishment and services and in addition by Directive 63/340 (60) on currency transfers where the services are limited only by restrictions on payments relating to them. Films form the subject of a directive under this Article (Directive 65/264). (61)

10.15 Article 66 applies the provisions of Articles 55 to 58 to the chapter on services. Services and establishment are closely related and at times it is difficult to distinguish between the two, particularly so in the case of the professions which are already governed by legislation under the right of establishment.

(58)   [1974] ECR 1405; [1975] 1 CMLR 320.
(59)   [1974] ECR 1299; [1975] 1 CMLR 298.
(60)   OJ 1963 64/31.
(61)   OJ 1965 85/1437.

CHAPTER 11

Taxation

Introduction

11.01 Customs duties and agricultural levies are charged on import into the Community (or in some cases on export from it), and constitute a fiscal fence within which the Community economy operates. They represent fully fledged Community taxes, imposed and varied by the Community legislature, and are the subject of directly applicable Regulations. Member States, however, impose taxation which is known as *internal taxation*. All types of internal taxation—an expression often interpreted widely to include any charge or levy which is compulsorily payable—are subject to the Treaty rules and to the general principles of Community law. Taxes charged by each Member State on the supply, production or import of goods are the types of internal tax most likely to be affected by the specific rules in Articles 95 to 99.

Fiscal neutrality

11.02 The principle of fiscal neutrality requires that tax legislation should as far as possible operate so as not to distort economic activity. It flows from the concept of a single market economy, and in Community law it manifests itself in a number of different contexts. It is seen first as one of the implications of the general prohibition against discrimination on grounds of nationality in Article 7 of the Treaty. Secondly, it is an underlying feature of the harmonised system of value added tax, which in general aims to be neutral as between different types of business activity. Thirdly, it is seen in the provisions of Articles 95–99 specifically on indirect taxation, which interlock with the prohibition in Articles 12 and 30 against customs duties and quantitative restrictions in trade between Member States. And finally, it is reflected in the Court's approach to tax avoidance.

(1) *Nationality discrimination*
11.03 Taking the broad concept of "tax" as any charge payable compulsorily, the Court held in *Case 293/83, Gravier v. City of Liège* (1),

(1) [1985] ECR 606; [1985] 3 CMLR 1.

that the imposition upon students from another Member State of a special tax for attending a vocational training course, which was not payable by Belgian nationals, was contrary to Article 7, and therefore recoverable by the students who had paid it. By contrast, a Member State which chooses to tax national production more heavily than imports does not infringe Community law: *Case 86/78, Grandes Distilleries Peureux* (2).

(2) Value added tax

11.04 The concept of value added tax is that of a turnover tax which discriminates as little as possible between one form of economic activity and another, and between businesses in one Member State and another; (3) it is thus in principle applicable to all supplies of goods or services, except those which are exempted, rather than being applicable only to defined categories of supply. It is, in its harmonised form, entirely compatible with the principles of Article 95 because it is levied on imported goods on the same basis, and at the same rate, as upon internally supplied goods. The following illustrations show how this concept has influenced the Court's approach to questions of construction of the Community legislation.

11.05 In *Case 269/86, Mol v. Inspecteur der Invoerrechten en Accijnzen* (4) and *Case 294/82, Einberger v. Hauptzollamt Freiburg*, (5) the question arose whether value added tax should be charged in one case on the supply, and in the other case on the import, of illegal drugs. Noting that the principle of tax neutrality opposed a general differentiation between lawful and unlawful transactions, the Court held that in the exceptional case of transactions which could in no circumstances be carried out lawfully no tax could be payable since the transactions were outside the contemplation of the Directive. In normal circumstances, therefore, neutrality requires that a breach of the law in the course of carrying out a transaction should not lead to its being treated differently for tax.

11.06 In *Case 50/88, Kuehne v. Finanzamt München* (6) the question arose whether depreciation on a car used by a lawyer, partly for professional use and partly for private use, could be charged to tax in circumstances in which the car had been acquired secondhand from a private individual, who had accordingly not charged tax on the price,

---

(2) [1979] ECR 897; [1980] 3 CMLR 337.
(3) Recitals to the First Directive 67/227 OJ English Special Edition, and to the Sixth Directive 77/388(29).
(4) (Not yet reported)
(5) [1984] ECR 1177; [1985] 1 CMLR 765.
(6) (Not yet reported).

and in respect of which therefore no input deduction could be claimed. Article 6(2) of the Sixth Directive on value added tax (7) provides that the use of goods forming part of the assets of a business by the taxable person for his private use is taxable if input tax on them is deductible. Member States, however, have the right to derogate from this provision on condition that the derogation does not lead to distortion of competition. But the Court held that the right to derogate from the rule in Article 6(2) could not be used to tax goods where the input on them was not deductible, since to do so would entail double taxation contrary to the principle of fiscal neutrality inherent in the Community system of value added tax.

(3) *The structure of internal taxation on goods*
11.07   It is in the context of the Treaty rules on internal taxation that the concept of fiscal neutrality has its clearest expression. The general principles are laid down in Articles 95 to 99, and in the extensive case law of the Court interpreting them. They are designed to prevent the effect of establishing the Customs Union and the Common Commercial Policy being lost as a consequence of Member States maintaining fiscal barriers to commerce within the Community. As noted above, the harmonised value added tax (established under the same Treaty chapter on taxation) complies with the basic requirements of a neutral tax; it is the first tax to do so to such a high degree, but Article 99 envisages similar harmonisation of excise duties and other indirect taxes.

11.08   Full harmonisation will involve approximating rates and the elimination of special derogations, matters which have not yet been achieved even in relation to value added tax. Very limited steps have been taken in relation to excise duty harmonisation by two directives on tobacco duties, Directive 72/464 (8) and Directive 79/32 (9). In the meantime, Articles 95 to 99 provide for internal taxation in which there is equality of treatment between goods from other Member States and similar or competing domestic products.

(4) *Equal taxation for similar products*
11.09   Article 95(1) prohibits Member States, directly or indirectly, imposing internal taxation on the products of other Member States in excess of that imposed on similar domestic products. Typically, but not always, taxation of goods from other Member States takes the form of import taxes which are designed to compensate for internal taxes on

(7)   OJ 1977 L 145/1.
(8)   OJ 1972 L 303/1, as last amended by Directive 86/246 OJ 1986 L 164/26.
(9)   OJ 1979 L 10/8.

home-produced goods. Although in this case the mechanism of charging at import may involve differences from that used for home produce: *Case 127/75, Bobie v. Hauptzollamt Aachen* (10), the effect of the prohibition is only that the burden of the charge may not be greater. In *Case 57/65, Lütticke v. Hauptzollamt Saarlouis* (11), Article 95(1) was held to have direct effect.

11.10 In an early decision which has been affirmed on many occasions, the Court in *Cases 2 & 3/62, Commission v. Belgium and Luxembourg* (12) laid down principles that: (a) an import charge with no internal counterpart would fall under Articles 9 and 12 on customs duties and charges having equivalent effect (see Chapter 3); and (b) an import charge would come under the provisions of Article 95 if a similar tax charge fell on national production. An internal charge for non-tax purposes would not justify an import charge by way of compensation. The concept of tax was given a wide interpretation (though consistent with the underlying objective of neutrality) in *Case 29/87, Dansk Denkavit Aps v. Landbrugs Ministeriet* (13), where it was held that a charge levied both on import and internally, for the purpose of financing the checking by the state of additives in feedingstuffs, satisfied the criteria of Article 95.

11.11 *Case 112/84, Delville v. Administration des Impôts* (14), illustrates the point that a discriminatory tax may not be chargeable at the moment of import. In that case, France levied a vehicle excise duty, by means of a licence displayed on the car, which was five times higher on cars with a capacity exceeding 16 cv than on those of a lower capacity. It happened that no cars of the higher capacity were made in France, and the Court held that the duty discriminated against products of other Member States (the car in question came from Italy) and was contrary to Article 95.

11.12 The case law on Article 95(1) has been considerable, dealing with the precise circumstances in which a charge falls under this Article or under Articles 9 and 12, the difficulties principally occurring on the identification of similar national products. This feature was considered in *Case 27/67, Fink-Frucht v. Hauptzollamt München* (15), where it was held that a guide to similarity was provided by the classification of

(10) [1976] ECR 1079.
(11) [1966] ECR 205; [1971] CMLR 674.
(12) [1962] ECR 425; [1963] CMLR 199.
(13) (Not yet reported).
(14) [1986] 2 CMLR 338.
(15) [1968] ECR 223; [1968] CMLR 228.

goods under the same fiscal, customs or statistical heading; the Court also commented that the absence of any item as a domestic product was not of itself a reason why the Member State should not impose a tax on it, even though the only goods to bear the tax would be those of another Member State.

(5) *Equal taxation for competing products*

11.13 Article 95(2), which has also been held to have direct effect (15), forbids the imposition of internal taxation on the products of other Member States of such a nature as to afford indirect protection to other products. This limb of the Article attacks taxes which cannot be said to be imposed on similar domestic products, and it marks the limit of a Member State's freedom to impose taxes at whatever level it wishes where there is no, or no significant, national production of the same item.

11.14 This is best illustrated by *Case 170/78, Commission v. United Kingdom* (16), in which the Commission successfully attacked the structure of British excise duties on wine and beer. The Court accepted that the two products were effectively in competition with each other, since consumers might in many circumstances choose to drink either, and it was established that the duty on wine was higher than that on beer. Wine being only to a minimal extent a home product, but beer a major domestic product, it followed that the effect of the level of duty on wine was to protect a domestic product (beer) against a competing product (wine) from other Member States. The taxation of wine produced in the United Kingdom at exactly the same rate as wine from elsewhere in the Community, while complying with Article 95(1), did not prevent the indirect protection of beer falling foul of Article 95(2).

(6) *Exports*

11.15 Article 96 permits repayment of internal tax on goods exported to other Member States, but makes it clear that the repayment must not exceed the amount of the internal taxation borne directly or indirectly. In *Case 45/64, Commission v. Italy* (17) the term "indirectly" was held not to include taxes borne by the business manufacturing the goods, but to be confined to taxes bearing on the goods themselves. Article 98, however, forbids export rebates (or countervailing charges on imports) of any direct tax, except as may be approved for a limited period by the council. When full harmonisation is achieved, indirect taxes will be

---

(16) [1983] ECR 2265; [1983] 3 CMLR 512.
(17) [1965] ECR 857; [1966] CMLR 97.

levied on a Community-wide basis and, at that point, export rebates and compensating import taxes will become unnecessary in intra-Community trade. Meanwhile, the Court held in *Case 142/77, Statens Kontrol med aedle Metaller v. Larsen* (18) that an export tax could infringe Article 95; but pending tax harmonisation, the Treaty contains no effective prohibition on double taxation on goods moving between Member States where, as in this case, domestic production and exports are taxed equally.

(7) *Tax avoidance*

11.16 Concern to ensure the neutral application of the tax provisions informed the Court's treatment of anti-avoidance provisions in *Cases 138 & 139/86, Direct Cosmetics v. Customs and Excise* (19). Here the question was whether Article 27 of Directive 77/388 ("the Sixth Directive") (7), allowing Member States to tax certain sales at market value, as opposed to the price at which they actually took place, was applicable. The provision was introduced to enable prevention of certain types of tax avoidance, but the facts of the case showed that the sales pattern in question existed for sound commercial reasons, unconnected with tax avoidance, though the effect was to avoid the full amount of tax that would have been payable but for it. The Court held that the intention of the taxpayer was irrelevant. What mattered was the objective fact of avoidance liable to prejudice the design of the tax as one in which the factors which might lead to distortions of competition at national and Community level were to be eliminated, and as a tax to be as neutral as possible covering all the stages of production and distribution.

11.17 In the field of international travel, where reliefs for travellers from excise and turnover taxes are provided under Directive 69/169, (20) the Court, in *Case 158/80, Rewe v. Hauptzollamt Kiel* (21), had to consider the effect of "butter cruises" in the Baltic Sea in which the passengers were able to buy butter tax-free and with the benefit of agricultural subsidies, and then to import the goods thus purchased free of tax. It held that the Directive must be interepreted as meaning that the reliefs were destined only for travellers coming from third countries and that, in the case of Community travellers, goods would only be eligible for the relief if they had been bought tax paid in a Member State.

(18)   [1978] ECR 1543; [1979] 2 CMLR 680.
(19)   [1988] STC 534.
(20)   OJ 1969 L 133/6, amended by Directive 87/197 OJ 1987 L 78/53.
(21)   [1981] ECR 1805; [1982] 1 CMLR 449.

11.18 In *Case 81/87, R. v. H. M. Treasury ex parte Daily Mail and General Trust plc*, (22) the taxpayer wished, for tax avoidance reasons, to move its residence to the Netherlands but was unable to do so under provisions of United Kingdom tax legislation which forbade a UK company to migrate outside the United Kingdom without Treasury consent. The Court held that this was not contrary to Articles 52–58 (guaranteeing the free right of establishment). Although *prima facie* a discrimination which was contrary to Article 58, the Court considered that, in the current state of Community law in which no provision had yet been made to regulate such a movement, the national restrictions in question were permissible. The object of the company's change of residence was, in any event, not a purpose for which freedom of establishment was provided.

Claims by taxpayers

11.19 It has been noted in Chapter 2 that, in relation to taxes and customs duties, the Court has developed a doctrine to deal with claims by taxpayers for reimbursement of taxes etc., paid to Member States but subsequently declared contrary to Community law. The Court affirmed in *Case 309/85, Barra v. Belgium and the City of Liège* (23), that unless it provides in a judgment indicating a tax's incompatibility with Community law that the judgment is to have prospective effect only, all payments of the wrongly levied tax in the past will in principle be reclaimable. The possibility of reclaim is, however, subject to two limitations.

11.20 The first concerns the way of making the repayment claim. This the Court has repeatedly affirmed must be by the national procedure and be governed by national time limits, there being as yet no Community provisions applicable. Nonetheless, Member States may not hedge that procedure round with so many limitations that, as a practical matter, it is impossible, or virtually impossible, for a taxpayer to make a repayment claim, even if the same restrictions apply to repayment claims where no element of Community law is involved: *Case 199/82, Amministrazione delle Finanze v. San Giorgio SpA* (24)

11.21 In *Case 240/87, Delville v. Administration des Impôts* (25), the taxpayer, who had imported a car from Italy, had paid tax on import

(22) [1988] 3 CMLR 713
(23) [1988] 2 CMLR 409.
(24) [1983] ECR 3595; [1985] 2 CMLR 658.
(25) (Not yet reported).

which the Court held was contrary to Article 95; after that decision, national legislation was introduced which had the effect of making back claims more difficult (and in M. Delville's case impossible). The Court ruled that Member States may not change the recovery rules to the detriment of the taxpayer in the aftermath of a decision by the Court from which it follows that a tax is contrary to Community law.

11.22 The second limitation concerns the doctrine, applicable in all cases of indirect taxation, of "passing on", under which a taxpayer's claim for repayment or remission may be refused by a Member State where the burden of the unlawful tax has been passed on to the taxpayer's customers. Member States are not obliged to adopt such a restriction but, if they do, it will also be subject to the rule that proof that there has been no passing on must not, in practical terms, be so difficult to provide that the right cannot effectively be relied upon. (24)

11.23 This permitted limitation may be affected by the decision of the Court in *Case 207/87, Weissgerber v. Finanzamt Neustadt* (26). In that case, it was held that an unimplemented provision of the Sixth Directive on value added tax (7), exempting credit negotiators from the tax, could be relied upon by the plaintiff as having direct effect. The taxpayer was accordingly not liable to be assessed for tax on credit commission, *provided* he had not passed the tax on to persons following him in the chain of supply by charging the tax as such. It was thus only in the case of the taxpayer having charged tax on the supply to his customer, and the customer being able to claim an input tax credit, that the taxpayer could be held to have passed on the burden of the tax.

Duties on capital

11.24 Indirect taxes affecting the movement of capital have been the subject of some degree of harmonisation in regard to duties on capital and share or stock certificates. Directive 69/335 (27) seeks to align provisions throughout the Community on company capital duty, and stamp duty on loan stock and shares, with a view to facilitating the free movement of capital and avoiding double taxation. The rules on capital duty apply to *capital companies*, which are defined as companies incorporated with limited liability, and any other profit-making bodies subjected to capital duty in a Member State.

(26)   (Not yet reported).
(27)   OJ Eng. Spec. Ed. Vol. 11, p. 17, as amended by Directives 73/79 OJ 1973 L 103/13; 74/553 OJ 1974 L 303/9, and 85/303 OJ 1985 L 156/23.

11.25   The basic principle therefore is that capital duty is payable once only and in one place only. This is to be in the Member State in which a capital company has its effective centre of management at the relevant time. Necessarily there are rules to cover cases in which effective management is outside the Community. Thus, where the company's registered office is within the Community, the state where that office is located is the one in which capital duty is levied; and where a company has a branch within the Community, but has both its registered office and its effective managment outside, the state where the branch has capital made available to it is the one in which duty may be levied.

11.26   The events which attract payment of duty in relation to a capital company are: incorporation or an increase in capital; the transfer of either effective management or registered office to the Community, when the other remains in a third country and the company is regarded as a capital company in the place of arrival; the transfer of either effective management from one Member State to another where the company is regarded as a capital company in the state to which transfer has been made, but is not so considered in the first Member State; the transfer, from one Member State to another, of the registered office where the effective centre of management remains outside the Community, and the company is regarded as a capital company in the state to which the transfer has been made, but is not so considered in the first Member State. Certain other operations taxed at 1% on 1 July 1984 may also continue to be subject to duty (see below).

11.27   Articles 5 and 6 of the directive lay down the permissible bases for the calculation of the duty, leaving some latitude to Member States: they are also given discretion with regard to charging duty at higher rates or granting exemptions for reasons of fiscal equity, social reasons or to take account of special situations—in this event, the Commission must be warned, and Article 102 of the Treaty applies. Subject to this, any dutiable event which on 1 July 1984 was exempt, or was taxed at a rate not exceeding 0.5%, is to be exempt thereafter. For the rest, the maximum rate of duty may not exceed 1%, and there are specific optional exemptions for public utility companies controlled by public authorities, and those pursuing only cultural, welfare or educational objectives.

11.28   Next, the directive prohibits any form of taxation on the creation, issue, or admission to a stock exchange of, or on any dealings with, stocks, shares, or certificates representing them, debentures or other negotiable securities, or in relation to the events which attract capital duty. Article 12, however, permits a number of derogations from these prohibitions (28). Thus, Member States are allowed to charge duty on transfers of securities (at a flat rate or *ad valorem*); duty on the transfer to a company or firm of businesses or immoveable property situated within the same state; duty on the transfer of any other assets to a company or firm for a consideration other than shares in the business; and duty on the creation, registration or discharge of mortgages or other charges. Also permitted are duties paid by way of fees or dues, and value added tax. The permitted duties may be levied irrespective of where the registered office or effective centre of management of the company or firm is located, provided that such duties are no greater than those applicable to like transactions in the Member State in question.

Value added tax

11.29   Value added tax is the harmonised form of the turnover tax now applicable throughout the Community, and it represents the vanguard of the tax harmonisation envisaged in Article 99 of the Treaty. It satisfies the basic criteria of neutrality as between Member States, in that it bears equally on domestic and imported products. It is in contrast both to the previously common "cascade" taxes, in which tax was cumulated at each stage of production or supply, and to single stage taxes or excises. The basic feature of value added tax is that it is economically neutral as between long and short chains of supply from manufacturer to consumer. This is achieved by allowing a set-off at each stage of the tax paid on the supply preceding (input tax) against tax payable on the supply onwards (output tax). In this way, the overall burden of tax is determined by the value of the final taxable supply.

11.30   The bulk of the relevant Community legislation is to be found in the Sixth Directive (29), referred to in this section as "the directive". The Community law is extensively implemented in the United Kingdom by the Value Added Tax Act 1983, subsequent Finance Acts and orders and regulations made thereunder. Under Article 33 of the directive, value added tax is now the only form of turnover tax permitted in the Community; in *Cases 93 & 94/88, Wisselink* (30) the Court considered a tax in the Netherlands, chargeable on imported and newly produced

---

(28)   The derogations are exhaustive: *Case 15/88, Maxi Di v. Bolzano* (Not yet reported).
(29)   Directive 77/388 OJ 1977 L 145/1, as last amended by Directive 88/498 OJ 1988 L 269/54.
(30)   (Not yet reported).

passenger cars–similar to the United Kingdom car tax–and held that, being a single stage tax, it was not a turnover tax and thus escaped the prohibition on other turnover taxes.

(1) *Scope*
11.31 Article 2 of the directive lays down the four elements of the tax as it applies within each country. There must be (i) a supply of goods or services for consideration, (ii) within the terrritory of the country, (iii) by a taxable person, (iv) acting as such. The tax is also chargeable on the importation of goods to a Member State, subject to exemptions. For the United Kingdom, the territory within which the tax is levied as a single area is Great Britain, Northern Ireland and the Isle of Man, but not the Channel Islands or the continental shelf outside territorial waters. Importation into that territory therefore gives rise to a charge to tax, whether the import comes from a Community country or a third country.

(2) *Supplies and consideration*
11.32 The concept of *supply* of goods and services is defined at length in Articles 5 and 6 of the directive. A supply of goods is defined essentially as being the transfer of the right to dispose of tangible property as owner, and the supply of services refers to any transaction which does constitute a supply of goods. With certain exceptions, tax is only chargeable where *consideration* for the supply is given. And the directive provides that a number of supplies are or may be treated by national legislation as having been made for consideration, when in reality they have not been. Thus, Article 5 of the directive provides that goods, on whose acquisition by a business input tax was wholly or partly deductible, are deemed to be supplied for consideration if they are applied by the taxable person (see below) for his own private use or that of his employees, or if they are gifted or applied for non-business purposes—an exemption is made for samples or small value business gifts.

11.33 The directive also allows Member States to regard as supplies for consideration (a) self-supplies of goods for use in a business where, if they had been acquired from another taxable person, input tax would not have been wholly deductible, (b) the retention of goods on the cessation of a business where input tax was deductible on their acquisition, and (c) the supply of goods in a non-taxable transaction by a taxable person where input tax has been wholly or partly deductible. A similar discretion exists to tax free supplies of services by a taxable person for his private use or that of his employees or for non-business purposes, and to tax as a supply of services the use similarly of business assets on which input tax was wholly or partly deductible.

11.34 Although the line between goods and services is to some extent left to Member States' discretion to define, some clarification of doubtful cases is provided in Articles 5 and 6 of the directive. The supply of goods is defined to include the supply of electric current, heat, refrigeration, certain interests in or over immovable property, goods sold on commission and goods sold on hire-purchase. Services include assignments of intangible property, the undertaking of an obligation to refrain from any act or to tolerate any act or situation, and the performance of services under an obligation to a public authority.

11.35 It was decided in *Case 154/80, Staatssecretaris van Financien v. CVCA* (31) that the term "consideration" as used in the directive must be interpreted by the Court as a matter of Community law, and that there must be a connection between the payment made and the supply rendered. In *Case 102/86, CEC v. Apple and Pear Development Council,* (32) the Court held that the (obligatory) payment by producers of a levy to promote the interests of the trade did not constitute consideration for the purposes of the tax. And in *Case 230/87, Naturally Yours Cosmetics v. Customs and Excise* (33) it was decided that where consideration is partly monetary and partly non-monetary, but capable of being given a monetary value, the total consideration is taxable. The term is defined in relation both to imports and internal supplies in Article 11 of the directive, referred to below.

(3) *Taxable persons*
11.36 The definition of *taxable person* in Article 4 focuses on the independent conduct of any of a number of specified economic activities, irrespective of their purpose or results. They include those of producers, traders and persons supplying services, and cover matters such as mining, agricultural activity and the practice of the professions. The exploitation of tangible or intangible property for the purpose of obtaining income from it is also a relevant activity. The supply, "on an occasional basis", of buildings prior to first occupation or of building land may be treated as a taxable activity.

11.37 Excluded from the concept of the "taxable person" are employees, and bodies governed by public law (33a) in respect of the

---

(31) [1981] ECR 445; [1981] CMLR 337.
(32) [1988] 2 CMLR 394; [1988] STC 221.
(33) [1989] 1 CMLR 797.
(33a) If transactions are subject to private law, the authority is *pro. tanto* a taxable person: *Cases 231/87 and 129/88, Fiorenzuola and Ors.* (Not yet reported).

activities in which they engage as public authorities, whether they collect payment for them or not; but there is again discretion left to the Member States to treat such activities as within the scope of the tax if not to do so would lead to significant distortions of competition. In any event, the supply of telecommunications, gas, water, electricity, steam, the transport of goods or passengers, port and airport services, the supply of new goods manufactured for sale, the transactions of agricultural intervention agencies, trade fairs, warehousing, commercial publicity, travel agency, co-operative type shops and canteens, and the commercial transactions of radio and television bodies are all within the scope of the tax, no matter who carries them out. In *Case 286/83, Rompelman v. Minister van Financien* (34), it was held that a person who carries out activities preparatory to economic activity is also within the definition.

(4) *Place of supply*

11.38 Articles 8 and 9 of the directive contain rules determining where a taxable supply has taken place, with a view to establishing its liability to tax in any given Member State. Goods are supplied where they are dispatched to the buyer, installed or handed over, as the case may be. The rules relating to services are more complex. The basic rule is that services are supplied where the taxpayer has established his business, or has a fixed establishment from which a service is supplied or, in default, where he has his permanent address or usual residence. Article 9 prescribes different rules for property and building services, transport and entertainment.

11.39 In the case of disposals of intellectual property, and the supply of certain services "exported" to customers or clients outside the Member State where the supplier is established, the Tenth Directive (84/386) (35) prescribes in general that where the customer is outside the Community or is a taxable person in another part of the Community, the place of the supply is where the customer has established his business, has a fixed establishment to which the service is supplied or where he resides. Discretions are given to the Member States to avoid situations of double taxation in respect of these services.

(5) *Time of supply*

11.40 Article 10 of the directive deals with the point at which the tax becomes chargeable. The normal tax points are when goods are delivered or services are performed, but earlier payment on account advances the tax point to the extent of the payment, and periodic supplies give rise

(34) [1985] ECR 656; [1985] 3 CMLR 202.
(35) OJ 1984 L 208/58.

to a tax point at the end of the relevant period. Member States are given discretion to provide for further alternative tax points for particular types of transaction or taxpayer: at the latest, the date of issue of an invoice or the receipt of the price, or the passing of a specified period from the basic tax point where there is no invoice. On import, the tax point occurs when goods enter the territory of the country, but may be assimilated to the point at which customs duty is payable on import or on release of goods for home use.

(6) *Basis of assessment*

11.41 Article 11A of the directive provides that the total of the consideration given or promised, whether by the purchaser or a third party, is the basis on which the tax is assessed. The purchase price of the goods, the cost of the goods or services or their open market value (as defined), are alternative bases in circumstances in which the directive deems there to have been a taxable supply for consideration. Early payment discounts and other rebates allowed at the time of supply together with disbursements made on behalf of customers are not included in the taxable amount, nor is interest awarded by a court on late payment: *Case 222/81, BAZ Bausystem v. Finanzamt München* (36). But interest contractually payable is included.

11.42 Article 27 permits other derogations from the rule of assessment being made on the actual consideration "to prevent certain types of tax evasion or avoidance". In *Cases 138 and 139/86, Direct Cosmetics v. Customs and Excise* (19), the Court affirmed the validity of Decision 85/369 (37) authorising the United Kingdom to require tax to be assessed on the open market value of a sale by retail in cases where the tax base for the last taxable sale would fall short of that level, as a result of the interposition of a non-registered supplier before the final sale to the customer. Other taxes, duties, levies and charges are included in the tax base, along with incidental expenses such as commission, packing and insurance charged by the supplier to the customer.

11.43 With regard to imports, Article 11B of the directive permits states to treat the tax as a customs duty, for the purpose of reckoning the tax base by reference to the customs valuation provisions in Regulation 1224/80. (38) Alternatively, the taxable amount may be the actual price paid where this is the only consideration, or otherwise the open market value: this latter concept is defined in Article 11B(1). Included

(36)   [1982] ECR 2527; [1982] 3 CMLR 688.
(37)   OJ 1985 L 199/60, now made permanent by Decision 89/534 OJ 1989 L280/54.
(38)   OJ 1980 L 134/1.

in the tax base are taxes, duties, levies and charges due by reason of the importation or outside the country of import, and incidental expenses such as commission, insurance and transport costs. Exclusions from the tax base are similar to those applicable to internal supplies.

11.44 Member States are given wide discretion to provide for bad debts, and it is provided that the taxable amount is to be reduced in cases where payment is refused or orders are cancelled, subject to conditions laid down by Member States. Currency conversions necessary are calculated by reference to the provisions in Regulation 1224/80 on customs valuation (38). The cost of returnable packaging is excluded from the tax base on condition that the packaging is returned.

(7) Tax rates
11.45 The rates at which the tax is charged vary considerably between the Member States, and are the subject of Commission harmonisation proposals. Article 12 of the directive requires that the rates applied must be those in force when the taxable supply takes place or, where different, when the tax becomes chargeable. Where Member States have assimilated tax on import to customs duties, the rate applicable is that when application is made for the goods to be released for home use, and must be the same as that to which internal supplies are subject. The directive then only prescribes that a standard rate shall be fixed by each Member State, the same for both goods and services, and that increased or reduced rates may be applied in certain cases. Reduced rates, however, should not result in input tax becoming non-deductible.

11.46 Zero rates (which are referred to not as rates, but as exemption with refund of tax at the preceding stage) are for the most part allowed on internal transactions under Article 28 of the directive only on a transitional basis until they are suppressed by the Council acting unanimously, but no later than the date on which tax on imports and refunds on exports within the Community are abolished. A number of other transitional provisions are contained in Article 28 relating to exemptions, reduced rates, blocked input tax, the taxation of buildings and building land, travel agents and transport. Both the termination of the transitional tolerances laid down in the directive and any new fiscal provisions require unanimity by the Council, under the terms of the directive itself and of Articles 99 and 100 of the Treaty.

11.47 A condition for the maintenance of zero rates is that they are confined to supplies to the final consumer (or supplies closely connected therewith), and are judged necessary for clearly defined reasons of social policy. In *Case 416/85, Commission v. United Kingdom* (39) the Court defined the "final consumer" as a person who does not use goods or services in an economic activity, and held that any supply otherwise than directly to such a person (or to a person sufficiently close to him in the supply chain for it to be able to enure to his benefit) may not be zero-rated under this provision. It was held accordingly that a variety of United Kingdom zero rates did not genuinely fulfil these criteria, and appropriate changes were made in the Finance Act 1989 to reflect this. Article 15 provides for the zero-rating of exports of goods and services.

(8) *Deduction of input tax*

11.48 Supplies within the scope of the tax are either positively rated or exempt; zcro-rating, which is categorised in the directive as exemption with refund of tax at the previous stage, is in effect treated as a positive rate of nil. As indicated above, the tax paid on supplies to a taxable person (the input tax) is set off against the tax due on supplies made by him (the output tax), and the excess of the latter over the former is alone payable to the tax administration. If the input exceeds the output, the taxable person receives a refund equal to the excess. An exempt input generates no tax credit, and an exempt output generates no tax liability, so that a person who makes nothing but exempt supplies is not liable to account for any tax.

11.49 The mechanism of offsetting input tax against output tax is dependent on a number of conditions being fulfilled, which are detailed in Articles 17 to 20 of the directive. The main condition is that the supply on which the input tax arose is one by another taxable person of goods or services for the purpose of the taxpayer's taxable transactions. This condition is also fulfilled where tax is payable on the import of goods, or where the taxpayer has made a self-supply on which input tax would—had the supply been made to him by another taxable person— have been only partly deductible. In these three cases the taxpayer must, respectively, hold a tax invoice for the supply addressed to him, an import document showing him as consignee or importer or comply with requirements laid down by the tax administration. Supplies to a tax- payer whose taxable transactions are exports are in general also eligible for input tax deduction. National legislation may not add requirements about tax invoices which make it "practically impossible or excessively difficult to exercise the right to deduct": *Cases 123 and 330/87, Jeune- homme.* (40)

(39) [1988] 3 CMLR 169.
(40) (Not yet reported).

11.50 In order to avoid credit being given for input tax on supplies which are not for the purpose of a taxable transaction, there must therefore be a relationship between the taxpayer's inputs and his outputs before the right to set off input tax against output tax will arise. This need occurs in particular when a proportion of the outputs is exempt. In this case, the rule is that only the input tax attributable to taxable (as opposed to exempt) outputs is deductable. Detailed provision is made in Article 19 for the calculation of the deductible proportion of inputs where—as is usual—direct attribution of inputs is not possible. Member States are given wide discretion to provide for mechanisms to attribute inputs to outputs to prevent over-deduction of input tax, and with regard to the deduction of input tax on capital goods. The right to deduct input tax arises when the tax on the supply in question becomes chargeable, but the United Kingdom has been authorised by Decision 87/400 (41) to derogate from this principle.

11.51 The Eighth Directive, 79/1072 (42), provides detailed harmonised procedures for taxable persons established in other Member States to be refunded tax on supplies made to them by taxable persons in the first Member State. It supplements the obligation contained in Article 17(4) of the Sixth Directive to refund tax on supplies to other Community traders. Applications duly made must be decided within six months, and appeals against refusal of an application must be provided for in the Member State in question on the same basis as similar internal appeals.

11.52 The Thirteenth Directive, 86/560 (43), provides the same in the case of third country traders, but it remains in Member States' discretion to make this conditional on the third country granting reciprocal treatment. Member States may also require third country traders to appoint a tax representative in their territory. Refunds may not be granted under conditions which are more favourable than those applicable to Community traders.

(9) *Exemptions*
11.53 Those supplies which are exempt are defined in Articles 13 to 16 of the directive, and in many cases are subject to compliance with conditions, sometimes selected at the discretion of Member States. Among the most important "public interest" types of exempt supply are: postal services, hospital and medical care, welfare services, education,

(41) OJ 1987 L 213/40.
(42) OJ 1979 L 331/11.
(43) OJ 1986 L 326/40.

services to their members by trade unions, political parties, religious bodies etc., and public service broadcasting. Member States may make these exemptions available to bodies which are not governed by public law subject to the condition that they do not aim systematically to make a profit.

11.54 Exemption is also provided for insurance, banking, finance and certain supplies in relation to land, although in certain cases Member States may allow taxpayers the option to elect for tax to be charged on such transactions. In *Case 348/87, Sufa* (44) the Court held that the exemptions in Article 13, since they constituted derogations from the general principle that turnover tax was charged on every supply of services for a consideration, were to be strictly interpreted. In general, exports of goods and services are exempt, with the right to a refund of the tax charged at the previous stage—see articles 15 and 17. Import exemptions are referred to below under "imports".

(10) Special schemes and simplification procedures
11.55 Articles 24 to 26 of the directive allow, at Member States' discretion, provision for special schemes for small undertakings and a common flat-rate scheme for farmers, and lay down special rules in relation to travel agents.

11.56 Provided there is no reduction in the amount of tax chargeable, simplified systems for charging and collection may, after consultation with the Community's value added tax committee, be provided for small businesses. Similarly, Member States may provide for a regressive system of relief from the charging of tax for small businesses. The states are also given discretion to exempt from the tax altogether businesses whose turnover is below a certain threshold (adjusted by the Council periodically); such businesses are then forbidden to deduct input tax or to show output tax on their invoices. Any business eligible for exemption in this way must have the option of electing for normal taxable status, or of taking advantage of any simplified small business scheme or graduated relief scheme available.

11.57 A further option, which has not been taken up by the United Kingdom, is granted for the taxation of farm businesses on a flat-rate basis. Travel agents (who include tour operators) are entitled to account for tax only on the margin of their profit on a supply to a client if they satisfy certain conditions laid down in Article 26 of the directive,

(44) (Not yet reported).

principally that they make use of services supplied by other taxable persons in the provision of travel services and act in their own name, and not as an intermediary charging clients for specific disbursements. Full deduction of input tax is accordingly not available to agents taxed on this basis.

11.58 Article 27 allows the Council to authorise derogations by Member States from the directive either for the purpose of introducing simplified procedures or for the purpose of preventing "evasion or avoidance" of the tax. The exercise of this power is subject to the proviso that the measures permitted must not, save to a negligible extent, affect the amount of tax due at the final consumption stage. Reference has been made at para 11.16 above to the Court's approach to the interpretation of this limitation. A number of derogations have been granted under this article to Member States, including the United Kingdom (45). Many transitional derogations permitted by Article 28 are being removed by Directive 89/465 (45a), starting on 1 January 1990.

(11) *Liability*
11.59 The basic liability for payment of the tax is imposed by Article 21 of the directive on taxable persons, in so far as tax due on transactions conducted within a Member State is concerned, and on the person or persons designated as being liable in the case of tax due on import. Where the taxable transaction is effected by a person resident outside the Member State in question, the Member States are given discretion to provide from whom the tax will be due e.g. a tax representative or the customer, who will be liable in the case of certain business services supplied by the non-resident taxable person. Any person who shows value added tax on an invoice is similarly liable for payment. Articles 22 and 23 empower Member States to make detailed provision regarding the time of payment, the keeping of records and the like.

Tax and excise duty reliefs on imports

11.60 Value added tax on the import of goods is chargeable as if the import was a supply, but without any of the other conditions in relation to internal transactions being required. Thus, whether the importer is a

---

(45) Including ones relating to: special schemes for retailers; trading stamps; non-registration of zero-rated suppliers; avoidance of tax on the retail margin; terminal markets; long stays in hotels; goods in warehouse; car fuel; avoidance of tax on supplies to connected exempt persons; cash accounting; gold and gold coins; buildings supplied before first occupation and related land.
(45a) OJ 1979 L 226/21.

taxable person or not, or is or is not making the importation for the purpose of a taxable business carried on by him, tax is chargeable. If tax has been paid in another Member State and not remitted on export, the state of import must give credit for it to a private importer: *Cases 15/81 and 47/84, Gaston Schul* (46). Imports of illegal drugs are not chargeable: *Case 294/82, Einberger v. Hauptzollamt Freiburg.* (47)

11.61 Article 14 of the Sixth Directive (29) details the exemptions to be granted on importation. They include cases in which an internal supply could be exempt and cases in which customs duty would not be exigible or be held in suspense. The Seventeenth Directive, 85/362, (48) is made pursuant to this article and provides for exemption from value added tax on goods, other than means of transport, which are temporarily imported. That directive applies to imports from other Member States and from third countries. In *Case 10/87, R. v. Customs and Excise ex parte Tattersalls Ltd* (49) it was held that goods whose supply is exempt in the exporting Member State are entitled to the exemption provided for by this directive. Directive 83/182 (50), relates to both value added tax and excise duties, and provides for relief for means of transport temporarily imported, but only from one Member State to another.

11.62 Directive 83/181 (51), however, contains extensive and detailed provision for the exemption from tax on final importation. The main categories of relief cover: personal property imported on a transfer of residence from outside the Community, goods imported on the occasion of marriage, personal property acquired by inheritance, certain property of students, capital goods imported on the transfer of a business, certain agricultural products and products for agricultural use, various medical goods, goods imported for charitable or welfare purposes, importers' samples, items used at trade fairs etc., and goods for examination, analysis or test purposes. Various other items are included in the lengthy list of exemptions. It will be seen that this list is similar to the list of reliefs applicable in the case of customs duties on import to the Community.

11.63 Permanent imports of personal property by private individuals, from one Member State to another, are relieved of value added tax and

(46) [1982] ECR 1409; [1982] 3 CMLR 229; [1985] ECR 1501.
(47) [1984] ECR 1177; [1985] 1 CMLR 765.
(48) OJ 1985 L 192/20.
(49) (Not yet reported).
(50) OJ 1983 L 105/59.
(51) OJ 1983 L 105/38, as last amended by Directive 89/219 OJ 1989 L 92/13.

excise duty by Directive 83/183 (52) if they are acquired tax paid in the first state and have had no export relief granted. Minimum periods of prior use are prescribed, as are various other conditions. Directive 74/651 (53) provides for tax and excise duty relief on imported goods in small non-commercial consignments from other Member States, and Directive 78/1035 (54) makes similar provision for goods imported from third countries, but the relief afforded may not exceed that available on imports from Community countries. Directive 68/297 (55) standardises Member States' provisions on the duty-free admission of fuel in the tanks of commercial vehicles.

11.64 Finally, Directive 69/169 (56) lays down exemptions from value added tax and excise duties for goods contained in the personal luggage of travellers coming both from third countries and from other Member States. In the case of third country imports, there is a lower permitted value (the values are periodically revised) than for Community goods, but the latter must already have been in free circulation before the relevant import and have been acquired tax paid in the Community. The states must set quantitative limits to the relief as it applies to tobacco, alcohol, coffee, tea and perfumes, with minimum age limits of seventeen, seventeen and fifteen respectively in the first three cases. The value of these restricted goods does not count towards a person's totals otherwise available for the relief.

Intra-Community tax enforcement

11.65 Under Directives 76/308 and 77/799 (57), provision is made for Member States to render each other mutual assistance in the recovery of value added tax, customs duty and agricultural levies, and for the exchange of information in relation to these matters and in relation to direct taxes.

11.66 *Exchange of information* is governed by Directive 77/779 (57), which is stated to apply to income tax, corporation tax, capital gains tax, petroleum revenue tax and value added tax, but also to any other taxes for the time being levied on income and capital. Member States are to exchange any information that may enable them to make correct

(52) OJ 1983 L 105/64, as amended by Directive 89/604 OJ 1989 L 348/28.
(53) OJ 1974 L 354/57, as last amended by Directive 88/663 OJ 1988 L 382/40.
(54) OJ 1978 L 366/34, as last amended by Directive 85/576 OJ 1985 L 372/30.
(55) OJ 1968 L 175/15, as last amended by Directive 85/347 OJ 1985 L 183/22.
(56) OJ 1969 L 133/6, as last amended by Directive 89/220 OJ 1989 L 92/15.
(57) OJ 1976 L 73/18, as last amended by Directive 79/1071 OJ 1979 L 331/10; and OJ 1977 L 336/15, as last amended by Directive 79/1070 OJ 1979 L 331/8.

assessments, either on the initiative of the state providing the information or at the request of another state. If necessary, enquiries are to be carried out to obtain information requested.

11.67 Information thus exchanged must be kept secret in the receiving state in the same manner as in the sending country, and may not be used other than for the assessment or recovery of tax; and it may only be disclosed at a public hearing if the state supplying the information raises no objection. But information may be used for all purposes for which it could be used in the sending state, if the latter so permits. In any case, information may be refused where its provision would lead to commercial, industrial or professional secrets being disclosed, or the disclosure would be contrary to public policy.

11.68 Directive 76/308 (57) governs the *recovery of taxes* (agricultural levies, intervention debts, customs duties and value added tax) by one Member State on behalf of another. These are all the duties in which the Community Treasury has an interest. The Directive similarly provides for the exchange of information useful in recovery action by any Member State, and there is a saving for information which would disclose commercial, industrial or professional secrets similar to that in the mutual assistance directives. The claims which a state may request another to recover on its behalf must not be contested in the former, and the recovery procedure available there must have been applied first.

11.69 It is not necessary for a court judgment for the debt to have been obtained in the requesting state, but only that an instrument permitting the enforcement of the debt in that state should have been in existence. Any dispute arising in the course of recovery action is to be settled according to the procedure of the requesting state, unless it concerns the validity of the procedure in the second state, when it is to be settled in accordance with the procedures of that state.

11.70 Claims may include sums for interest and costs, and are to be recovered in the currency of the requested state, but are not to be treated as preferred debts there. Limitation is governed solely by the law of the requesting state, and the actions of the requested state are accordingly deemed to have occurred in the requesting state for the purpose of reckoning any question of limitation under the law of that state. The requested state may refuse to take recovery action if to do so would create serious social or economic difficulties. Detailed provisions enlarging upon those in the main Directive are contained in Directive 77/794 (58).

11.71 United Kingdom implementing legislation is contained in the Finance Act 1977 section 11, the Finance Act 1978 section 77 and the Finance Act 1980 section 17. It provides for the recovery of other Member States' claims to be effected by treating them as if they were Crown debts, and proceeding accordingly.

European Economic Interest Groupings (EEIGs)

11.72 EEIGs are provided for by Regulation 2137/85 (59), which is discussed in Chapter 13. They are a new form of business entity set up by enterprises (which may be companies or individuals) in two or more Member States. They may be formed for the purpose of activities which are ancillary to those of the EEIG's members, but not in order to make profits for the grouping itself. The regulation stipulates that national tax law is to apply to an EEIG's activity in a Member State, but that profits or losses are to be taxable only in the hands of its members. Legislation to give effect to those requirements in the United Kingdom will be contained in the Finance Act 1990, but operative from 1 July 1989, when the regulation took effect. (60)

---

(58)   OJ 1977 L 333/11, as last amended by Directive 86/489 OJ 1986 L 283/23.
(59)   OJ 1985 L 199/1.
(60)   Inland Revenue press release, 13 April 1989.

CHAPTER 12

Insurance, Banking and Capital Movements

INSURANCE

12.01 The only specific mention of insurance in the EEC Treaty is in Article 61, which provides that the liberalisation of banking and insurance services connected with movement of capital shall be effected in step with the progressive liberalisation of movement of capital. This is so because movements of capital are involved in a very large proportion of insurance business.

12.02 The existing Community legislation concerning insurance is based on the provisions of the Treaty covering the freedom of establishment and the freedom to render services. Article 54 of the Treaty calls on the Council to draw up a general programme for the abolition of existing restrictions on freedom of establishment within the Community, and it goes on to mandate the Council to issue directives accordingly. The first requirement of Article 54 is implemented by the enactment of the General Programme for the Abolition of Restriction on Freedom of Establishment of 18 December 1961 and by the enactment of Directive 64/225 (1) on the abolition of restrictions on freedom of establishment and on freedom to provide services in respect of reinsurance and retrocession.

12.03 Article 59 of the Treaty calls for the abolition of restrictions on freedom to provide services and extends the provisions of the Chapter on Services to nationals of a third country who provide services and who are established in the Community, should the Council so decide (see Article 16(3) of the Single European Act). Article 60, which covers insurance, states that the person providing a service may, in order to do so, temporarily pursue his activity in the State where the service is provided, under the same conditions as are imposed by that State on its own nationals.

12.04 Two directives were enacted dealing with direct insurance. First, Council Directive 73/239 (2), made under Article 57(2), on the coordination of laws, regulations and administrative provisions relating to the

(1) OJ 1964 56/878.
(2) OJ 1973 L 228/3.

taking up and pursuit of the business of direct insurance other than life insurance, last amended by Directive 87/343 (3), made the commencement of the business of direct insurance subject to an official authorisation and requirements for obtaining such authorisation. It contained various rules as to the conditions insurance companies must comply with and referred to the solvency margin represented by free assets which insurance companies must maintain. In addition there is a provision for a guarantee fund equivalent to one third of the solvency margin. The rules also apply to third country insurers operating in the Community, specific rules applying to agencies or branches whose head offices are outside the Community.

12.05 The principles governing the freedom to provide insurance services were considered in *Case 205/84, Commission v. Federal Republic of Germany* (4), where the requirements of authorisation and of permanent establishment under the German Insurance Supervision Law came under scrutiny. The Court emphasised that authorisation must be granted on request to any undertaking established in another Member State which meets the conditions of the legislation of the State in which the service is provided. The requirement of authorisation under domestic law might be maintained only if it was justified on grounds relating to the protection of policy-holders. The Court, however, took the view that it was not in a position to lay down the limits of that distinction with sufficient precision in order to determine individual cases in which the need of protection did not justify the requirement of an authorisation. The necessity for permanent establishment was considered clearly as a negation of the freedom to provide services. Both requirements under the Insurance Supervision Law in relation to Community co-insurance (for authorisation and permanent establishment) were found to be contrary to Directive 78/473 (5) and Articles 59 and 60 of the Treaty. In three other cases considering Directive 78/473 (5) and Community co-insurance, the Court held that France (*Case 220/83*) (6), Ireland (*Case 206/84*) (7) and Denmark (*Case 252/83*) (8) were in breach of the Treaty by requiring that Community co-insurers be established in these Member States in order to provide co-insurance services there as leading insurers.

12.06 The other directive enacted under the General Programme was Directive 73/240 (9) abolishing restrictions on freedom of establishment

---

(3) OJ 1987 L 185/72.
(4) [1986] ECR 3755; [1987] 2 CMLR 69.
(5) OJ 1978 L 125/125.
(6) *Commission v. France* [1986] ECR 3663; [1987] 2 CMLR 113.
(7) *Commission v. Irish Republic* [1986] ECR 3817; [1987] 2 CMLR 150.
(8) *Commission v. Denmark* [1986] ECR 3713; [1987] 2 CMLR 169.
(9) OJ 1973 L 228/20.

in the business of direct insurance other than life insurance. Further directives following the general tendency to enlarge the freedom of establishment and services are Directive 77/92 (10) on measures to facilitate the effective exercise of freedom of establishment and freedom to provide services in respect of the activities of insurance agents and brokers, Directive 78/473 (5) making provisions for Community co-insurance and Directive 87/344 (11) dealing with legal expenses insurance.

12.07 The scope of these directives is extended by the Second Council Directive 88/357 (12), supplementing and amending Directive 73/239 (2). Articles 2 to 4 define "undertaking", "establishment", "Member State where the risk is situated", "Member State of establishment" and "Member State of provision of services" and provide that any permanent presence of an undertaking in the territory of a Member State shall be treated in the same way as an agency or branch, even if it is only an office managed by an undertaking's own staff or an independent person with authority to act. Article 5 is supplementary to Directive 73/239 (2) in that it adds to Article 5 of that Directive a definition of "large risks". Article 7 determines the law applicable to contracts of insurance. Article 8 sets out rules whereby insurance undertakings may offer and conclude compulsory insurance contracts. Article 9 abolishes as a general rule the notification of special policy conditions and scales of premiums, subject to various qualifications. Article 10 deals with powers of supervisory authorities and Article 11 with transfers of portfolios of contracts. Articles 12 to 26 deal with the provision of services and specific rules which affect the freedom to provide services in the field of insurance. The Directive contains transitional provisions for Greece, Ireland, Spain and Portugal. The Directive also amends Directive 78/473 (5) so that the criteria defining "large risks" in Article 5 (above) should also define risks to be covered under Community co-insurance arrangement.

12.08 The subject of life insurance is tackled by the First Council Directive 79/267 (13) on the taking up and pursuit of the business of direct life insurance. The legislation shows a distinction between life insurance and other insurance and it could well be that it shows a distinction between services connected with the movement of capital and services not so connected, a distinction made by the Treaty itself. Here Directive 88/361 (14) on movements of capital becomes relevant by abolishing restrictions on movement of capital in respect of transfers in

(10) OJ 1977 L 26/14.
(11) OJ 1987 L 185/77.
(12) OJ 1988 L 172/1.
(13) OJ 1979 L 63/1.
(14) OJ 1988 L 178/5.

performance of insurance contracts and dealing with premiums and payments in respect of life assurance (Section X of Annex I of the Directive).

12.09 A separate category seems to be made for automobile liability insurance (Council Directive 72/166 (15) as amended by Directive 72/430) (16). National automobile liability insurance is made compulsory on a Community basis and in effect the official associations of insurance companies in each Member State become the agents for all insurance companies from other Member States for the purpose of handling claims. This has done away with the border check of certificates of insurance (the so-called "green cards"). These two directives maintained the existing disparities between the laws of the different Member States concerning the extent of the obligation of insurance cover and so Second Council Directive 84/5 (17) aims at the reduction of such disparities. It lays down the minimum requirements for compulsory insurance cover against damage to property and against personal injury. Member States must establish or authorise a body to provide compensation at least up to the limits of the compulsory insurance obligation in respect of damage or injury caused by unidentified or uninsured vehicles. Member States have to ensure that any statutory provision or any contractual clause contained in an insurance policy issued in accordance with Directive 72/166 (15) which excludes certain categories of vehicle users from insurance is deemed to be void as against third party accident victims. Members of the family of any person liable under civil law and covered by insurance referred to in this Directive must not be excluded from insurance in respect of their personal injuries by virtue of that relationship. Three Commission Decisions (88/367, 88/368, 88/369) (18) further relate to the application of Directive 72/166. (15)

BANKING

12.10 The basis of the existing EEC legislation in relation to banking and credit institutions rests on the principles of freedom of establishment and of freedom to provide services. The latter assumes the liberalisation of banking and insurance services. This liberalisation connected with movements of capital attaches it in terms (Article 61(2) of the EEC

(**15**)   OJ 1972 L 103/2.
(**16**)   OJ 1972 L 291/162.
(**17**)   OJ 1984 L 8/17.
(**18**)   OJ 1988 L 181/45, 46, 47.

Treaty) to the progressive liberalisation of movement of capital. However the banking legislation of the EEC has its philosophical origins in the aims of the Treaty. Article 54(3) of the Treaty, which is cited in the preamble as one of the *vires* for the first Directive of consequence (19) on the activities of banks, talks of priority treatment to be given by the Council and Commission to action where freedom of establishment makes a particularly valuable contribution to the development of production and trade. This Directive on the abolition of restrictions on freedom of establishment and freedom to provide services for self-employed activities of banks and other financial institutions.

12.11   The main provisions in Article 3 of the Directive require Member States to abolish restrictions which prevent banks from establishing themselves or from providing services in the host country under the same conditions and with the same rights as nationals of that country. The Directive goes on to prohibit restrictions existing because of administrative practices which result in treatment being applied to beneficiaries that is discriminatory when compared to that for nationals. The Article then deals with specific restrictions in named Member States. The United Kingdom was required to abolish provisions existing in the Prevention of Fraud (Investments) Act 1958 and corresponding provisions in Northern Ireland whereby any company which intends to exercise the activity of manager and trustee of a unit trust must be constituted in the United Kingdom. Other provisions of the Directive give the right to join professional and trade organisations under the same conditions and with the same rights and obligations as the nationals of a Member State. The Directive also deals with the use of the title "bank", "banker" and "savings bank". The banking sector comprises not only banks but also financial institutions such as finance companies, savings and loan institutions and consortia. Excluded are the activities of stockbrokers and the supply of services by intermediaries who, while remaining established in one Member State, move to another Member State to provide services.

12.12   The decisions of the European Court, since the promulgation of the Directive, that Articles of the EEC Treaty dealing with freedom of establishment and freedom to provide services are directly applicable go further in their application than the Directive.

12.13   The First Council Directive 77/780 (20) on the co-ordination of laws, regulations and administrative provisions relating to the business

(19)   Directive 73/183, OJ 1973 L 194/1.
(20)   OJ 1977 L 322/30.

of credit institutions based on Article 57 of the EEC Treaty was the first serious attempt to make it easier to conduct business by eliminating obstructive differences between the laws of the Member States and, as its preamble indicates, it was intended only as a first step, to be followed eventually by a variety of additional measures until uniform authorisation requirements applied to comparable types of credit institutions, thus avoiding the need for additional authorisations when credit institutions in one Member State wish to set up branches in another Member State. Article 3 of this Directive provides for Member States to require those credit institutions subject to the Directive to obtain authorisation before commencing their activities. It lays down the requirements for this authorisation: the credit institution must possess separate and adequate minimum own funds and it must be managed by at least two persons who are of good repute and have sufficient experience to perform their duties. It must also submit a programme of operations setting out the types of business envisaged and the structural organisation of the institution.

12.14 The Directive also establishes an Advisory Committee of Member State and Commission representatives, its task being to assist the Commission in insuring the proper implementation of both this Directive and the 1973 Directive. The Directive does not regulate branches of credit institutions which have their headquarters in third countries but provides that such branches may not receive more favourable treatment than branches of institutions with headquarters in a Member State.

12.15 The provisions of the Directive were implemented in the United Kingdom by the Banking Act 1979. However, the criteria for recognition as a bank and for a full licence under the Act were more stringent than those laid down in the Directive. Every person who is a director, controller or manager of the institution must be a fit and proper person to hold that position; thus the "good repute" and "sufficient experience" of the Directive was transformed into "fit and proper person". These requirements were further enlarged by the Banking Act 1987.

12.16 The 1977 Directive was supplemented by Directive 83/350 (21) on the supervision on a consolidated basis of credit institutions. The need for this Directive arose from the fact that many banks may be subsidiaries of other banking institutions or own other such institutions and their finances are affected by the financial health of all the related institutions. Under the Directive, which is based on Article 57(2) of the EEC Treaty, Member State banking authorities must supervise credit institutions which have a shareholding of at least 25 per cent in another

(21) OJ 1983 L 193/18.

institution by including in their ambit the financial situation of all such other institutions in which the institution subject to supervision participates. The duty to supervise is imposed upon the Member State where the institution concerned has its head office. A distinction is made between majority and minority shareholdings and the supervisory authority has a wide element of discretion. Directive 89/299 (22) further deals with own funds of credit institutions.

12.17 EEC company law legislation (see Chapter 13) formerly allowed Member States to exempt banks from the accounting requirements applied to companies in general. This gap was filled in 1986 by Directive 86/635 (23) on annual accounts and consolidated accounts of banks and other financial institutions. The Directive provides that the rules of the Fourth Company Directive are to be followed except in those specified instances where different terminology, valuation rules, contents of items in balance sheets and profit and loss accounts are considered necessary to reflect the special position of banks. Undisclosed reserves are dealt with as well as maturity analyses.

12.17.1 All these directives have been complemented by the Second Council Directive 89/646 (23a) which amends the First Directive (20) and deals with harmonisation of authorisation conditions and with conditions for pursuit of banking business. Freedom of establishment and freedom to provide services are important concerns of the Second Directive. Complementary to it is Directive 89/647 (23b) on solvency ratios for credit institutions.

12.18 This Directive is supplemented by Directive 89/117 (24) on the obligations of branches established in a Member State of credit institutions and financial institutions having their head office outside that Member State regarding the publication of annual accounting documents. This supplementing Directive provides for branches to supply the supervising authorities with copies of the annual report and accounts drawn up by their head office in accordance with the main Directive (23) and it places strict limits on the specific information concerning the branch that foreign bank branches can be required to disclose. It also allows Member States to insist that branches of non-Community banks publish branch accounts, should the accounts of their head office not conform with accounts drawn up in accordance with Directive 86/635. (23)

(22) OJ 1989 L 124/16.
(23) OJ 1986 L 372/1.
(23a) OJ 1989 L 386/1.
(23b) OJ 1989 L 386/14.
(24) OJ 1989 L 44/40.

12.19 Since banking involves consumer credit, Directive 87/102 (25) for the approximation of laws, regulations and administrative provisions of the Member States concerning consumer credit covers all credit agreements made with a consumer, subject to a maximum limit of 20,000 ECU, except lending for property, short-term agreements and hiring agreements. It deals with advertising, canvassing, written documentation, repossession of goods, rebates for early settlement, negotiable instruments, liability for defective goods or services and licensing requirements. The annual rate of interest must be quoted in all cases, but the Directive leaves the rules concerning the true cost-of-credit formula to the Member States pending the introduction of Community methods for calculating the annual rate. The Directive also contains provisions for authorisation and monitoring of persons granting credit or offering credit arrangements. In the United Kingdom the Consumer Credit Act 1974 reflects generally the provisions of the Directive.

CAPITAL MOVEMENTS

12.20 The programme for the liberalisation of capital movement proposed by the Commission in 1986 looks to the removal of financial and monetary impediments to the establishment of a Community-wide financial area. Articles 67 to 73 of the EEC Treaty lay down the ground rules for free movement of capital. This area is one in which Community law is less developed than it is in regard to other "freedoms" (free movement of goods, free movement of workers, freedom to provide services and freedom of establishment). In view of its close relationship with the economic policy of Member States, it has to be considered at the same time as the provisions of the Treaty dealing with economic policy, especially Articles 104 to 109. The Single European Act of 1986 replaced the unanimity requirement in Council voting on Article 70(1) (co-ordination of exchange policies of Member States concerning capital movements between those States and third countries), by a system of qualified majority voting.

12.21 Article 67 is the principal source for the provisions on free movement of capital. Article 67(1) provides that Member States during the transitional period and to the extent necessary to ensure the proper functioning of the common market progressively abolish between themselves all restrictions on the movement of capital belonging to persons resident in Member States, and any discrimination based on the nationality or on the place of residence of the parties or on the place where

(25)   OJ 1987 L 42/48.

such capital is invested. This of course relates to companies and firms within the definition of Article 58.

12.22 In *Case 203/80, Casati* (26) the Court of Justice observed that, while Articles 3 and 67 of the Treaty show that the free movement of capital constitutes, alongside that of persons and services, one of the fundamental freedoms of the Community, capital movements necessarily have close links with the economic and monetary policy of the Member States; thus at present the possibility exists of complete freedom of movement in relation to capital undermining a state's economic policy or creating an imbalance in its balance of payments and jeopardising the proper functioning of the Common Market. This factor will vary with time and will depend on an assessment of the requirements of the Common Market. This is a matter, first and foremost, for the Council. The judgment therefore means that Member States remain free for the time being to impose control on capital movements, even where there are Community rules requiring the Member States to liberalise such transactions.

12.23 The earliest directive implementing Article 67 was the First Directive of 11 May 1960 (27) amended by Directives 85/583 (28) and 86/566 (29), designed to complete the first stage of the programme for the liberalisation of capital movements in the Community. The First Directive divides capital movements into four groups listed A to D.

12.24 *List A*, as now amended, covers:

(a) direct investments,

(b) operations in securities and their admission to the capital market,

(c) investments in real estate,

(d) grants and repayments of credits in connection with commercial transactions or the provision of services,

(e) transfers in performance of insurance contracts,

(f) sureties and other guarantees,

(g) personal capital movements such as inheritances, gifts, insurance payments and authors' royalties,

(h) invisible transactions of certain kinds (such as payments of damages and royalties for patents etc.), and

(i) credits granted in connection with the performance of services.

Article 1 of the Directive requires Member States to grant the requisite foreign exchange authorisations for capital movements of these kinds at

(26) [1981] ECR 2595; [1982] 1 CMLR 365.
(27) OJ 1959–62/49.
(28) OJ 1985 L 372/39.
(29) OJ 1986 L 322/22.

foreign exchange authorisations for capital movements of these kinds at the normal exchange rates. The Monetary Committee set up under Article 105 is entrusted with the task of monitoring the exchange rates applied.

12.25 *List B* covers:

(a) the aquisition of securities quoted on a stock exchange,

(b) credits in connection with transactions in which no resident is participating, and

(c) other payments not covered by List A.

Article 2 of the Directive provides for complete freedom in respect of these transfers, but the monetary conversion safeguard mentioned in Article 1(2) is not included, the Member States being required only to try and ensure that transfers are made at rates which do not differ from those ruling for payments relating to current transactions. The Commission is authorised to make recommendations after consulting the Monetary Committee.

12.26 *List C* contains a third group of transactions which are only slightly liberalised:

(a) placement of securities on capital markets,

(b) transactions in securities not traded upon securities exchanges, and

(c) the granting of long and medium-term credits.

Article 3 of the Directive requires Member States to allow foreign exchange authorisation for List C transactions, but permits Member States to maintain or re-introduce restrictions existing when the Directive took effect if the liberalisation of these transactions is likely to interfere with its economic policy.

12.27 Certain transactions have not been liberalised at all and Member States retain freedom of action. They are described in *List D* and include:

(a) short-term investments in Treasury notes,

(b) the establishment and maintenance of deposits with financial institutions,

(c) the importation and exportation of securities not included in List B and of gold and of means of payment of any kind, and

(d) all other movements of capital not specifically listed elsewhere.

For List C and D transactions, where the degree of liberalisation reached is at best partial, Article 6 requires Member States to endeavour to impose no new exchange control restrictions affecting capital movements which were free when it came into force, and not to make existing provisions more restrictive. Article 5 of the Directive permits Member States to verify the nature and *bona fides* of transactions and transfers, so that capital frauds may be kept in check. The Second Directive 63/21 (30) removes a restriction upon the liberalisation of transactions in previously issued securities and adds certain "invisible" transactions to List A.

12.28 Four more directives must be noted at this stage. The First Directive, 63/474, (31) liberalised transfers in respect of invisible transactions not connected with the movement of goods, services, capital or persons (not already liberalised under Article 106). Directive 72/156 (32), based on Articles 70 and 103, regulates international capital flows and neutralises their undesirable effects on domestic liquidity. Directives 85/583 (28) and 86/566 (29) amended the First Directive, thus completing the first part of the Commission's 1986 programme to liberalise capital movements in the Community. This further liberalisation relates to long-term credits in commercial transactions, acquisition of securities not dealt on the stock exchange and admission of securities of an undertaking in one Member State to the capital market of another.

12.29 The position changes considerably on 1 July 1990 with the coming into force of Directive 88/361 (33) for the implementation of Article 67 of the Treaty and repealing the First Directive of 11 May 1960 and Directive 72/156 (32) with effect from 1 July 1990. Article 1 of Directive 88/361 (33) provides that Member States shall abolish restrictions on movements of capital taking place between residents of Member States. Under Article 4 Member States have the right to take all requisite measures to prevent infringements of their laws and regulations (*inter alia* in the field of taxation and prudential supervision of financial institutions) or for declaration of capital movements for statistical purposes.

12.30 Capital movements are now classified in accordance with the Nomenclature in Annex I of the Directive. It covers:

(a) direct investments,
(b) investments in real estate,
(c) operations in securities normally dealt in on the capital market,
(d) operations in units of collective investment undertakings,
(e) operations in securities and other instruments normally dealt in on the money market,

(30) OJ 1963–64/5.
(31) OJ 1963–64/45.
(32) OJ 1972 296.
(33) OJ 1988 L 178/5.

(f) operations in current and deposit accounts with financial institutions,

(g) credits related to commercial transactions or to the provision of services in which a resident is participating,

(h) financial loans and credits,

(i) securities, other guarantees and rights of pledge,

(j) transfers in performance of insurance contracts,

(k) personal capital movements,

(k) physical import and export of financial assets, and

(m) other capital movements.

The Annex contains also detailed explanatory notes.

12.31 Article 3 of the Directive allows the Community to authorise Member States, in cases of severe strains on foreign exchange markets and movements leading to serious disturbances in the conduct of monetary and exchange rate policies, to take protective measures determined by the Commission in respect of capital movements listed in Annex II. Annexes III and IV list special provisions for Spain, Portugal, Greece and Ireland.

12.32 Article 68(1) provides that Member States shall be as liberal as possible in granting such exchange authorisations as are still necessary after the entry into force of the Treaty. Under Article 71, Member States must endeavour to avoid introducing any new restrictions on movements of capital and current payments connected with such movements and must endeavour not to make existing rules more restrictive. Article 71 does not, it seems, impose on the Member States an unconditional obligation which can be relied upon by individuals: *Casati*. (26)

12.33 Article 68(2) provides that where Member States apply to capital movements domestic rules governing the capital market and the credit system they must do so in a non-discriminatory manner; this appears to be directly applicable. Under Article 68(3) loans for the direct or indirect financing of a Member State or its regional or local authorities may not be issued or placed in other Member States unless the States concerned have reached agreement on this, although this does not preclude the European Investment Bank from borrowing on the capital markets of Member States.

12.34 Article 72 requires Member States to keep the Commission informed of any capital movements to and from third countries which

come to their knowledge, and if movements of capital lead to disturbances in the functioning of the capital market in any Member State, the
Commission is empowered by Article 73 to authorise Member States to
take protective measures in the field of capital movements. In cases of
urgency or secrecy a Member State may act on its own initiative, but the
Commission has power to direct such measures to be amended or
abolished, and both it and the other Member States must be informed of
them.

12.35 The Community when dealing with capital movements was
conscious of the balance of payments difficulties of its members and
provided for a machinery if support of balances of payments were
necessary. Regulation 1969/88 (34) establishes a single facility providing
medium-term financial assistance for member States' balances of payments, repealing previous acts. The amount of loans to be granted under
this facility is limited to 16,000 million ECU and the Commission is to
contract loans on the capital markets or with financial institutions.

(34)   OJ 1988 L 178/1.

CHAPTER 13

Company Law

Freedom of establishment

13.01 Community legislation dealing with companies has its background in the provisions of the Treaty concerned with Right of Establishment. Article 52 calls for abolition of restrictions on the freedom of establishment of nationals of a Member State in the territory of another Member State. This freedom of establishment includes the right to take up and pursue activities as self-employed persons and to set up and manage undertakings, in particular companies or firms within the meaning of the second paragraph of Article 58. Article 58 states that companies or firms formed in accordance with the law of a Member State (and having their registered office, central administration or principal place of business within the Community) shall be treated in the same way as natural persons who are nationals of Member States. In the second paragraph it defines "companies or firms" as companies or firms constituted under civil or commercial law, save for those which are non-profit-making.

13.02 In *Case 81/87, The Queen v. HM Treasury and Commissioners of Inland Revenue ex parte Daily Mail and General Trust PLC* (1) the Court of Justice ruled that in the present state of Community Law, Articles 52 and 58 of the Treaty, properly construed, confer no right on a company incorporated under the legislation of a Member State and having its registered office there to transfer its central management and control to another Member State.

13.03 Article 54 calls for a general programme for the abolition of existing restrictions on freedom of establishment within the Community, and for co-ordinating the safeguards which, for the protection of the interests of members and others, are required by Member States of companies or firms within the meaning of the second paragraph of Article 58 with a view to making such safeguards equivalent throughout the Community.

(1)   [1988] 3 CMLR 713.

Company Directives

13.04   These provisions are the basis for Community legislation which commenced in 1968 with the First Directive (68/151) (2) concerned with disclosure, validity of company acts and nullity. The Directive applies to public and private companies and provides for mandatory publication of certain documents and information, eg company statutes, names of directors and officers, subscribed capital, balance sheet and profit and loss account of public companies, details of winding up, liquidators and termination of a liquidation. (The provisions dealing with accounts were further extended by the Fourth Directive (78/660). (3)) The First Directive further provides for establishment of company registries in each Member State; validation of obligations entered by companies including a prohibition against the doctrine of *ultra vires* applying against a third party contracting in gooth faith; and definition of occasions when nullity of a company may be claimed. In *Case 136/87, Ubbink Isolatie BV v. Dak- en Vandtechniek BV* (4) the Court of Justice held that the rules on the nullity of companies contained in the First Directive do not apply where the acts involved were performed in the name of a private limited liability company which was not registered in the public register because the formalities for incorporation required by national law had not been completed. The First Directive is now implemented in the United Kingdom by Section 35 of the Companies Act 1985 (formerly Section 9 of the European Communities Act 1972). The doctrine of *ultra vires* is restricted by the Act when it provides that: (a) in favour of a person dealing with a company in good faith, any transaction decided on by the directors is deemed to be one which it is within the capacity of the company to enter into, and the power of the directors to bind the company shall be deemed to be free of any limitation under the memorandum or articles of association; and (b) a party to a transaction so decided on shall not be bound to enquire as to the capacity of the company to enter into it or as to any such limitations on the power of the directors, and shall be presumed to have acted in good faith unless the contrary is proved. Section 36(4) of the 1985 Act, implementing Article 7 of the Directive, establishes liability for contracts entered prior to the formation of the company by those concerned with its incorporation. The concept of "nullity" in the Directive is unknown to United Kingdom law. Section 15(1) of the Companies Act 1948 provided that the certificate of incorporation is conclusive evidence of the due formation of the company.

(2)   OJ 1968 L 65/8.
(3)   OJ 1978 L 222/11.
(4)   (Not yet reported).

13.05   The Second Directive, 77/91 (5), deals with public companies, their formation and the maintenance of their capital. The major requirements of the Directive include a minimum capital of 25,000 ECU, differentiation in name between public and private companies, restrictions on the payment of dividends, virtual prohibition of issuing shares at a discount, the necessity for an expert's report on the value of non-cash consideration to be paid for new shares, sundry provisions relating to share capital and the requirement for a shareholders' meeting if accumulated losses exceed at most 50% of subscribed capital. This Directive was implemented by the Companies Act 1980 (now the Companies Act 1985). A public company is defined as a company limited by shares or guarantee or having a share capital whose memorandum must state it to be a public company. Its name must end with the words "public limited company". The minimum issued share capital in the UK must be £50,000 (as opposed to 25,000 ECU in the Directive). In defining the non-cash consideration to be paid for new shares the Act employs a concept of money or money's worth in place of the Directive's assets "capable of economic assessment".

13.06   The Third Directive, 78/855 (6), applies to public companies and deals with mergers between two companies both subject to the laws of the same Member State. It is intended to pave the way for rules applying to mergers between companies subject to the laws of different states. The term "merger" in the Directive relates to a total merger involving the legal transfer of all the assets and liabilities. The provisions of the Directive are intended to protect not only shareholders but also creditors and employees. (The interests of employees are specifically dealt with in Directive 77/187 (7)). The Sixth Directive 82/891 (8) on splitting up of public limited liability companies covers cases where a public company, in the course of reconstruction, divides up and transfers to more than one other company all its assets and liabilities in exchange for the issue of shares in those companies. The detailed provisions of this Directive are designed to complement those of the Third Directive. The Directives do not embrace most "mergers" as the term is generally understood in the United Kingdom, that is the acquisition for shares of one company by another, but without subsequent transfer of assets and liabilities. The Companies Act 1985 is presumed to cover the rare eventualities arising out of the Directives. (See also para. 14.64 below.)

(5)   OJ 1977 L 26/1.
(6)   OJ 1978 L 295/36.
(7)   OJ 1977 L 61/26.
(8)   OJ 1982 L 378/47.

13.07   The Fourth Directive, 78/660 (3), on annual accounts applies to
public and private companies with the exception of banks and insurance
companies. It deals with the layout of annual accounts, valuation
methods to be adopted for their preparation, contents of the annual
report and provisions concerning publication of the accounts. It does not
cover the preparation of consolidated accounts. The Directive applies to
all limited liability companies, although less strict requirements are
imposed on small and medium-sized companies. New thresholds for
smaller companies were adopted by the Council in Directive 84/569 (9)
in place of those in Article 11 of the Fourth Directive. For the purposes
of the main Directive annual accounts shall comprise the balance sheet,
the profit and loss account and the notes to the accounts. The accounts
shall give a true and fair view of the company's assets, liabilities and
financial position. The Directive sets out in considerable detail the
information required to be disclosed, the layout and grouping of balance
sheet and profit and loss account headings. It defines in detail the nature
of items to be included under certain headings, eg land and buildings etc.
A section dealing with valuation rules sets out certain basic concepts. The
Directive concerns itself with the rules relating to historical cost accounting. In the United Kingdom the Directive is implemented by the
Companies Act 1985. Company accounts have to comply with the
requirements of Schedule 4. The Schedule is based on the Directive and
the Annexes I and II (layout of the balance sheet and layout of the profit
and loss account) of the Directive. The general principles of the Directive
are incorporated in the Act.

13.08   The Seventh Company Directive 83/349 (10) on consolidated
accounts covers the areas omitted by the Fourth Directive. It requires the
consolidation of finanacial statements where either the parent undertaking or the subsidiary is established as a public company limited by shares
or by guarantee or as a private company limited by shares or by
guarantee. The Directive exempts from consolidation parent undertakings which are not established as one of the forms of company mentioned
above. Member States may exempt financial holding companies (ie
companies which are not involved in the management of the undertakings
in which they acquire holdings) from the provisions of the Directive. The
Directive deals in detail with the nature and form of consolidated
accounts.

13.09   The Seventh Directive is implemented in the United Kingdom by
the Companies Act 1989 (in section 5 and Schedule 2), which inserts new

(9)   OJ 1984 L 314/28.
(10)   OJ 1983 L 193/1.

sections 227–230 into the Companies Act 1985. The new section 227 contains the obligation to prepare group accounts and prescribes their form; the new section 228 makes exemptions from the obligation; and the new section 229 requires that subsidiary undertakings should be included in consolidated accounts subject to exceptions set out in that section. The new section 230 makes concessions in respect of individual profit and loss accounts where group accounts are prepared. Schedule 2 of the 1989 Act, which will become Schedule 4A to the 1985 Act, lays down the detailed rules for the form and content of group accounts, including the accounting methods and valuation rules prescribed by the Seventh Directive. The Fourth and Seventh Directives on annual accounts and consolidated accounts respectively have made the role of the auditor extremely important.

13.10 The Eighth Directive 84/253 (11) deals with the professional qualifications of statutory auditors. Auditing under the Directive must be carried out by approved persons only. The Directive is mainly concerned with educational and professional training and examination requirements. It has provisions relating to the independent status of auditors and to arrangements for persons entitled to carry out audits who do not fulfil the requirements of the Directive. In the United Kingdom the authority to grant approval is regulated by Section 389 of the Companies Act 1985 and the Directive is implemented by Part II of the Companies Act 1989.

13.11 Directive 88/627 (12) specifies the information to be published when a major holding in a listed company is acquired or disposed of. When, following acquisition or disposal of a holding, a person or a legal entity holds voting rights exceeding or falling below a specified proportion he has to notify the company and at the same time the competent authority within seven calendar days. Reference ought to be made to the Convention on the Mutual Recognition of Companies and Bodies Corporate signed in 1968 by the original six Member States under Article 220 of the Treaty. The United Kingdom acceded to the Convention under the Act of Accession of 1972, but the original Convention has not entered into force because of failure of the necessary number of ratifications. Since the Treaty itself provides for non-discrimination of Community companies and for all intents and purposes the benefits foreseen by the Convention are already available, it is open to doubt whether the Convention will enter into force.

(11) OJ 1984 L 126/20.
(12) OJ 1988 L 348/62.

European Economic Interest Groupings

13.12 Pending further developments leading to the harmonisation of Company law in the Community, the Council adopted in 1985 Regulation 2137/85 (13) on the European Economic Interest Grouping (EEIG), providing for the formation of groupings of firms in the Community, with the aim stated in the Regulation "to facilitate or develop the economic activities of members and to improve or increase the results of those activities; its purpose is not to make profits for itself." These firms will co-operate in joint ventures, provide for research and development, join in submission of tenders outside the Community, arrange for bulk purchases and provide joint services. All these activities do not affect the legal and economic independence of the members of the grouping. An EEIG can best be described as a form of incorporated partnership of companies at Community level. It has legal capacity, its formation depends upon a contract drawn up by its members; there is no requirement for any capital and the liability of its members is unlimited.

13.13 The activity of the Grouping must be related to the economic activities of its members and must not be more than ancillary to those activities. It must pursue an activity which each of its members has in common, thus forming a logical basis for the creation of a grouping. Each member must have a link with the Community and carry on an economic activity within the Community, being taxable within the Community by trading through a permanent establishment. EEC subsidiaries of a non-EEC parent may become members. An EEIG should have at least two members from at least two different Member States. The Regulation prescribes the terms in which the groupings are formed. The formation contract must be registered in the Member State in which the official address is located; the formation of the EEIG must also be notified in the Official Journal. EEIGs must be registered in one Member State and that state may require the number of members to be limited to 20. EEIGs can be formed with or without capital, they may not employ more than 500 people and when employing more than 100 people, a statutory auditor is required. From the date of registration the EEIG has the capacity to have rights and obligations, to enter into contracts and to sue and be sued. It may hold shares but not in any of its members and may not become a member of another EEIG. The acts of managers are binding on the Grouping, even if they go beyond the EEIG's objectives. For the purposes of taxes on profits, the Regulation provides

(13)   OJ 1985 L 199/1.

that an EEIG is to be fiscally transparent. The entity itself will not be taxed but its profit or losses will be apportioned among the members and taxed or relieved in their hands. The headquarters of an EEIG will constitute the permanent establishment in the Member State in which it is located. Hence each member of an EEIG will be exposed to tax in that state. The Regulation deals in detail with the contents of the formation contract and with the internal machinery of the EEIG. It further prescribes the procedure of winding up and liquidation which are governed by national law. The regulation applies from 1 July 1989.

CHAPTER 14

The Competition Rules of the EEC Treaty

14.01 The Community competition rules are found in the policy section of the EEC Treaty. Chapter 1 which deals with rules on competition is divided into 3 parts; the first deals with the rules governing undertakings, the second with anti-dumping and the last with state aids.

14.02 Articles 85 and 86 of the EEC Treaty form the core of the rules relating to undertakings and until recently were the provisions most commonly encountered in a commercial context. Coal and steel are dealt with under a different regime in the ECSC Treaty, which contains detailed rules governing the operations of certain coal and steel producers and distributors. Dumping from third countries is dealt with as part of the common commercial policy (Chapter 4). It is only intra-Community dumping which is considered as part of the Community Competition law and is dealt with under Article 91.

14.03 The Commission has been empowered by the Council to act in a number of areas, but the Commission's legislation, decisions in individual cases and informal notices are all subject to review by the Court. The Commission is responsible for the policing of the Community's competition policy and has been given wide powers including the power to impose significant fines for breaches of the rules. The way in which the Commission exercises its powers is subject to review by the Court of Justice under Article 173 of the Treaty, and the Court retains primary responsibility for ensuring that the law is observed in the interpretation and application of the EEC Treaty. If the Court decides that the Commission's view of the law is wrong it has shown that it is prepared to overrule it, even though the view has been accepted for some time: *Case 65/86, Bayer & Hennecke v. Sulhoffen.* (1)

14.04 Article 85 is essentially concerned with agreements and concerted practices which do or may affect competition in a particular fashion. Article 86 is concerned with abusive conduct by an enterprise in a dominant position. It will generally be more difficult to show a breach of Article 86 than a breach of Article 85, as in the case of Article 86 it will

---

(1) [1988] 4 CMLR 881 (no challenge clauses in licences).

be necessary to show that the enterprise concerned actually was in a dominant position. However, if there is no agreement or form of concerted practice, for instance if there is a refusal to supply, then it will be necessary to consider Article 86. Nevertheless, Articles 85 and 86 have a number of features in common, so that the Court's ruling on one Article may be useful when considering the other, if common features are concerned.

14.05   The Court generally uses the purposive method of interpretation of the Treaty and it has interpreted both Articles 85 and 86 in the light of the objectives set out in Articles 2 and 3. An example of this was *Cases 6–7/73, ICI and Commercial Solvents Corporation v. Commission.* (2) Here the Court was concerned with Article 86 which it construed in the light of the general aims set out in Articles 2 and 3 of the Treaty. Article 2 of the Treaty provides as follows:

> "The Community shall have as its task, by establishing a common market and progressively approximating the economic policies of Member States, to provide throughout the Community a harmonious development of economic activities, a continuous and balanced expansion, an increase in stability, an accelerated raising of the standard of living and closer relations between the States belonging to it."

14.06   A number of specific aims are set out in Article 3, but those of particular interest in relation to the Competition Rules are set out in Article 3(b), (f) and (g). Article 3 provides as follows:

> "For the purposes set out in Article 2, the activities of the Community shall include, as provided in this Treaty and in accordance with the timetable set out therein:
> . . . .
> (b) the establishment of a common customs tariff and of a common commercial policy towards third countries;
> . . . .
> (f) the institution of a system ensuring that competition in the common market is not distorted;
> (g) the approximation of the laws of Member States to the extent required for the proper functioning of the common market. . . ."

14.07   Recently the Court has also relied on Articles 90 and 5 when considering cases under Articles 85 and 86. In *Case 66/86, Ahmed Saeed Flugreisen and Silver Line Reisebüro GmbH v. Zentrale zur Bekampfung unlauteren Wettbewerbs EV,* (3) a case involving price fixing on regular flights, the Court stated that Articles 90 and 5 of the Treaty obliged the

(2)   [1974] ECR 223; [1974] 1 CMLR 309.
(3)   (Not yet reported). Also see Chapter 15.

national authorities not to approve or do anything to encourage airlines to adopt pricing structures which breached Articles 85 and 86.

14.08 In *Case 23/67, Brasserie de Haecht v. Wilkin and Janssen* (4), when considering the question of effect upon trade between Member States, the Court was concerned with the problems of achieving the "economic inter-penetration" which is aimed at by the Treaty. Ten years later in a similar vein in *Case 27/76, United Brands Co. & United Brands Continental v. Commission* (5), the Court ruled that any practice which affects inter-state commerce is likely to hinder the attainment of the Treaty objective of economic inter-penetration.

Article 85

14.09 Article 85 contains three sections. The first part specifies prohibited types of agreements. The second part declares that any agreements or decisions which fall within Article 85(1) shall be automatically void. The third then provides that in certain circumstances Article 85(1) can be declared inapplicable in individual cases, or categories of cases, provided certain criteria are fulfilled.

14.10 Article 85 provides as follows:

"(1) The following shall be prohibited as incompatible within the common market: all agreements between undertakings, decisions by associations of undertakings, and concerted practices which may affect trade between Member States and which have as their object or effect the prevention, restriction or distortion of competition within the common market, and in particular those which:

(a) directly or indirectly fix purchase or selling prices or any other trading conditions;
(b) limit or control production, markets, technical development or investments;
(c) share markets or sources of supply;
(d) apply dissimilar conditions to equivalent transactions with other trading parties, thereby placing them at a competitive disadvantage;
(e) make the conclusion of contracts subject to acceptance by the other parties of supplementary obligations which, by their nature or according to commercial usage, have no connection with the subject of such contracts.

(2) Any agreements or decisions prohibited pursuant to this Article shall be automatically void.

(4) [1967] ECR 407 [1968] 7 CMLR 26.
(5) [1978] ECR 207; [1978] 1 CMLR 429.

(3) The provisions of paragraph (1) may, however, be declared inapplicable in the case of:

(a) any agreement or category of agreements between undertakings;
(b) any decision or category of decisions by associations of undertakings;
(c) any concerted practice or category of concerted practices;

which contributes to improving the production or distribution of goods or to promoting technical or economic progress, while allowing consumers a fair share of the resulting benefit, and which does not:

(a) impose on the undertakings concerned restrictions which are not indispensable to the attainment of these objectives;
(b) afford such undertakings the possibility of eliminating competition in respect of a substantial part of the products in question."

Agreements, decisions and concerted practices
14.11 As can be seen, the scope of Article 85(1) is very wide. It catches formal and informal agreements; gentlemen's understandings; concerted practices and other forms of consensual behaviour. In *Cases No. 48–57/69, ICI Ltd v. EEC Commission (Dye Stuffs)* (6) the Court explained the scope of Article 85 as follows:-

". . . If Article 85 distinguishes the concept of "concerted practice" from that of "agreements between enterprises" or "decisions of associations of enterprises" this is done with the object of bringing under the prohibitions of this Article a form of co-ordination between undertakings, which without going so far as to amount to an agreement properly so called, knowingly substitutes a practical co-operation between them for the risks of competition.

By its very nature then, the practice does not combine all the elements of an agreement, but may, *inter alia*, result from a co-ordination which becomes apparent from the behaviour of the participants."

14.12 While parallel conduct is not a concerted practice, it can be evidence that such a practice is in existence. (7)

14.13 The list of conduct in Article 85 is a non-exhaustive catalogue of examples of particularly anti-competitive behaviour. The list does not limit the scope of the Article (8). Further, Article 85, like Article 86, is concerned with the effects of actions and not the forms in which they are executed. Thus unlike the Restrictive Trade Practices Act in the United Kingdom which is forms-based, it is unlikely that it will be possible to draft round Community competition provisions.

(6) [1972] ECR 619–933; [1972] CMLR 557.
(7) *Ibid.*
(8) *Continental Can* [1972] ECR 157; [1973] 12 CMLR 199, para 26.

It may be possible though to frame an agreement so that it can benefit from one of the block exemptions provided for under Article 85(3) of the Treaty (see paras 14.42 *et seq.*)

Undertakings and associations of undertakings
14.14   Article 85 is concerned with the behaviour of natural and legal persons, but only if they have a reasonable degree of independence. Accordingly, a subsidiary which is completely under the control of its parent is not regarded as an enterprise for the purposes of Article 85. (9) It follows that a restrictive agreement between a non-autonomous subsidiary and its parent or between two non-autonomous subsidiaries of the same parent will not breach Article 85. In *Case 16/74, Centrafarm BV and De Peijper v. Winthrop BV* (10) the Court ruled as follows:

> "Article 85 does not apply to agreements or concerted practices between undertakings belonging to the same group in the form of parent company and subsidiary, if the undertakings form an economic unit within which the subsidiary does not have real autonomy in determining its line of conduct on the market and if the agreement or practices have the aim of establishing an internal distribution of tasks between the undertakings. . ."

14.15   The corollary has also been applied and in *Cases 6–7/73, Commercial Solvents* (11) it was decided that a parent in the US which owned and controlled a subsidiary within the EEC could be regarded as doing business within the EEC, and the Commission had power to order it to supply certain raw materials to a competitor.

14.16   If Article 85 does not apply because of a parent/subsidiary relationship, it may nevertheless be the case that Article 86 may do so if as a group the parties are in a dominant position in the product market. The existence of a restrictive intra-group agreement may in itself constitute an abuse of a dominant position.

14.17   The extra-territorial application of Article 85 to enterprises established outside the Community has now been confirmed in the joined *Case 89/85, Re Woodpulp Cartel* (12). In considering this question of extra-territorial jurisdiction the Court adopted an effects-based approach. Agreements which were entered into by enterprises outside the EEC, but which were implemented within it, were held to be subject to Article 85.

(9)   *Re Christiani & Nielsen*, Decision 69/195, OJ 1969 L 165/12.
(10)   [1974] ECR 1183; [1974] 2 CMLR 480.
(11)   [1974] ECR 223; [1974] 1 CMLR 309.
(12)   [1988] 4 CMLR 901.

14.18 In a further application of the independence test under Article 85 the Court has drawn a distinction between the position of an independent distributor and a commercial traveller. An agreement between an undertaking and its distributor may well breach Article 85 and there have been a number of cases involving distribution agreements. The Court has taken the view, however, that an agreement between a principal and an agent of the commercial traveller sort does not involve Article 85 (13). In 1962 the Commission issued its so-called Christmas message on exclusive dealing contracts with commercial agents (14). The notice sets out the views of the Commission upon the distinctions between an independent trader and an agent who acts as no more than an extension of the principal. The criteria for distinguishing between the two are concerned with the acceptance of commercial risk. Directive 86/653 on commercial agents (15) does not deal specifically with this distinction between independent trader and agent.

Effect on trade between Member States
14.19 An agreement which does not affect trade between Member States is not caught by Article 85. In *Cases 56/64 and 58/64, Consten and Grundig v. Commission* (16) the Court stated that the purpose of the requirement of an effect on trade between Member States was to separate the respective fields of application of national and community law.

> "It is to the extent to which an agreement may affect trade between Member States that the alteration in competition provoked by the agreement relates to the prohibitions in community law of Article 85, whereas in the contrary case, it escapes."

14.20 The importance of this distinction between the application of national cartel law and Community law can be seen in the discussions which have gone on within the Community for a number of years on the regulation for control of mergers. Those countries with developed competition systems of their own have been keen to preserve national autonomy both on grounds of principle and also on pragmatic grounds, namely that the Commission would be unable to cope if all the mergers currently dealt with at a national level were referred to it for consideration.

14.21 There is sufficient effect on intra-community trade to bring Article 85 into operation if an agreement hinders the attainment of the

(13) *Consten and Grundig v. Commission* [1966] ECR 299, 385; [1966] CMLR 418, 470.
(14) OJ 1962 L 39/2921.
(15) OJ 1986 L 328/17.
(16) [1966] ECR 299, 385; [1966] CMLR 418, 472.

Treaty's aims. Thus in *Consten and Grundig* (17) the Court considered that the vital question was whether:

> "the agreement is capable of endangering, either directly or indirectly, in fact or potentially, freedom of trade between Member States in a direction which could harm the attainment of the objects of a single market between States."

14.22   Article 85 is not breached if there is only a negligible effect on trade between Member States. In *Case 5/69, Volk v. Vervaercke* (18) the Court ruled that an agreement did not fall within Article 85 when in view of the weak position of the parties in the market for the products involved its effect on the market was insignificant. The Commission has published a *de minimis* notice which sets out specific thresholds for the application of Article 85. The Court, however, has merely stated that an agreement must affect competition between Member States in a non-negligible fashion and has not set out quantitative criteria.

14.23   It is not necessary to show an actual effect on trade; it is sufficient if it may exist. In *Case 56/65, Société Technique Minière v. Maschinenbau Ulm GmbH* (19) the Court said that the necessary effect on trade would be present if it allows:

> "one to expect, with a sufficient degree of probability, that it would exercise a direct or indirect, actual or potential, effect on the eddies of trade between Member States."

14.24   While an obvious example of a provision which will affect trade between Member States is an export ban, the necessary effect can also be found in other less obvious forms. It is sufficient if a provision may have an effect on trade entering or leaving a Member State. Thus the granting of an exclusive territory to a distributor may affect Member States' trade if someone else has to import goods from another Member State as a result.

14.25   To the cynical it may sometimes appear that the element of an effect on intra-community trade is readily detected in cases which involve particularly anti-competitive behaviour. In the *Commercial Solvents* case (11) the Court ruled that trade within the common market was affected where the complained of conduct involved the elimination of a competitor. The repercussions of the elimination upon the competitive structure within the common market were said to show the necessary effect on trade between Member States. (20)

(17)   *Ibid.*
(18)   [1969] ECR 285; [1969] CMLR 273.
(19)   [1966] ECR 235; [1966] CMLR 357, 375.
(20)   *Commercial Solvents* [1974] ECR 223; [1974] 1 CMLR 309.

Prevention, restriction or distortion

14.26 Article 85 applies to both vertical and horizontal agreements. It can apply to exclusive supply or distribution arrangements, selective distribution arrangements, joint ventures, research and development agreements, intellectual property licences, restraint of trade clauses, loyalty rebates, differential pricing and the application of dissimilar conditions to equivalent trading transactions. Until recently it appeared that any form of exclusive territorial protection, was likely to come within Article 85(1). However in *Case 27/87, SPRL Louis Erauw-Jacquery v. La Hesbignonne* (21) the Court upheld an agreement which gave the licensor, who was the holder of plant breeder's rights, absolute territorial protection as the customer restrictions were necessary to protect the licensor's rights.

Competition

14.27 The Treaty does not define competition. One commentator defines it as follows: (22)

> "Competition is the freedom to compete with others for business opportunities on whatever terms appear desirable. Competition is restrained when that freedom is limited, either because of the parties to the agreement, decision, or concerted practice, or because any other non-party is limited in his freedom to deal with others. A person who merely sells a 100 tonnes of wheat to someone else is not restraining competition, because the freedom of the contracting parties to buy or sell wheat elsewhere and that of others to sell wheat to the purchaser remains unaffected. On the other hand, requirements and output contracts restrain competition, because they limit the freedom of the purchaser to buy his requirements, and that of the seller to sell his output, elsewhere."

The Court has ruled in *Case 56/65, Société Technique Minière* (23) that:

> "the competition in question should be understood within the actual context in which it would occur in the absence of the agreement in question."

Within the Common Market

14.28 In all competition problems, the definition of the market is crucial. Thus a supplier may have 90% of the UK market for red pencils, 20% of the EEC market for such pencils, but only 5% of the UK market for all pencils and 0.5% of the EEC market for all pencils.

14.29 It follows that it is necessary to consider the market on more than one level. First a product market must be arrived at, then a

(21) [1988] 4 CMLR 576.
(22) *The Law of the European Communities,* Smit & Herzog.
(23) [1966] ECR 235; [1966] CMLR 357, 375.

geographical market, and lastly it may be necessary to consider the particular point in the chain of manufacture and supply which is involved. Market share is relevant in considering both whether there is any distortion of competition under Article 85 as well as under Article 86 in deciding whether an undertaking is in a dominant position. It is usually in the interests of the parties to argue that the market is defined as widely as possible, both in terms of product and area. However, certain differences may be detected between the general position in respect of market definition as adopted by the Court and the definitions of product and geographical market adopted by the Commission in its Minor Agreements Notice.

14.30 The classic statement of the Court in respect of market definitions is to be found in *Case 27/76, United Brands* where the Court ruled (24):

> "It is necessary to define (the) market both from the stand-point of the product and from the geographic point of view ... (and) to have regard to the particular features of the product in question and with reference to a clearly defined geographic area in which it is marketed and where the conditions of competition are sufficiently homogeneous for the effect of the economic power of the undertaking concerned to be able to be evaluated."

Product market
14.31 The tendency has been for the Commission to have regard to fairly narrowly defined product markets. In *Brass Band Instruments Ltd v. Boosey & Hawkes plc* (25) the market was brass band instruments; in *Case 22/78, Hugin Kassenregister AB – Hugin Cash Registers Ltd v. Commission* (26) the market was said to be that of spare parts for a particular type of cash register. In the *Commercial Solvents* case (27) the Commission defined the market as that of raw materials for a particular therapeutic drug which was used for the treatment of tuberculosis and it did not look at a wider market for all drugs for tuberculosis; in *Case 85/76, Hoffman-La Roche & Co. AG v. Commission* (28) the Commission looked at separate markets in respect of particular vitamins.

14.32 However, the Commission's definition of the market in the *Continental Can Case* (29), namely of cans for meat and fish and can closures, was rejected by the Court, which considered that insufficient

(24) [1978] ECR 207; [1978] 1 CMLR 429.
(25) Decision 87//500, OJ 1987 L 286/36.
(26) [1979] ECR 1869; [1979] 3 CMLR 345.
(27) [1974] ECR 223; [1974] 1 CMLR 309.
(28) [1979] ECR 461; [1979] 3 CMLR 211.
(29) [1972] ECR 157; [1973] CMLR 199.

consideration had been given to the possibility of product substitutes and of the entry into the market of manufacturers of different types of cans. Similarly in *Cases 19 and 20/74, Kali & Salz v. Commission* (30) the Court rejected the argument of the Commission that the market was for pure potash fertilisers, as it found that such substances were in competition with compound potash fertilisers.

14.33 In *United Brands* (31) the Court considered consumer substitutes. It considered whether bananas had any special features which distinguished them from other fruits when considering whether they were interchangeable with those others. As bananas are not seasonal fruits the question of interchangeability from the consumers viewpoint was considered over the whole year. Price fluctuations caused by the availability of seasonal fruits were considered. The Court concluded that bananas were sufficiently distinct from other fresh fruits to form a separate market as they were only exposed to competition from other fruits in a barely perceptible fashion.

Geographic market
14.34 In considering the geographic market in *United Brands* the Court said that it was essential to be able to define a substantial part of the Common Market where the effects were felt and where the objective conditions of competition applying are the same for all traders.

14.35 Further consideration was given to the question of a geographic market in *Case 247/86, Alsatel v Novasam* (32). This case involved the telecommunications company for Alsace and Lorraine. The Court ruled that although Alsatel had a very substantial share of the market in Alsace and Lorraine, those areas could not constitute a separate geographical market for the purposes of the application of Article 86 on the facts of the case.

Invalidity
14.36 Agreements in breach of Article 85(1) are declared automatically void by Article 85(2). The Court decided in the *Société Technique Minière* case (33) that it is appropriate to use a blue pencil approach and it is only necessary to strike out those provisions which have been declared void under Article 85(2). The Court will not rule upon the effect upon the whole agreement of the nullity of some parts. That is a

(30) [1975] ECR 499; [1974] ECR 337, 787; [1975] 2 CMLR 154.
(31) [1978] ECR 207; [1978] 1 CMLR 429.
(32) [1988] 4 CMLR 882.
(33) [1966] ECR 235; [1966] CMLR 357.

matter for the national courts of the Member States to decide in accordance with the general principles applied by them. In the *Consten and Grundig* case (34) the Court said an agreement would only be wholly void if the offending parts could not be severed.

Exemptions
14.37 An agreement or practice which falls within Article 85(1) of the EEC Treaty may nevertheless be exempted from the operation of Article 85(1) and thus from the effects of Article 85(2), i.e. voidness, and the possibility of fines if it can satisfy all the four parts to Article 85(3). These consists of two positive and two negative tests. They are as follows:

(1) The agreement or practice must contribute to improving the production or distribution of goods or promoting technical or economic progress; and

(2) It must also allow consumers a fair share of the resulting benefit; and

(3) It must not impose on the undertakings concerned any restrictions which go beyond the positive aims of the agreement; and

(4) It must not result in the elimination of competition in respect of a substantial part of the products in question.

14.38 Article 85(3) provides for the issue of exemptions both for individual agreements or practices and for categories of agreements.

14.39 The machinery for notification of individual agreements and for making application for exemption is contained in Regulation 17/62 of the Council (35) which provides that, subject to review by the Court, the Commission has the sole power to declare Article 85(1) inapplicable pursuant to Article 85(3). It also confers upon the Commission various powers relating to enforcement and fines.

14.40 Commission decisions under Article 85(3) granting individual exemptions are issued for a limited period and may be subject to the fulfilment of conditions and obligations. A decision can be renewed on further application if Article 85(3) continues to be satisfied. The Commission may revoke or amend a decision granting individual exemption in certain circumstances.

14.41 Categories of agreements are exempted from Article 85(1) by means of regulations known as block exemptions which grant class relief.

(34) [1966] ECR 299; [1966] CMLR 418.
(35) OJ 1962 L 3/204 (Special Edition 1959–62 p87).

Block exemptions

14.42 The Commission has been empowered by the Council to issue block exemptions in a number of areas, and to date has issued them variously for exclusive distribution agreements (Regulation 1983/83 (36)), exclusive purchasing agreements (Regulation 1984/83 (37)), patent licensing agreements (Regulation 2349/84 (38)), motor vehicle distribution and servicing agreements (Regulation 123/85 (39)), specialisation agreements (Regulation 417/85 (40)), research and development agreements (Regulation 418/85 (41)), know-how agreements (Regulation 556/89 (42)) and franchising arrangements (Regulation 4087/88 (43)). It has also granted certain other exemptions in the transport field.

14.43 In practice, the block exemptions are extremely useful and much used. A contract which falls squarely within the terms of a block exemption does not have to be notified to the European Commission and there is no danger that the contracting parties will be fined for breach of Article 85. Although most of the block exemptions contain provisions which permit the Commission to withdraw the benefit of a block exemption from particular agreements, to date this power has not been used.

14.44 Each of the block exemptions contains its own individual criteria which must be satisfied in all respects. Certain of the block exemptions are mutually exclusive, and care must be taken to ensure that an agreement does not fall partly within one block exemption and partly within another with the result that it cannot benefit from either; cf *DDD v. Delta* (44) where this happened. In certain instances, however, more than one block exemption can be relied upon at the same time. Thus, the research and development block exemption permits reliance on the other block exemptions relating to patent licensing or exclusive distribution or exclusive supply.

14.45 A block exemption generally will only apply to an agreement with no more than two parties. However, in counting heads for this purpose all connected undertakings can be treated as one party.

(36)   OJ 1983 L 173/1.
(37)   OJ 1983 L 173/5.
(38)   OJ 1984 L 219/15.
(39)   OJ 1985 L 15/16.
(40)   OJ 1985 L 53/1.
(41)   OJ 1985 L 53/5.
(42)   OJ 1989 L 61/1.
(43)   OJ 1988 L 359/46.
(44)   [1989] 4 CMLR 535.

"Connected undertakings" are defined in the block exemptions and are companies which are in the same group provided the linkage between each company involves 50% ownership or control. If more than one party to an agreement jointly has such a degree of control or ownership over a third party, then that third party is considered as being connected with each of them. The block exemptions tend to follow a pattern in which certain clauses, which may not in fact fall under Article 85 at all, are specifically permitted (the white clauses). Certain other provisions which always restrict or distort competition are expressly forbidden if the agreement is to benefit from block exemption from Article 85 (the black clauses). Some of the block exemptions contain a further category of clauses which require the agreement to be notified to the Commission under the opposition procedure (the grey clauses). Under the opposition procedure the Commission has 6 months in which to take action in respect of notified agreements and if at the end of that period it has not acted, then the agreement notified under the procedure is deemed to have qualified for block exemption.

14.46 If an agreement includes a "black" clause, then the parties cannot rely upon a severance clause, or use of a blue pencil to bring the agreement within the scope of the block exemption. (45)

Individual exemption
14.47 Procedural matters relating to the operation of Regulation 17/62 (46) are dealt with under Regulation 27/62 (47). Under those procedures an application for individual exemption must be made on the form specified, Form A/B. As it is notification which has the effect of preventing fines from accruing and of stopping fines which may already be running, it is usual to notify at the same time as the application for individual exemption is made. Form A/B operates both as notification and as application for exemption.

14.48 There is no need to notify an agreement which falls within Article 4(2) of Regulation 17/62. This provision is of very limited application. It relates to certain specialisation, and research and development agreements and to agreements relating to standards where: (1) there are only two parties; (2) there are no import or export ramifications; (3) the terms either relate only to the terms of resale or to the use or the application of certain industrial property rights; (4) the products do not represent more than 15% of the volume of business done in such

(45)   Commission Notice 84/C101/02 OJ 1984 C 101/2.
(46)   OJ 1962 13/204.
(47)   OJ 1962 35/1118 (Special Edition 1959–62 p132).

products in a substantial part of the European Communities; and (5) the total annual turnover of the participating undertakings does not exceed 200 million units of account.

14.49 Form A/B must be submitted in multiple copies which as a rule of thumb will be the number of Member States for the time being plus one. The application for exemption must be accompanied by all relevant documents and information relating to the relevant markets. Detailed guidance notes are issued with the Form A/B as to the types of information required.

14.50 It is necessary under United Kingdom provisions (48) to notify the Office of Fair Trading at the same time as the Form A/B is submitted. Any negative clearance or exemption granted by the Commission must also be notified to the Office of Fair Trading. Negative clearance or exemption will not relieve the United Kingdom parties of their obligations under the Restrictive Trade Practices Act 1976. There is provision in section 21(1) of that Act which permits the Director-General of Fair Trading to refrain from referring agreements to the Restrictive Practices Court where the relevant restrictions have benefited from exemption from Article 85.

Article 86

14.51 Article 86 of the EEC Treaty provides as follows:

> "Any abuse by one or more undertakings of a dominant position within the common market or in a substantial part of it shall be prohibited as incompatible with the common market in so far as it may affect trade between Member States.
> Such abuse may, in paticular, consist in:
> (a) directly or indirectly imposing unfair purchase or selling prices or other unfair trading conditions;
> (b) limiting production, markets or technical development to the prejudice of consumers;
> (c) applying dissimilar conditions to equivalent transactions with other trading parties, thereby placing them at a competitive disadvantage;
> (d) making the conclusion of contracts subject to acceptance by the other parties of supplementary obligations which, by their nature or according to commercial usage, have no connection with the subject of such contracts."

14.52 Article 86 is concerned with the conduct of dominant undertakings. Like Article 85, it starts with a general statement of prohibition

---

(48) Registration of Restricted Trading Agreements (EEC) (Documents) Regulations 1973, SI 1973 No. 950.

which is supported by examples. The examples are very similar to those set out in Article 85 and a number of factors, already considered in relation to Article 85, apply equally to Article 86. Thus, Article 86 involves a consideration of both geographical and product markets and the criterion of effect on trade between Member States must also be satisfied.

Dominant position

14.53 Unlike the position in the United Kingdom, where monopoly control commences once undertakings have a market share of 25% or more, there is no specific level at which Article 86 comes into operation. Market share is merely treated as one of a number of factors which must be considered in assessing whether or not a particular undertaking is in a position of dominance within the Common Market. Thus in *Case 26/76, Metro SB–Grossmarkte GmbH & Co. KG v. Commission* (49) the Court held that an enterprise holding between 5% and 10% of the relevant market did not necessarily have a dominant position. In the *Sugar Cases 40 to 48, 50, 54, to 56, 111, 113 to 114/73* (50) the Court found that the enterprise, which provided 85% of Belgian sugar production, was in a dominant position as imports of sugar into Belgium were negligible. It concluded that as the enterprise was able to impede effective competition in the market in question it occupied a dominant position.

14.54 There is no doubt now that the Court has stated the classic test for assessing the existence of a dominant position. The leading case is *Case 27/76, United Brands* (51) where the Court defined a "dominant position" as:

> "... a position of economic strength enjoyed by an undertaking which enables it to prevent effective competition being maintained on the relevant market by giving it the power to behave to an appreciable extent independently of its competitors, customers and ultimately of its consumers."

14.55 While a number of factors are taken into account in assessing whether a dominant position exists, an undertaking can only have a dominant position if it occupies a large part of the market. In the *United Brands* case the Court said that the fact that United Brands had between 40% and 45% of the market did not of itself lead to a conclusion that United Brands controlled that market. However, in the particular

(49) [1977] ECR 1875; [1978] 2 CMLR 1.
(50) [1975] ECR 1663; [1976] 1 CMLR 295.
(51) [1978] ECR 207; [1978] 1 CMLR 429.

circumstances of that case, where United Brands owned its own plantations, its own fleets and subjected its distributors, who also acted as its ripeners, to stringent and restrictive agreements, the Court found that it *was* in a dominant position. In fact the United Brands Group was the largest supplier of bananas worldwide with over 30% of the banana market. In addition to all its other advantages United Brands' technology was in advance of its competitors and the facts before the Court showed consumer preference for its "Chiquita" brand of bananas.

14.56 In a case involving Italian manufacturers of flat glass (52), the Commission had treated a cartel as a collective abuse of a dominant position. This notion of joint dominant position occupied by a number of companies was specifically rejected by the European Court in *Case 66/86, Ahmed Saeed* (53). As concerted practices and parallel conduct are in any event caught by Article 85 as forms of consensual behaviour, it would seem that the approach of the Court is to be preferred to that of the Commission.

14.57 In *Case 22/78, Hugin Cash Registers* (54) the Court decided that Hugin occupied a dominant position in relation to the supply of spare parts for its own cash registers. It is not clear whether this decision would be followed by the Court again as it was not referred to in the subsequent decision of the Court relating to spare parts for motor vehicles dealt with below at para. 14.72.

Abuse
14.58 To establish a breach of Article 86 it is not sufficient merely to show that an undertaking is in a dominant position; it is necessary to go on and show some abusive conduct on the part of the dominant undertaking. Whether or not an abuse exists is essentially a matter of fact. In the *United Brands* case the Court found a number of separate abuses, namely differential pricing, refusal to supply and the operation of a selective distribution system involving blanket prohibitions on re-sale which had the effect of partitioning the market.

14.59 In *Case 6/72, Continental Can* (55) the Court had ruled that the acquisition by a company in a dominant position of a competitor could consititue an abuse for the purpose of Article 86.

(52) OJ 1989 L 33/44.
(53) (Not yet reported). See also Chapter 15.
(54) [1979] ECR 1869; [1979] 3 CMLR 345.
(55) [1972] ECR 157; [1973] 12 CMLR 199.

14.60   Further instances of abuse have involved the use of loyalty rebates and other rebates which are not justified on normal commercial terms (56), arbitrary refusals to supply (57), excessive pricing (58) and the refusal to supply spare parts for motor cars to independent repairers or the fixing of their prices at an unfair level or the decision to cease production of such spare parts. (59)

14.61   On the other hand, the Court has consistently ruled that the mere existence of intellectual property rights does not of itself constitute an abuse under Article 86. See paras. 14.70 ff.

14.62   Other factors also involved in the consideration of Article 86 have already been dealt with in relation to Article 85 at paras. 14.19 to 14.35 above.

Mergers, acquisitions and joint ventures

14.63   In the 1960s the Commission issued a notice expressing its view that Article 85 had no application in the field of merger control. Events have moved on and the Commission made a number of efforts to obtain some degree of control over mergers, notably in a draft regulation on merger control which came into existence a number of years ago. The draft regulation seemed doomed to remain a draft until it received considerable impetus in the Court judgement in *Cases 142 and 156/84, British-American Tobacco Co. Ltd–R. J. Reynolds Industries Inc. v. Commission* (60) ("the Tobacco case"). There it was finally decided that Article 85 can apply to acquisitions of shareholdings. The Court had already ruled in *Continental Can* (61) in 1973 that Article 86 could apply to a merger which resulted in the acquisition of a competitor by an undertaking in a dominant position. In the Tobacco case the Court held that while:

> ". . . the acquisition by one company of an equity interest in a competitor does not in itself constitute conduct restricting competition, such an acquisition may nevertheless serve as an instrument for influencing the commercial conduct of the companies in question so as to restrict or distort competition on the market on which they carry on business."

---

(56)   *Hoffman-La Roche & Co. v. Commission* [1979] ECR 461; [1979] 3 CMLR 211; *San Pellegrino Spa v Coca-Cola Export Corporation* [1989] 4 CMLR 137.
(57)   *Commercial Solvents* [1974] ECR 223; [1974] 1 CMLR 309.
(58)   *Bodson v Pompes Funèbres*, judgement 4 May 1989; *Ahmed Saeed*, judgement 11 April 1989 (Not yet reported).
(59)   *Case 238/87, Volvo v Veng* [1989] 4 CMLR 122.
(60)   [1986] ECR 1899; [1988] 4 CMLR 24.
(61)   [1972] ECR 157; [1973] 12 CMLR 199.

14.64 Following the decision of the Court in the Tobacco case an amended proposal for a merger control regulation was submitted to the Council. A merger control regulation has now been agreed and will apply from September 1990. The rationale behind the regulation is that Community control will only extend to those mergers which have a Community dimension and that smaller mergers will be left for control by national authorities. A Community dimension is found where the joint turnovers of the parties worldwide exceed 5 billion ECU and the Community turnover of each of at least two of the parties exceeds 250 million ECU. Where the parties each achieve over two-thirds of their turnover in a single Member State, the merger will not usually have a Community dimension.

14.65 The merger control regulation (62) defines a concentration as taking place either where two or more undertakings merge or where one or more persons already controlling at least one undertaking or one or more undertakings acquire direct or indirect control of the whole or part of one or more undertakings. Thus the definition is sufficiently wide to catch certain forms of joint venture.

14.66 Mergers which fall within the merger control regulation are to be subject to a system of pre-notification to the Commission.

Joint ventures
14.67 By their very existence joint ventures tend to fall within Article 85(1) and a very large percentage of joint venture agreements are potentially notifiable under Article 85. Most notified joint ventures obtain exemption under Article 85(3).

14.68 Until quite recently it was believed that joint ventures between undertakings which did not operate within the same field were not notifiable. The recent Commission decision in *BBC Brown Boveri and NGK Insulators Ltd* (63) suggests that this view may no longer be accurate. The joint venture involved two parents in completely different fields and yet was held to breach Article 85. However, the two parent organisations entered into licensing arrangements worldwide which in effect foreclosed competition and this may be the true rationale behind the decision.

14.69 The position would appear to be, however, that until the block exemption on joint ventures currently planned by the Commission is

(62) Agreed 21.12.1989.
(63) OJ 1988 L 301/68.

available, large numbers of joint ventures will require notification to the Commission. The presence of any restraints on trade on the parents are likely to bring Article 85 into operation but the absence of such restraint cannot in itself be treated as a reason for not notifying the joint venture.

Intellectual and industrial property rights

14.70 Competition law potentially comes into direct conflict with the national law of various Member States in the area of the monopoly protection of intellectual and industrial property rights. Many of the cases on intellectual property rights have involved consideration of Articles 30 and 36 of the Treaty and the free movement of goods, but the principles decided in them are usually of equal application when considering the competition rules.

14.71 The approach of the Court has been to permit the exercise of national industrial property rights in the absence of any community harmonisation or regime provided the exercise of such rights is carried out in a non-discriminatory way and does not involve the partitioning of the Common Market. (64)

14.72 It was held in the *Case 96/75, EMI Records Ltd v. CBS Schallplatten* (65) that the mere ownership of intellectual property rights does not import the existence of a dominant position. Even if the owner does occupy a dominant position, the mere exercise of its rights to prevent infringement will not necessarily constitute abuse: *Case 707/76, Hoffman-La Roche v. Centrafarm* (66). In *Case 119/75, Terrapin v. Terranova* (67) the Court followed the earlier cases and held that a trade mark owner was not necessarily in a dominant position and was entitled to rely upon his rights to prevent imports into a protected territory without being guilty of an abuse under Article 86. In *Case 238/87, Volvo v. Veng UK* (68) the failure by Volvo to grant licences under its United Kingdom registered designs was held not to be an abuse of a dominant position even though as a consequence Volvo had a total monopoly in the product concerned. The Court stated that other conduct such as arbitrary refusal to supply or excessive pricing, not alleged before it, could in those circumstances have constituted abusive conduct.

(64) *Case 144/81, Keurkoop v Nancy Kean Gifts* [1983] 2 CMLR 47.
(65) [1976] ECR 913; [1976] 2 CMLR 000.
(66) [1979] ECR 461.
(67) [1976] ECR 1039; [1976] 2 CMLR 482.
(68) [1989] 4 CMLR 122.

14.73 The rationale for the approach of the Court in intellectual property cases can be found in *Case 24/67, Parke Davis & Co. v. Probel* (69) where the Court said that a patent:

"results from a legal status granted by a State to products meeting certain criteria and thus avoids the elements of contract or concert mentioned by Article 85(1)".

It decided Article 85(1) would operate if a patent was used in concert by more than one undertaking in a situation which was covered by the Article. It ruled that Article 86 would only operate if a patent was used in such a way that it could degenerate into improper exploitation of the protection accorded to the patent owner.

14.74 Progress toward harmonisation in areas of intellectual property has been slow so far. A first directive on trade marks 89/104 (70) has been agreed and this provides for the first stages of harmonisation of trade marks throughout the Community. While there is a Directive 87/54 (71) on the protection of semiconductor topography and a draft directive on the protection of computer programs (72), at present Community proposals on copyright generally have proceeded no further than a Green Paper. (73)

14.75 The United Kingdom is signatory to the European Patent Convention, as are most of the other members of the European Community. However, at present a European patent is not available uniformly throughout the Community. This can lead to difficulties in respect of protection of technology in the countries which are not signatories. Perhaps a greater difficulty, however, is the problem which can arise in preventing parallel imports from countries within the Community where the holder of the patent has not perhaps for financial reasons, obtained patent protection. In the light of the decision of the Court in *Case 187/80, Merck & Co. Inc. v. Stephar BV* (74) and in *Case 193/83, Windsurfing* (75) it has been argued that the holder of the patent right in (say) the United Kingdom would be unable to prevent the importation of goods made without his consent in a Member State where he had not obtained patent protection, if such protection was available there.

(69)   [1968] ECR 55; [1968] 4 CMLR 47.
(70)   OJ 1989 L 40/1.
(71)   OJ 1987 L 24/36.
(72)   OJ 1989 C 91/4.
(73)   COM. (88) 172 final. Brussels 7 June 1988.
(74)   [1981] ECR 2063; [1981] 3 CMLR 463.
(75)   [1986] 3 CMLR 489.

Commission notices

14.76   The Commission has issued a number of notices relating to the application of Articles 85 and 86 to particular types of agreements.

14.77   The most widely known and one of the most useful is the Commission Notice on Agreements of Minor Importance (76). The most recent revision of that notice was published in September 1986. The Notice has never been considered by the Court and is subject to review by it. The Notice provides that in cases that fall within its scope it is unlikely that Article 85 will be breached because the necessary effect upon trade between Member States is not present. The Notice does not apply to Article 86 as by definition an undertaking in a dominant position cannot benefit from its provisions. The Notice applies to contracts for the supply of goods or services where each of the following two criteria is satisfied:

(1) The aggregate annual worldwide turnover of all participating enterprises (taking into account the connected undertakings definition) does not amount to more than 200 million ECU; and

(2) The participating enterprises (and all connected undertakings) do not account for more than 5% of the total market for the contract goods or services.

14.78   The connected undertakings rule is that all enterprises connected by *de facto* or *de jure* ownership or control of 50% or more must be brought into the equation when considering the application of the Notice.

14.79   The Notice also helps by providing its own definition of the product and geographical markets. It should be noted that these two definitions are not necessarily the same as the definitions adopted by the Court when considering these matters. The product market will be the market for the contract goods and all other goods which are regarded by users as functional equivalents, having regard to their characteristics, price and use. The geographical market will be the entire Common Market save where the contract goods are not bought and sold freely in any part of the market, when that part must be disregarded.

14.80   There are marginal provisions in the Minor Agreements Notice so that an agreement may still benefit from it even though it exceeds the criteria set out at para. 14.77 above by no more than 10% for no more than two consecutive years. It follows that where the Minor Agreements Notice is relied upon as a method of avoiding notification, the progress

(76)   OJ 1986 C 231/2.

of the parties must be kept under review, in particular to check how market shares are progressing. Once the parties can no longer rely on it, their agreement must be notified.

Notice on Sub-Contracting Agreements

14.81 This notice (77) provides that sub-contracting agreements will not fall within the scope of Article 85(1) of the Treaty where a contractor entrusts the manufacture of goods, the supply of services or the performance of work under its instructions to a sub-contractor. Certain clauses relating to protection of the contractor's technology and equipment are declared not to breach Article 85. However, it is essential that the agreement does not restrict the sub-contractor from using his own technology and equipment or technology and equipment that are freely available.

Notice on Co-operation between Enterprises

14.82 This notice (78) lists a number of agreements which the Commission states are not by their nature to be regarded as anti-competitive. The notice deals with a large number of agreements relating to matters as diverse as joint market research, co-operation in accounting matters, joint use of production facilities, and the use of a common label to designate a certain quality.

Enforcement powers of the Commission

14.83 Regulation 17/62 (79) gives the Commission power to fine undertakings which infringe Article 85 or Article 86 intentionally or negligently. The Commission may impose fines of no more than 10% of the total turnover in the previous business year of each of the undertakings concerned in an infringement. The Court has the power to review and alter the fines imposed by the Commission.

14.84 The Commission has wide powers to require information to be supplied to it. It may impose further fines in the event of a failure to provide the information or of the provision of inaccurate information. The Commission is also empowered by Article 14 of Regulation 17/62 to search premises and take away copies or extracts of records.

14.85 Member States are required by both Article 89 of the Treaty and by Regulation 17/62 to render assistance to the Commission in carrying

(77)   OJ 1979 C 1/2.
(78)   OJ 1968 C 75/3 as amended.
(79)   OJ 1962 L 3/204.

out its duties under the Treaty. The Commission must observe national legislation procedures in its investigations. *Cases 46/87 and 227/88, Hoechst AG v. Commission* (80) are now the leading authority on the exercise by the Commission of its powers of search.

14.86 Individuals may complain to the Commission about alleged breaches of the competition provisions of the Treaty. Complaints may be made informally, but a formal, well-documented complaint, made on Form C published by the Commission is preferable. The Commission has power to investigate such complaints and initiate proceedings in respect of them as well as initiating proceedings at its own instance.

State aids

14.87 State aids are dealt with in the third section of Chapter 1 of the Treaty, and complete the Chapter relating to the competition rules.

14.88 Article 92 of the Treaty provides that any aid granted by a Member State or through State resources in any form whatsoever which distorts or threatens to distort competition by favouring certain undertakings or the production of certain goods shall be incompatible with the common market insofar as it affects trade between Member States. The Article exempts from its operation social aid granted to individual consumers where there is no discrimination as to the origin of products; aid for natural disasters and exceptional occurrences and certain aid granted in the Federal Republic of Germany.

14.89 There is a further provision for certain other forms of aid also to be exempted from Article 92. These essentially relate to promotion of standards of living in areas where economic development is low; the promotion of important projects of Community interest; the development of certain activities and other categories as may be specified from time to time by the Council.

14.90 Under Article 93 of the Treaty the Commission has a duty to keep under constant review all forms of aid existing in the Member States. Where a Member State does not comply with a decision of the Commission that its aid is incompatible with the Treaty, the Commission or any other interested State may refer the matter to the European Court of Justice.

14.91 The Council may decide under Article 93 that a particular form of State aid may be permissible in derogation from the normal provisions.

(80) (Not yet reported).

CHAPTER 15

Transport

15.01 The objectives of the common market and the physical nature of the Community combine to make a common transport policy an essential part of the machinery of making the Community work. Article 3 of the EEC Treaty, in defining the activities of the Community, specifies in subparagraph (e) the adoption of a common policy in the sphere of transport. Title IV of Part Two of the Treaty deals with Transport in Articles 74 to 84. And so Article 74 states that the objectives of the Treaty shall, in matters governed by this Title, be pursued by Member States within the framework of a common transport policy. The Court of Justice found the Council (in *Case 13/83, European Parliament v. Council*) (1) infringing the Treaty by failing to ensure freedom to provide services in the sphere of international transport and to lay down conditions under which non-resident carriers may operate transport services in a Member State.

15.02 The common transport policy in relation to rail, road and inland waterways is to be implemented by Article 75 which provides for the Council to lay down common rules applicable to international transport to or from the territory of a Member State or passing across the territory of one or more Member States, the conditions under which non-resident carriers may operate transport services within a Member State and any other appropriate provisions. Article 75 constitutes the legal basis for most of the secondary legislation issued in the transport field. In *Case 22/70, Commission v. Council* (2) the Court ruled that in the areas in which the Community has developed a common policy the competence to negotiate international agreements passed from Member States to the Community. Article 75 is part of this legal authority to negotiate. One of the first steps in developing a common transport policy was the Council Decision of 21 March 1962 (3), amended by Decision 73/402 (4), which lays down an obligation by member States to submit to the Commission draft laws and measures which may substantially affect the implementation of the common transport policy for

(1) [1985] ECR 1556; [1986] 1 CMLR 138.
(2) [1971] ECR 263; [1971] CMLR 335.
(3) OJ 1962 23/720.
(4) OJ 1973 L 347/48.

purposes of consultation and examination. Within two months of the receipt of the draft the Commission must make a recommendation or comment.

Carriage of goods by road

15.03   Carriage of goods by road lent itself most readily to Community action to liberalise it with the object of enabling freight firms in Member States to carry goods in the entire Community without requiring authorisation from the Member States involved. The first step along that road was Regulation 1018/68 (5) which allocated to Member States quotas of Community-wide permits. Each permit was valid for one vehicle at one time and enabled the holder to carry goods between Member States. The quota system was intended to permit authorised road hauliers to convey and pick up freight destined for other Member States in the Community, but excluded internal carriage within other Member States. The basic legislation aiming at this effect was contained in Regulation 2829/72 (6), which was extended in Regulation 3164/76 (7). Regulation 3024/77 (8) increased the Community quota and simplified record sheets for transport operations. Regulation 3062/78 (9) increased by 10% the Community quota. Quotas were increased again in 1979 when an experimental system of short-term Community authorisation was issued. This was made permanent by Regulation 3515/82 (10) with the ceiling of short-term authorisations being 15% of the total quotas of the Member States. The quotas under Regulation 3164/76 (7) are amended each year. Regulation 3621/84 (11) authorised an increase in quotas for the subsequent five years. Regulation 3677/85 (12) amended Regulation 3164/76 (7) to allow for accession of Spain and Portugal. The system worked by annual increases in quotas, pending their replacement by "qualitative criteria regarding market access, containing the basis for future organisation of the market for the carriage of goods by road between Member States" (draft Regulation proposed by the Commission in 1983). These annual and additional increases brought extra Community authorisations for 1987, 1988 and 1989.

15.04   Again common rules for international carriage of goods exempt certain types of carriage from any transport quota or exempt other types

(5)   OJ 1968 L 175/13.
(6)   OJ 1972 (30–31 Dec.) 43.
(7)   OJ 1976 L 357/1.
(8)   OJ 1977 L 358/4.
(9)   OJ 1978 L 366/5.
(10)   OJ 1982 L 369/2.
(11)   OJ 1984 L 333/61.
(12)   OJ 1985 L 354/46.

from quotas but subject them to authorisation (First Council Directive of 23 July 1962) (13). This exemption has been extended several times, last by Directive 84/647 (14), which allows for use of vehicles hired without drivers for the carriage of goods by road. Regulation 1841/88 (15) amending Regulation 3164/76 (7) increases the Community quota by 40% for 1988 and 1989 and replaces the present national bilateral and Community quota systems from 1 January 1993 by qualitative criteria for access to the international road haulage market.

Rate regulation
15.05 The Common Market calls for some uniformity in rate regulation. Regulation 1174/68 (16) introduced a flexible system of rate regulation and a system of compulsory brackets for tariffs for carriage of goods by road. The competent authorities laid down and published bracket tariffs fixing transport rates and conditions, the rate being freely negotiated within the fixed maximum and minimum. The spread of the bracket was to be 23% of the maximum. Regulation 2831/77 (17) replaced this regulation, it being in turn replaced by Regulation 3568/83 (18) which was intended to cover the period up to the end of 1988. This last Regulation is amended by Regulation 1991/88 (19). Rates here are formed under a system of non-compulsory reference tariffs. Two or more Member States may introduce compulsory brackets for tariffs instead of reference tariffs. This system was prolonged until the end of 1989. From January 1989 however Member States have agreed to abolish the compulsory tariffs.

Road passenger transport

15.05.1 The basic Regulation on the carriage of passengers by road is Regulation 117/66 (20) which establishes common definitions for international services and a system largely free from authorisation for occasional passenger services. Regulation 516/72 (21) deals with shuttle services by coach and bus between Member States and Regulation 517/72 (22) with regular and special regular services. Shuttle services are

(13)   OJ 1962 70/2005.
(14)   OJ 1984 L 335/72.
(15)   OJ 1988 L 163/1.
(16)   OJ 1968 411.
(17)   OJ 1977 L 334/22.
(18)   OJ 1983 L 359/1.
(19)   OJ 1988 L 516/5.
(20)   OJ 1966 2688.
(21)   OJ 1972 L 67/13.
(22)   OJ 1972 L 67/19.

defined as the transportation of previously formed groups of travellers from one point to another point without break and their return transportation at some subsequent time. The Agreement on international carriage of passengers by road by means of occasional coach and bus services (ASOR) was signed in 1982 by the Community and certain other European States (Decision 82/505). (23)

Drivers' hours

15.06 Road transport drivers' hours and records were originally based on Regulation 543/69 (24), amended several times. The position is now governed by Regulation 3820/85 (25), which introduced an element of flexibility. This Regulation applies to carriage by road within the Community. The European Agreement concerning the Work of Crews of Vehicles in International Road Transport of 1 July 1970 (AETR Agreement), which entered into force on 5 January 1976), covers Community drivers travelling to or transiting other countries which are signatories to the Agreement, including the journey within the Community, instead of the rules in the Regulation. Certain vehicles are exempted from the Regulation and AETR. There is an element of discretion left to Member States to exempt vehicles in certain circumstances. Minimum ages are laid down for drivers, for drivers' mates and conductors. Rest periods and total driving periods over specific periods are also stipulated. Payments to wage-earning drivers related to distances travelled or the amount of goods carried are prohibited. In the case of regular services a service timetable and duty roster has to be drawn up. The latter provisions do not apply to drivers of vehicles fitted with tachographs under Regulation 3821/85 (26). This Regulation governs the use of tachographs from 29 September 1986 and prescribes in detail the rules of construction, installation, use and testing of tachographs. The definitions used in Regulation 3820/85 (25) apply to this Regulation and Member States must check on compliance and penalties to be imposed in case of breach. Directive 88/599 (27) lays down minimum conditions for checking the correct and uniform application of both Regulations. Minimum levels of training for drivers are laid down in Directive 76/914. (28)

(23)   OJ 1982 L 230/39.
(24)   OJ 1969 L 77/49.
(25)   OJ 1985 L 370/1.
(26)   OJ 1985 L 370/8.
(27)   OJ 1988 L 325/55.
(28)   OJ 1976 L 357/36.

Qualifications

15.07 The occupations of road haulage operator and road passenger transport operator are the subject of Directives 74/561 (29) and 74/562 (30) respectively. Both specify good repute, appropriate financial standing and technical competence as conditions for the exercise of these occupations. Technical competence involves skills in law, business, financial management, legislation, technical standards and road safety and these subjects are listed in the Annexes to the Directives. Mention should be made of Directive 77/796 (31) on mutual recognition of diplomas and other evidence of qualifications for these two kinds of operator. These three directives were amended by Directive 89/438 (32) which provides for measures intended to encourage the effectiveness of operators. Directive 80/1263 (33) calls for the introduction of a national driving licence based on a Community model.

15.08 The Customs Convention on the International Transport of Goods under a TIR carnet has been adopted by the Community and Regulation 3237/76 (34) as amended by Regulation 2112/78 (35) and Regulation 3020/81 (36) have transposed the Convention into Community law. The International Convention for Safe Containers is dealt with in Recommendation 79/487 (37).

Vehicle standards

15.09 Vehicles themselves became subject to Community legislation with the passing of Directive 85/3 (38), as amended by Directives 86/360 (39), 86/364 (40) on vehicle plating and 88/218 (41) which specifies maximum dimensions and maximum weights for various types of vehicle and associated trailers. Directive 85/3 (38) was modified by Directive 89/338 (42) in respect of standard weight and size and by Directive 89/461 (43) dealing with articulated vehicles. Temporary exemptions have been made for the United Kingdom from the operation

(29) OJ 1974 L 308/18.
(30) OJ 1974 L 308/23.
(31) OJ 1977 L 334/37.
(32) OJ 1989 L 212/101.
(33) OJ 1980 L 375/1.
(34) OJ 1976 L 368/1.
(35) OJ 1978 L 252/1.
(36) OJ 1981 L 302/6.
(37) OJ 1979 L 308/18.
(38) OJ 1985 L 2/14.
(39) OJ 1986 L 217/19.
(40) OJ 1986 L 221/48.
(41) OJ 1988 L 98/48.
(42) OJ 1989 L 142/3.
(43) OJ 1989 L 226/7.

of Directive 85/3, the latest derogation being in Directive 89/46 (44). Roadworthiness for large vehicles is laid down in Directive 77/143 (45). Tread depth of tyres is subject of Directive 89/459 (46) and lateral protection (sideguards) of motor vehicles of Directive 89/297. (47)

Railways and waterways

15.10   Railway systems of the Member States do not, on the whole, operate outside their own country and so there is not much effective competition between them. They do compete with other means of transport however and this forces them to co-operate in order to offer effective competition to these other modes of transport. Such co-operation is of importance to the really effective common market. A series of Resolutions has called for such co-operation. The state of finances of the railways led to Decision 75/327 (48), designed to attain an overall financial balance on the railways, independence on administrative, economic and accounting matters, activity and investment plans and to investigate measures to promote co-operation to integrate at Community level. Regulation 2830/77 (49), called for railway undertakings to produce their national accounts in the form of annual accounts as shown in the Annex to the Regulation. Under Regulation 2183/78 (50) the cost of international carriage of freight must be calculated in accordance with uniform costing principles. Decision 82/529 (51) dealt with the fixing of rates for international carriage of goods by rail between Member States so as to maximise returns and Decision 83/418 (52) was concerned with the commercial independence of the railways in management of international traffic. The aims of Decision 75/327 (48) gave rise to Recommendation 84/646 (53), which contained measures on the commercial management of international services, rail tariffs, train movements, the simplification of frontier crossing procedures and combined transport.

15.11   The inland waterway system is an important part of the Community transport system, particularly in relation to heavy industry. The Rhine plays a great part in the system. Directive 76/135 (54) provided for mutual recognition of navigability licences issued for vessels using

(44)   OJ 1989 L 226/5.
(45)   OJ 1977 L 47/47.
(46)   OJ 1989 L 226/4.
(47)   OJ 1989 L 124/1.
(48)   OJ 1975 L 152/3.
(49)   OJ 1977 L 334/13.
(50)   OJ 1978 L 258/1.
(51)   OJ 1982 L 234/5.
(52)   OJ 1983 L 237/32.
(53)   OJ 1984 L 333/63.
(54)   OJ 1976 L 21/10.

inland waterways, if the licence contained the minimum information set out in the Directive. Directive 82/714 (55) dealt with technical standards for the construction of inland waterway vessels and safety of the crews' accommodation. Directive 87/540 (56) lays down conditions for becoming a carrier of goods on the Community waterways. Navigation on the Rhine, which involves the Member States and Switzerland, is governed by an international agreement, the Act of Mannheim, which the Community adopted.

Sea transport

15.12 Article 84 of the EEC Treaty, in its first sub-paragraph, applies the provisions of the Title dealing with Transport to transport by rail, road and inland waterway. Sea and air transport is subject to the second subparagraph, authorising the Council, acting by a qualified majority, to make appropriate provisions. In addition, following the decision of the Court of Justice in *Case 167/73, Commission v. French Republic*, (57) the general provisions of the Treaty apply to sea and air transport.

15.13 Sea transport forms the basis of the Community's external trade. This by itself, apart from other factors, would call for action on a Community basis in this sphere. This action started with several Decisions dealing with consultation procedures and collection and exchange of information. The United Nations Convention on a code of conduct for Liner Conferences (sharing of cargo) was given effect in the Community by Regulation 954/79 (58). In the area of safety at sea and sea pollution Directive 79/115 (59) deals with pilotage by deap-sea pilots in the North Sea and English Channel and Directive 79/116 (60) lays down requirements for tankers entering and leaving Community ports. A considerable step in the field of common sea transport policy is represented by Regulation 4055/86 (61) introducing the concept of freedom to provide services to maritime transport between Member States and Member States and third countries. By way of derogation there is a timetable for phasing out unilateral national restrictions: by Regulation 4056/86 (62), which lays down rules for the application of Articles 85 and 86 (competition Articles) to maritime transport, certain technical agreements and certain agreements between carriers in scheduled

(55) OJ 1982 L 301/1.
(56) OJ 1987 L 322/1.
(57) [1974] ECR 359; [1974] CMLR 216.
(58) OJ 1979 L 121/1.
(59) OJ 1979 L 33/32.
(60) OJ 1979 L 33/33.
(61) OJ 1986 L 378/1.
(62) OJ 1986 L 378/4.

services are exempted from the prohibition in Article 85, and conditions are attached to the latter exemption. Decision 78/774 (63) is the legal basis for Community monitoring of unfair pricing practices by third country shipowners. Evidence of such practices led to Regulation 4057/ 86 (64) which deals with unfair pricing practices by third-country shipowners which cause disruption of the freight patterns and threaten to cause or cause injury to Community shipowners and Community interests. In case of major injury redressive duty may be applied by Regulation 4058/86 (65), intended to safeguard the access to cargoes in ocean trade. Details of the procedures relating to competition hearings in relation to sea transport were laid down in Regulation 4260/88. (66)

Air transport

15.14 *Case 167/73, Commission v. French Republic* (57) decided that air transport is subject to the general rules of the EEC Treaty. This was specifically confirmed in joined *Cases 209-213/84, Ministère Public v. Asjes and Others* (67) in relation to air tariffs and rules of competition. However, in the absence of specific legislation (Regulation 141/62 (68) exempted transport from the application of Regulation 17/62 (69), which forms the basic secondary legislation on the subject of competition), the principle pronounced in *Case 13/61, De Geus v. Bosch* (70) renders agreements concerning air tariffs valid until a finding that they are contravening Article 85 of the Treaty. Following the judgment in the *Asjes* case the EEC Commission officially alleged that Community airlines had infringed the Community competition rules and required them to stop the infringements. Other action in the field of air transport is represented by Decision 80/50 (71) (consultation procedure), Decision 80/51 (72) (limitation of noise emission from subsonic aircraft), and Directive 80/1266 (73) (co-operation and mutual assistance in air accident investigations). Directive 83/416 (74), amended by Directive 89/463 (75), deals with scheduled inter-regional air services between Member States. Then in 1987 three important measures were taken in

(63) OJ 1978 L 258/35.
(64) OJ 1986 L 378/14.
(65) OJ 1986 L 378/21.
(66) OJ 1988 L 376.
(67) [1986] ECR 1425; [1986] 3 CMLR 173.
(68) OJ 1962 124/2751.
(69) OJ 1962 13/204.
(70) [1962] ECR 45; [1962] CMLR 1.
(71) OJ 1980 L 18/24.
(72) OJ 1980 L 18/26.
(73) OJ 1980 L 375/32.
(74) OJ 1983 L 237/19.
(75) OJ 1989 L 226/14.

the aviation section, namely Regulation 3975/87 (76) laying down a procedure for the application of competition rules to the sector (Regulation 4261/88 passed in December of 1988 (77) provides for the procedure on the hearings dealing with such application), Regulation 3976/87 (78) applying Article 85(3) of the Treaty (exemptions of certain types of agreement from the competition rules) and Decision 87/602 (79) on the sharing of passenger capacity and on access of carriers to scheduled air routes in the Community. Directive 87/601 (80) was concerned with fares for scheduled services. Commission Regulations 2671/88 (81), 2672/88 (82) and 2673/88 (83) dealt with the application of Article 85(3) to agreements concerned with sharing of revenues, computer reservation systems and ground handling services respectively. The exemption of computerised reservation systems from the provisions of Article 85 called in turn for a code of conduct for such systems which was provided by Council Regulation 2299/89. (84)

15.15 All these legislative instruments enacted in 1987 and 1988 were the subject of a decision by the Court of Justice in *Case 66/86, Ahmed Saeed Flugreisen and another v. Zentrale zur Bekampfung Unlauteren Wettbewerbs eV* (85), where it was held that bilateral or multilateral agreements fixing tariffis for international flights between Community airports which did not satisfy the conditions for exemption laid down in Regulation 3975/87 (76) were automatically void by virtue of Article 85(2) of the Treaty. The application of tariffs arising from bilateral or multilateral agreements to scheduled flights might, in certain circumstances, constitute an abuse of a dominant position where the conditions laid down by Article 86 were fulfilled.

Investment and co-ordination

15.16 One of the main aims of the common transport policy is co-ordination among Member States, and so the Council created a consultation procedure for transport infrastructure investment. Under Decision 78/174 (86) Member States must inform the Commission of their plans and

(76)   OJ 1987 L 374/1.
(77)   OJ 1988 L 378/10.
(78)   OJ 1987 L 374/9.
(79)   OJ 1987 L 374/19.
(80)   OJ 1987 L 374/12.
(81)   OJ 1988 L 239/9.
(82)   OJ 1988 L 239/13.
(83)   OJ 1988 L 239/17.
(84)   OJ 1989 L 220/1.
(85)   (Not yet reported).
(86)   OJ 1987 L54/16.

programmes for developing transport infrastructure and of projects of Community interest. Under Decision 64/389 (87) a survey was organised of infrastructure costs in road, rail and inland waterway transport which was followed by Regulation 1108/70, (88), as amended, instituting an accounting system within this Decision. There have been a series of Regulations granting financial support for infrastructure from 1982 onwards. The commission monitored the market for the carriage of goods by rail, road and inland waterway and as a result Directive 75/130 (89) governs multi-modal (combined road/rail) systems, Member States having to liberalise multi-modal transport systems from all quota systems and systems of authorisation.

15.17 An example of another necessary harmonisation is the harmonisation of different national systems for summertime (daylight saving). Directive 88/14 (90) on summertime arrangements provides for summertime in 1989 with the United Kingdom and Ireland able to terminate their summertime exceptionally at a later date than other Community states. Similar arrangements will apply for 1990-92 (Fifth Directive 89/47) (91). Another aim of the Community is facilitation of physical inspection and administrative formalities in respect of carriage of goods between Member States which found expression in Directive 83/643 (92) with the aim of elimination of certain frontier checks leading ultimately to the completion of the internal market. This Directive was amended by Directive 87/53. (93)

Abolition of subsidies and other distortions to trade

15.18 Until the provisions referred to in Article 75(1) have been laid down, Article 76 introduces a standstill obligation, whereby carriers from other Member States are protected against a worsening of their position in relation to that of domestic carriers. Article 77 allows for subsidies if they meet the needs of coordination of transport or if they represent reimbursement for the discharge of certain obligations inherent in the concept of a public service. Article 92 of the Treaty contains a general prohibition of governmental subsidies which may lead to distortion in the common market with a list of exceptions. Article 77 provides an independent exception to the principle. The concept of a public

(87)   OJ 1964 102/1598.
(88)   OJ 1970 L 130/4.
(89)   OJ 1975 L 48/31.
(90)   OJ 1988 L 6/38.
(91)   OJ 1989 L 17/57.
(92)   OJ 1983 L 359/8.
(93)   OJ 1987 L 24/33.

service obligation is defined in Regulation 1191/69 (94) and in *Case 36/73, NV Nederlandse Spoorwegen v. Minister van Verkeer en Waterstaat* (95). Regulation 1107/70 (96) limits the kinds of subsidies that may be granted in order not to create distortions of competition.

15.19 Article 78 provides that any measures taken within the framework of the Treaty in respect of transport rates and conditions shall take account of the economic circumstances of the carriers. When measures are enacted, consideration must be given not only to the needs of the economy as a whole, but also to the needs of transport enterprises.

15.20 Article 79 calls for the abolition of discrimination which takes the form of carriers charging different rates and imposing different conditions for the carriage of the same goods over the same transport links on the grounds of origin or destination of goods. The Article thus eliminates rates adopted for protectionist purposes. Article 79 is implemented by virtue of its subparagraph (3) by Regulation 11/60 (97) concerning the abolition of discrimination in transport rates and conditions, as amended by Regulation 3626/84 (98). Regulation 2988/74 (99) deals with the appropriate sanctions. The burden of showing that their actions do not violate Article 79 is placed on the carriers.

15.21 Another aspect of the defences of the common market is contained in Article 80, which prohibits Member States imposing freight rates supporting specific enterprises or industries. Transportation by enterprises on their own behalf falls outside the scope of the Article. The Commission may in a specific case grant exemption from the provisions of the Article.

15.22 Article 81 demands that charges or dues charged by the carrier in addition to the transport rates on the crossing of frontiers should be at a reasonable level and be progressively reduced by Member States. With the TIR Convention this has become much less significant. Article 82 allows the Federal Republic of Germany to take measures to counteract economic disadvantages caused by the division of Germany to the economy of certain areas. Article 83 creates an Advisory Committee of experts attached to the Commission, to be consulted on transport matters.

(94)   OJ 1969 L 156/1.
(95)   [1973] ECR 1299; [1974] 2 CMLR 148.
(96)   OJ 1970 L 130/1.
(97)   OJ 1960 1121.
(98)   OJ 1984 L 335/4.
(99)   OJ 1974 L 319/1.

15.23   Outside the Title of the Treaty dealing with transport there are provisions dealing with the rail, road and inland waterway transport in the ambit of the competition rules. Decision 65/271 (100) deals with harmonisation of competition in relation to this kind of transport by aiming at the removal of the differences between Member States in the field of taxation, social legislation and State aids. Double taxation of motor vehicles is abolished, the basis for calculation of goods vehicle taxes is to be harmonised for road and inland waterways and so are the provisions on duty-free import of fuel in vehicle tanks. Directives 68/297 (101) and 85/347 (102) standardise provisions concerning the duty-free entry of fuel in the tanks of commercial vehicles. While Regulation 17/62 (69) did not apply to transport, Regulation 1017/68 (103) applied competition rules to transport by rail, road and inland waterway.

(100)   OJ 1965 88/1500.
(101)   OJ 1968 L 175/15.
(102)   OJ 1985 L 183/22.
(103)   OJ 1968 L 175/1.

CHAPTER 16

Consumer Protection, Public Health and the Environment

16.01   The concept of consumer protection is inherent in the principles of the EEC Treaty. The preamble to the Treaty calls for balanced trade and free competition. The objectives of free movement of goods and a common market involve these two requirements and in turn involve measures of harmonisation of standards in manufacture, sale and use of goods, thus eliminating trade barriers and affording consumer protection, and of product liability legislation. Direct specific references to the consumer are in Article 39, where one of the objectives of common agricultural policy shall be "... to ensure that supplies reach consumers at reasonable prices" and in Article 86, where an abuse of a dominant position may, in particular, consist in "... limiting production, markets or technical development to the prejudice of consumers."

16.02   Most of the legislation in the field of consumer protection is based on Article 100, which provides for the Council issuing directives for the approximation of such provisions laid down by law, regulation or administrative action in Member States as directly affect the establishment or functioning of the Common Market. Again Article 235 is used in the field of consumer protection when it enables the Council to take appropriate measures if action by the Community should prove necessary to attain, in the course of the operation of the common market, one of the objectives of the Community and the Treaty has not provided the necessary powers. In pursuance of these objectives the Council passed a resolution in 1975 on a preliminary programme of the EEC for consumer protection and information policy. It was followed by a submission by the Commission of a draft directive and an explanatory memorandum in 1976. The memorandum points to the divergences in law of the Member States when it comes to the extent of liability for defective products and to the nature of compensation for the injured consumer. The divergences may distort competition, and the liability rules imposed on producers of defective products lead to differences in costs for the economies of the various Member States. The draft was finally turned into Directive 85/374 (1) on the approximation of the

(1)   OJ 1985 L 210/29.

laws, regulations and administrative provisions of the Member States concerning liability for defective products.

The Product Liability Directive

16.03 This Directive is far-reaching in laying down the principle of liability irrespective of fault: Article 1 provides that the producer shall be liable for damage caused by a defect in his product. The definition of "producer" in Article 3 is very wide. It includes the manufacturer of a finished product or of a component part and any person who presents himself as the producer. An importer is deemed to be a producer. When the producer of the product cannot be identified each supplier is treated as its producer; and the same applies in the case of imports if the product does not identify the identity of the importer. The provisions of Article 3 are wide enough to cover undertakings such as mail order firms which have products manufactured by unspecified undertakings and sell them under their own name. Article 2 defines "product" as meaning all moveables, even though incorporated into another moveable or into an immoveable, with the exception of primary agricultural products and game. Product includes electricity. Article 6 of the Directive in defining a product as defective states that a product shall not be considered defective for the sole reason that a better product is subsequently put into circulation. Article 7 provides that the producer shall not be liable as a result of the Directive if he proves that he did not put the product into circulation or that having regard to the circumstances it is probable that the defect which caused the damage did not exist at the time when the product was put into circulation by him or that this defect came into being afterwards. It is a defence if the producer proves that the state of scientific and technical knowledge at the time when he put the product into circulation was not such as to enable the existence of the defect to be discovered. Each Member State may by way of derogation legislate to make the producer liable even if he is covered by this exception (Article 15). The new legislation derogating from Article 7 is subject to the Community stand-still procedure in order, as the Recital to the Directive states, "to raise if possible the level of protection in a uniform manner throughout the Community". The rights of an injured party on grounds other than that provided for in the Directive remain unaffected by the Directive, which in the Recital refers to the special liability system and the effective protection of consumers in the sector of pharmaceuticals products already obtained in a Member State under a special liability system. The Directive does not apply to injury or damage arising from nuclear accidents and covered by international conventions ratified by the Member States. The Recital suggests that liability for nuclear injury or damage is already covered by adequate special rules in all Member States. Proceedings for the recovery of damages under the Directive are subject to a limitation period of three years. The liability of the producer arising from the Directive may not in relation to the injured person be limited or excluded by a provision limiting his liability or exempting him from the liability.

16.04 The Directive is implemented in the United Kingdom by the Consumer Protection Act 1987. Part I of the Act under the heading "Product Liability" puts into effect the provisions of the Directive and in fact section 1(1) states that "this part shall have effect for the purpose of making such provision as is necessary in order to comply with the product liability Directive and shall be construed accordingly." Section 2 re-enacts the provisions of the Directive as to the persons liable for the damage and who are deemed to be producers, but goes further than the Directive in setting out the steps which may be necessary for the consumer to take in order to identify the person liable. Again section 3, while following the Directive, is more explicit in the definition of defect. Section 5 provides that no damages shall be awarded in respect of any loss or damage to property if the amount which would fall to be awarded does not exceed £275.

Misleading advertising

16.05 Another aspect of the protection of consumers is seen in the Directive 84/450 (2) on misleading advertising. Advertising can nowadays be transmitted across frontiers and community-wide legislation was deemed necessary to protect consumers or trade competitors. The Directive defines misleading advertising as any advertising which in any way, including its presentation, deceives or is likely to deceive the persons to whom it is addressed or whom it reaches and which, by reason of its deceptive nature, is likely to affect their economic behaviour or which injures or is likely to injure a competitor. The Directive goes into details to be considered when determining whether an advertisement is misleading. Member States must ensure that adequate and effective means exist for the control of misleading advertising, including ultimate recourse to the courts. In the United Kingdom the Directive is implemented by the functioning of the Advertising Standards Authority and by enforcement of the Trade Descriptions Act 1968. Sections 20–26 of the Consumer Protection Act 1987 on misleading price indications have now replaced section 11 of the Trade Descriptions Act 1968.

(2) OJ 1984 L 250/17.

Doorstep selling

16.06 Directive 85/577 (3) deals with the element of surprise inherent in selling away from the business premises (doorstep selling); the consumer is now entitled to have the contract of sale reconsidered. The directive applies to contracts which are concluded during a visit by a trader where the visit does not take place at the express request of the consumer. Traders are required to give consumers written notice of their right of cancellation. This directive was considered by the Court of Justice in *Case 382/87, Buet and another v. Ministère Public* (4), when it referred to the preamble of the directive which recognised that Member States might adopt or maintain in force a total or partial ban on concluding contracts outside commercial establishments and ruled that the application to imported products of a prohibition against door-to-door selling of educational material was not incompatible with Article 30 of the Treaty. Directive 87/102 (5) is concerned with consumer credit. (See Chapter on Banking).

Harmonisation of provisions on health and safety

16.07 The concept of common market and consumer protection in the Community involves not only the right to protection of economic interests but also the right to protection of health and safety. This involves the principle that products (whether manufactured or not) and services in the Community must not constitute a risk to health and safety. As a result the Community has adopted a very large number of measures harmonising standards in manufactured goods and eliminating technical barriers to trade. An example of this approach is Community legislation in relation to motor vehicles represented by a large number of directives covering minute details connected with the safety of the vehicle and creating a Community type-approval procedure. Another example of this approach are directives harmonising the laws on foodstuffs e.g. dealing with authorised colouring matters, and preservatives, and on medicinal products, on labelling of paints and on cosmetics. There are many more covering all aspects of safety of consumer products. The common internal market, public health and interests of an individual consumer are inextricably tied up as a reason and basis for the Community legislation. The Community approach is indicated by Decision 84/133 (6) providing for exchange of information relating to dangers arising out of use of consumer products. This concept of consumer

(3)   OJ 1985 L 372/31.
(4)   (Not yet reported).
(5)   OJ 1987 L 42/48.
(6)   OJ 1984 L 70/16.

protection in its widest sense is indicated by the subjects of Community legislation. It falls under the category of health and safety or the internal market. The principle of the internal market has called for legislation on motor vehicles, agriculture and forestry, tractors, metrology (measurement), electrical materials, foodstuffs, proprietary medicinal products, cosmetics, dangerous substances, fertilisers and other subjects which call for approximation of laws in the Community. In the field of agriculture there is a large quantity of detailed legislation dealing with approximation of laws in relation to health measures (see Chapter 6). A list of basic legislative instruments in the other fields is annexed at the end of this Chapter.

Protecting the environment

16.08 The protection of human life and long-term availability of all the resources which determine the quality of life were considered as part of the objectives of the Community's environment policy (Council Resolution in 1983). Before 1987 the legislation in matters concerning the environment was under the umbrella of the general aims of the Treaty and specifically within the realm of consumer protection. The Single European Act of 1986 introduced a new Title to the EEC Treaty, (Title VII), the Title on the environment, containing three new Articles. Article 130r states that the objectives of action by the Community are to preserve, protect and improve the quality of the environment, to contribute towards protecting human health and to ensure a prudent and rational utilisation of natural resources. Article 130s empowers the Council to take action and Article 130t does not exclude more stringent protective measures compatible with the Treaty being maintained or introduced by any Member State. In *Case 302/86, Commission v. Denmark* (7) the Court observed that it had already held that environmental protection is "one of the Community's essential objectives" which as such may justify certain limitations to the principle of free movement of goods. In the particular circumstances of the case the Danish system of returnable containers was found in its operation to be disproportionate to the objective pursued and the restriction to 3000 hl per producer per annum of beer and soft drinks on imports in non-approved containers to be contrary to Article 30 of the Treaty.

Public health
16.09 Most of the existing appropriate legislation was enacted in the field dealing with public health and a good example is water. Drinking

(7) [1989] 1 CMLR 619.

water was the concern of Directive 75/440 (8) and Directive 80/778 (9). This last Directive was the subject of *Case 228/87, Criminal proceedings against persons unknown* (10), when the Court held that the authorisation to exceed the maximum admissible concentrations of substances shown in Annex I to the Directive relating to the quality of water intended for human consumption, as provided by Article 10 of that Directive, must be granted only in the event of an emergency in which national authorities suddenly have to cope with difficulties in connection with the supply of water for human consumption; further, such authorisation must be limited to the time normally necessary in order to restore the quality of water affected, must not pose any unacceptable risk to public health and may be granted only if the supply of water for human consumption cannot be maintained in any other way. Fish and shellfish breeding water became the subject of Directive 79/923 (11), Directive 76/160 (12) concerns the quality of bathing water and Directive 80/68 (13) with pollution of groundwater. Marine pollution became the subject of Directive 78/176 (14) which dealt with pollution caused by waste from the titanium dioxide industry, in addition to a Resolution dealing with oil pollution.

Atmospheric pollution
16.10 Air pollution was dealt with by several Decisions providing for exchange of information and data regarding air pollution, and by Directive 84/360 (15) which dealt with air pollution from industrial plants. It listed the most important polluting substances and in accordance with it Directive 88/609 (16) established limits of emissions from large combustion plants. Directive 89/369 (17) deals with prevention of air pollution from new municipal waste incinerating plants. Directive 89/427 (18), amending Directive 80/779 (19), prescribes air quality limit values and guide values for sulphur dioxide and suspended particulates. A significant step in this context is Directive 85/210 (20), amended by Directive 87/416 (21), under which Member States must ensure that unleaded petrol is available and distributed from 1 October

(8) OJ 1975 L 194/26.
(9) OJ 1980 L 229/11.
(10) (Not yet reported).
(11) OJ 1979 L 281/48.
(12) OJ 1976 L 31/1.
(13) OJ 1980 L 20/43.
(14) OJ 1978 L 54/19.
(15) OJ 1984 L 188/20.
(16) OJ 1988 L 336/1.
(17) OJ 1989 L 163/32.
(18) OJ 1989 L 201/53.
(19) OJ 1980 L 229/30.
(20) OJ 1985 L 96/25.
(21) OJ 1987 L 225/33.

1989. This was followed by Directive 88/77 (22) dealing with measures to be taken against the emission of gaseous pollutants from diesel engines in vehicles and Directive 88/76 (23) concerned with air pollution by gases from engines in motor vehicles. A far-reaching measure to deal with car pollution is Directive 89/458 (24), which after referring to many previous instruments limiting emissions of carbon monoxide and unburnt hydrocarbon, prescribes new standards for emissions from cars below 1.4 litres cylinder capacity. These standards apply to new models from 1 July 1992 and all new cars after 31 December 1992. Sulphur content of gas oil was prescribed by Directive 75/716 (25) with new levels introduced by Directive 87/219. (26)

Disposal of waste
16.11 Disposal of waste is another of the subjects which fall within the ambit of public health and other aspects of environment. Directive 75/442 (27) dealt with waste generally, its objectives being specified as being in the area of the protection of health and the environment. The extent of rights conferred by this Directive upon individuals was considered by the Court of Justice in *Case 380/87, Knichem Base and others v. Comune di Cinisello Balsamo* (28). Directive 75/439 (29) dealt with waste oils (which may affect water, soil and air), Directive 76/403 (30) with disposal of polychlorinated biphenyls and polychlorinated terphenyls, and Directive 78/319 (31) with toxic and dangerous waste. Directive 84/631 (32) introduces the supervision and control of trans-frontier shipment of hazardous waste, being amended in detail by Commission Directive 87/112 (33). Regulation 1734/88 (34) is concerned with the export from and import into the Community of certain dangerous chemicals. Directive 89/428 (35) has the purpose of harmonising the programmes for the reduction and eventual elimination of pollution caused by waste from the titanium dioxide industry.

(22)   OJ 1988 L 36/33.
(23)   OJ 1988 L 36/1.
(24)   OJ 1989 L 226/1.
(25)   OJ 1975 L 207/22.
(26)   OJ 1987 L 91/19.
(27)   OJ 1975 L 194/39.
(28)   (Not yet reported).
(29)   OJ 1975 L 194/23.
(30)   OJ 1976 L 108/41.
(31)   OJ 1978 L 84/43.
(32)   OJ 1984 L 326/31.
(33)   OJ 1987 L 48/31.
(34)   OJ 1988 L 155/2.
(35)   OJ 1989 L 201/56.

Noise

16.12 Noise is another subject of Community legislation. As early as 1970 the Council passed directive 70/157 (36) relating to the sound level and the exhaust system of motor vehicles and Directive 78/1015 (37) relating similarly to motorcycles. Directive 80/51 (38) covers noise of subsonic aircraft and Directive 84/538 (39) noise of lawnmowers. Directive 86/549 (40) is concerned with airborne noise of household appliances and there is legislation limiting noise of specific items of industrial and road-making machinery.

(36) OJ 1970 L 42/16.
(37) OJ 1978 L 349/21.
(38) OJ 1980 L 18/26.
(39) OJ 1984 L 300/171.
(40) OJ 1986 L 344/24.

ANNEX TO CHAPTER 16

List of Principal EC Directives
Internal Market: Approximation of Laws

M indicates an amending instrument
C indicates a supplementary instrument

GENERAL PROGRAMME

Directive 83/189 on procedure for the provision of information in the field of technical standards and regulations (OJ 1983 L 109/8)
  M by Directive 88/182 (OJ 1988 L 81/75)

MOTOR VEHICLES

Directive 70/156 on type-approval of motor vehicles and their trailers (OJ 1970 L 42/1)
  M by Directive 80/1267 (OJ 1980 L 375/34)
  M by Directive 87/358 (OJ 1987 L 192/51)
  C by Directive 87/403 (OJ 1987 L 220/44)

Directive 70/157 on permissible sound levels and exhaust systems of motor vehicles (OJ 1970 L 42/16)
  M by Directive 84/424 (OJ 1984 L 238/31)
  M by Directive 87/354 (OJ 1987 L 192/43)

Directive 70/220 on measures to be taken against air pollution by gases from positive-ignition engines of motor vehicles (OJ 1970 L 76/1)
  M by Directive 83/351 (OJ 1983 L 197/1)
  M by Directive 88/76 (OJ 1988 L 36/1)
  M by Directive 88/436 (OJ 1988 L 214/1)

Directive 70/221 on liquid fuel tanks and rear protective devices for motor vehicles and their trailers (OJ 1970 L 76/23)
  M by Directive 79/490 (OJ 1979 L 128/22)

Directive 70/222 on the space for mounting and fixing of rear registration plates on motor vehicles and their trailers (OJ 1970 L 76/25)

Directive 70/311 on steering equipment for motor vehicles and their trailers (OJ 1970 L 133/10

Directive 70/387 on the doors of motor vehicles and their trailers (OJ 1970 L 176/5)

Directive 70/388 on audible warning devices for motor vehicles (OJ 1970 L 176/12)
  M by Directive 73/101(01) (OJ 1973 L 2/1)
  M by Directive 87/354 (OJ 1987 L 192/43)

240

Directive 71/127 on rear-view mirrors of motor vehicles (OJ 1971 L 68/1)
  M by Directive 86/562 (OJ 1986 L 327/49)
  M by Directive 87/354 (OJ 1987 L 192/43)
  M by Directive 88/321 (OJ 1988 L 147/77)

Directive 71/320 on braking devices of certain categories of motor vehicles and of their trailers (OJ 1971 L 202/37)
  M by Directive 85/647 (OJ 1985 L 380/1)
  M by Directive 88/194 (OJ 1988 L 92/47)

Directive 72/245 on suppression of radio interference produced by spark-ignition engines fitted to motor vehicles (OJ 1972 L 152/15)

Directive 72/306 on measures to be taken against the emission of pollutants from diesel engines for use in vehicles (OJ 1972 L 190/1)

Directive 74/60 on interior fittings of motor vehicles (interior parts of the passenger compartment other than the interior rear-view mirrors, layout of controls, the roof or sliding roof, the backrest and rear part of the seats) (OJ 1984 L 38/2)
  M by Directive 78/632 (OJ 1978 206/26)

Directive 74/61 on devices to prevent the unauthorised use of motor vehicles (OJ 1974 L 38/22)

Directive 74/297 on the interior fittings of motor vehicles (the behaviour of the steering mechanism in the event of an impact) (OJ 1974 L 165/16)

Directive 74/408 on the interior fittings of motor vehicles (strength of seats and of their anchorages) (OJ 1974 L 221/1)
  M by Directive 81/577 (OJ 1981 L 209/34)

Directive 74/483 on the external projections of motor vehicles (OJ 1974 L 266/4)
  M by Directive 87/354 (OJ 1987 L 192/43)

Directive 75/443 on the reverse and speedometer equipment of motor vehicles (OJ 1975 L 196/1)

Directive 76/114 on statutory plates and inscriptions for motor vehicles and their trailers, and their position and method of attachment (OJ 1976 L 24/1)
  M by Directive 78/507 (OJ 1978 L 155/31)
  M by Directive 87/354 (OJ 1987 L 192/43)

Directive 76/115 on anchorages for motor vehicle safety belts (OJ 1976 L 24/6)
  M by Directive 81/575 (OJ 1981 L 209/30)
  M by Directive 82/318 (OJ 1982 L 139/9)

Directive 76/756 on the installation of lighting and light-signalling devices on motor vehicles and their trailers (OJ 1976 L 262/1)
  M by Directive 83/276 (OJ 1983 L 151/47)
  M by Directive 84/8 (OJ 1984 L 9/24)

Directive 76/757 on reflex reflectors for motor vehicles and their trailers (OJ 1976 L 262/32)
  M by Directive 87/354 (OJ 1987 L 192/43)

Directive 76/758 on end-outline marker lights, front position (side) lights, rear position (side) lights and stop lights for motor vehicles and their trailers (OJ 1976 L 262/54)
  M by Directive 87/354 (OJ 1987 L 192/43)

Directive 76/759 on direction indicator lights for motor vehicles and their trailers (OJ 1976 L 262/71)
  M by Directive 87/354 (OJ 1987 L 192/43)
  M by Directive 89/277 (OJ 1989 L 109/25)

Directive 76/760 on rear registration plate lights for motor vehicles and their trailers (OJ 1976 L 262/85)
  M by Directive 87/354 (OJ 1987 L 192/43)

Directive 76/761 on motor-vehicle headlamps which function as main-beam and/or dipped-beam headlights, and on incandescent electric filament lamps for such headlamps (OJ 1976 L 262/96)
  M by Directive 87/354 (OJ 1987 L 192/43)

Directive 76/762 on front fog lamps for motor vehicles and filament lamps for such lamps (OJ 1976 L 262/122)
  M by Directive 87/354 (OJ 1987 L 192/43)

Directive 77/143 on roadworthiness tests for motor vehicles and their trailers (OJ 1977 L 47/47)
  M by Directive 88/449 (OJ 1988 L 222/10)

Directive 77/389 on motor-vehicle towing devices (OJ 1977 L 145/41)

Directive 77/538 on rear fog lamps for motor vehicles and their trailers (OJ 1977 L 220/60)
  M by Directive 87/354 (OJ 1987 L 192/43)

Directive 77/539 on reversing lights for motor vehicles and their trailers (OJ 1977 L 220/72)
  M by Directive 87/354 (OJ 1987 L 192/43)

Directive 77/540 on parking lights for motor vehicles (OJ 1977 L 220/83)
  M by Directive 87/354 (OJ 1987 L 192/43)

Directive 77/541 on safety belts and restraint systems of motor vehicles (OJ 1977 L 220/95)
  M by Directive 82/319 (OJ 1982 L 139/17)
  M by Directive 87/354 (OJ 1987 L 192/43)
  M by Directive 88/366 (OJ 1988 L 181/40)

Directive 77/649 on the field of vision of motor-vehicle drivers (OJ 1977 L 267/1)
  M by Directive 81/643 (OJ 1981 L 231/41)
  M by Directive 88/366 (OJ 1988 L 181/40)

Directive 78/316 on the interior fittings of motor vehicles (identification of controls, telltales and indicators) (OJ 1978 L 81/3)

Directive 78/317 on defrosting and demisting systems for the glazed surfaces of motor vehicles (OJ 1978 L 81/27)

Directive 78/318 on the windscreen wiper and washer systems of motor vehicles (OJ 1978 L 81/49)

Directive 78/548 on heating systems for the passenger compartment of motor vehicles (OJ 1978 L 168/40)

Directive 78/549 on the wheel guards of motor vehicles (OJ 1978 L 168/45)

Directive 78/932 on head restraints on the seats of motor vehicles (OJ 1978 L 325/1)
   M by Directive 87/354 (OJ 1987 L 192/43)

Directive 78/1015 on permissible sound levels and exhaust systems of motor-cycles (OJ 1978 L 349/21)
   M by Directive 87/56 (OJ 1987 L 24/42)
   M by Directive 89/235 (OJ 1988 L 98/1)

Directive 79/490 on the liquid fuel tanks and rear underrun protection of motor vehicles and their trailers (OJ 1979 L 128/22)
   M by Directive 81/333 (OJ 1981 L 131/4)

Directive 80/780 on rear-view mirrors for two-wheeled motor vehicles with or without a sidecar and on their fitting to such vehicles (OJ 1980 L 229/49)

Directive 80/1268 on the fuel consumption of motor vehicles (OJ 1980 L 375/36)

Directive 80/1269 on the engine power of motor vehicles (OJ 1980 L 375/46)
   M by Directive 88/195 (OJ 1988 L 92/50)

Directive 81/643 on the field of vision of motor vehicle drivers (amending 77/649/EEC) (OJ 1981 L 231/41)

Directive 82/244 on the installation of lighting and light-signalling devices on motor vehicles and their trailers (amending 76/756/EEC) (OJ 1982 L 109/31)

Directive 82/318 on anchorages for motor vehicle safety belts (amending 76/115/EEC) (OJ 1982 L 139/9)

Directive 82/319 on safety belts and restraint systems of motor vehicles (amending 77/541/EEC) (OJ 1982 L 139/17)

Directive 84/8 on the installation of lighting and light-signalling devices on motor vehicles and their trailers (amending 76/756/EEC) (OJ 1984 L 9/24)

Directive 85/3 on the weights, dimensions and certain other characteristics of certain road vehicles (OJ 1985 L 2/14)
   M by Directive 88/218 (OJ 1988 L 98/48)

Directive 85/647 on the braking devices of certain categories of motor vehicles and their trailers (amending 71/320/EEC) (OJ 1985 L 380/1)

Directive 86/364 on proof of compliance with Directive 85/3/EEC on the weights, dimensions and certain other technical characteristics of certain road vehicles (OJ 1986 L 221/48)

Directive 88/77 on measures to be taken against the emission of gaseous pollutants from diesel engines for use in vehicles (OJ 1988 36/33)

AGRICULTURAL AND FORESTRY TRACTORS

Directive 74/150 on the type-approval of wheeled agricultural or forestry tractors (OJ 1974 L 84/10)
  M by Directive 82/890 (OJ 1982 L 378/45)
  M by Directive 88/297 (OJ 1988 L 126/52)

Directive 74/151 on certain parts and characteristics of wheeled agricultural or forestry tractors (OJ 1974 L 84/25)
  M by Directive 82/890 (OJ 1982 L 378/45)
  M by Directive 88/410 (OJ 1988 L 200/27)

Directive 74/346 on rear-view mirrors for wheeled agricultural or forestry tractors (OJ 1974 L 191/1)
  M by Directive 82/890 (OJ 1982 L 378/45)

Directive 86/415 on the installation, location, operation and identification of the controls of wheeled agricultural or forestry tractors (OJ 1986 L 240/1)

METROLOGY

Directive 71/316 on common provisions for measuring instruments and methods of metrological control (OJ 1971 L 202/1)
  M by Directive 83/575 (OJ 1983 L 332/43)
  M by Directive 87/354 (OJ 1987 L 192/43)
  M by Directive 87/355 (OJ 1987 L 192/46)
  M by Directive 88/665 (OJ 1988 L 382/42)

Directive 71/317 on 5 to 50 kg medium accuracy rectangular bar weights and 1 to 10 kg medium accuracy cylindrical weights (OJ 1971 L 202/14)

Directive 71/318 on gas volume meters (OJ 1971 L 202/21)
  M by Directive 78/365 (OJ 1978 L 104/26)
  M by Directive 82/623 (OJ 1983 L 252/5)

Directive 71/319 on meters for liquids other than water (OJ 1971 L 202/32)

Directive 71/347 on measuring the standard mass per storage volume of grain (OJ 1971 L 239/1)

Directive 71/348 on ancillary equipment for meters for liquids other than water (OJ 1971 L 239/9)

Directive 71/349 on the calibration of the tanks of vessels (OJ 1971 L 239/15)

Directive 73/360 on non-automatic weighing machines (OJ 1973 L 335/1)
  M by Directive 76/696 (OJ 1976 L 236/26)
  M by Directive 82/622 (OJ 1982 L 252/2)

Directive 73/362 on material measures of length (OJ 1973 L 335/56)
  M by Directive 78/629 (OJ 1978 L 206/8)
  M by Directive 85/146 (OJ 1985 L 54/29)

Directive 74/148 on weights of from 1 mg to 50 kg of above-medium accuracy (OJ 1974 L 84/3)

Directive 75/33 on cold-water meters (OJ 1975 L 14/1)

Directive 75/107 on bottles used as measuring containers (OJ 1975 L 42/14)

Directive 75/410 on continuous totalling weighing machines (OJ 1975 L 183/25)

Directive 76/764 on clinical mercury-in-glass maximum-reading thermometers (OJ 1976 L 262/139)
  M by Directive 83/128 (OJ 1983 L 91/29)
  M by Directive 84/414 (OJ 1984 L 228/25)

Directive 76/765 on alcoholometers and alcohol hydrometers (OJ 1976 L 262/143)
  M by Directive 82/624 (OJ 1982 L 252/8)

Directive 76/766 on alcohol tables (OJ 1976 L 262/149)

Directive 76/891 on electrical energy meters (OJ 1976 L 336/30)

Recommendation 76/223 on units of measurement referred to in patent conventions (OJ 1976 L 43/22)

Directive 77/95 on taximeters (OJ 1977 L 26/59)

Directive 77/313 on measuring systems for liquids other than water (OJ 1977 L 105/18)
  M by Directive 82/625 (OJ 1982 L 252/10)

Directive 78/1031 on automatic check-weighing and weight-grading machines (OJ 1978 L 364/1)

Directive 79/830 on hot-water meters (OJ 1979 L 259/1)

Directive 80/181 on units of measurement, and on repeal of 71/354/EEC (OJ 1980 L 39/40)
  M by Directive 85/1 (OJ 1985 L 2/11)

Directive 86/217 on tyre pressure gauges for motor vehicles (OJ 1986 L 152/48)

ELECTRICAL EQUIPMENT

Directive 73/23 on electrical equipment designed for use within certain voltage limits (OJ 1973 L 77/29)

Directive 76/117 on electrical equipment for use in potentially explosive atmospheres (OJ 1976 L 24/45)

Directive 76/889 on radio interference caused by electric household appliances, portable tools and similar equipment (OJ 1976 L 336/1)
  M by Directive 87/308 (OJ 1987 L 155/24)
  M by Directive 89/336 (OJ 1989 L 139/19)

Directive 76/890 on suppression of radio interference with regard to fluorescent lighting fitments fitted with starters (OJ 1976 L 336/22)
  M by Directive 82/500 (OJ 1982 L 222/42)
  M by Directive 87/310 (OJ 1987 L 155/27)
  M by Directive 89/336 (OJ 1989 L 139/19)

Directive 79/196 on electrical equipment for use in potentially explosive atmospheres employing certain types of protection (OJ 1979 L 43/20)
    M by Directive 88/571 (OJ 1988 L 311/46)
    M by Directive 88/665 (OJ 1988 L 382/42)

Directive 82/130 on electrical equipment for use in potentially explosive atmospheres in mines susceptible to firedamp (OJ 1982 L 59/10)
    M by Directive 88/35 (OJ 1988 L 20/28)

Recommendation 82/490 on the certificates provided for in Directive 76/117/ EEC on electrical equipment for use in potentially explosive atmospheres (OJ 1982 L 218/27)

Directive 83/447 adopting measures provided for in Art. 3(3) of Directive 76/889/EEC on radio interference caused by electrical household appliances, portable tools and similar equipment, and of Directive 76/890/EEC on the suppression of radio interference with regard to fluorescent lighting fitments fitted with starters (OJ 1983 L 247/10)

Directive 84/539 on electro-medical equipment used in human or veterinary medicine (OJ 1984 300/179)

Directive 88/35 amending 82/130/EEC on electrical equipment for use in potentially explosive atmospheres in mines susceptible to firedamp (OJ 1988 L 20/28)

Recommendation 88/41 on the involvement and improvement of consumer participation in standardisation (OJ 1988 L 23/26)

FOODSTUFFS

Directive 62/2645 on colouring matters authorised for use in foodstuffs intended for human consumption (OJ 1962 L 115/2645)
    C by Directive 81/712 (OJ 1981 L 257/1)
    M by Directive 85/7 (OJ 1985 L 2/22)

Directive 64/54 on preservatives authorised for use in foodstuffs intended for human consumption (OJ 1964 12/161)

Directive 65/66 laying down specific criteria of purity for preservatives authorised for use in foodstuffs intended for human consumption (OJ 1965 22/373)
    C by Directive 86/604 (OJ 1986 L 352/45)

Directive 68/420 amending 64/54/EEC on preservatives authorised for use in foodstuffs intended for human consumption (OJ 1968 L 309/25)

Directive 70/357 on antioxidants authorised for use in foodstuffs intended for human consumption (OJ 1970 L 157/31)
    M by Directive 80/608 (OJ 1980 L 170/33)
    M by Directive 85/7 (OJ 1985 L 2/22)
    M by Directive 87/55 (OJ 1987 L 24/41)

Directive 73/241 on cocoa and chocolate products intended for human consumption (OJ 1973 L 228/23)
    M by Directive 80/608 (OJ 1980 L 170/33)
    M by Directive 85/7 (OJ 1985 L 2/22)

Directive 73/437 on certain sugars intended for human consumption (OJ 1973 356/71)

Directive 74/329 on emulsifiers, stabilisers, thickeners and gelling agents for use in foodstuffs (OJ 1974 L 189/1)
   M by Directive 85/7 (OJ 1985 L 2/22)
   M by Directive 86/102 (OJ 1986 L 88/40)

Directive 74/409 on honey (OJ 1974 L 221/10)

Directive 75/726 on fruit juices and certain similar products (OJ 1975 L 311/40)
   M by Directive 79/168 (OJ 1979 L 37/27)
   M by Directive 81/487 (OJ 1981 L 189/43)

Directive 76/118 on certain partly of wholly dehydrated preserved milks for human consumption (OJ 1976 L 24/49)
   M by Directive 83/635 (OJ 1983 L 357/37)

Directive 76/621 on fixing of the maximum level of erucic acid in oils and fats intended as such for human consumption and in foodstuffs containing added oils or fats (OJ 1976 L 202/35)

Directive 76/893 on materials and articles intended to come into contact with foodstuffs (OJ 1976 L 340/19)
   M by Directive 80/1276 (OJ 1980 L 375/77)
   M by Directive 85/7 (OJ 1985 L 2/22)
   M by Directive 89/109 (OJ 1989 L 40/38)

Directive 77/94 on foodstuffs for particular nutritional uses (OJ 1977 L 26/55)
   M by Directive 85/7 (OJ 1985 L 2/22)

Directive 77/436 on coffee and chicory extracts (OJ 1977 L 172/20)
   M by Directive 85/7 (OJ 1985 L 2/22)
   M by Directive 85/573 (OJ 1985 L 372/22)

Directive 78/142 on materials and articles which contain vinyl chloride monomer and are intended to come into contact with foodstuffs (OJ 1978 L 44/15)

Decision 78/663 laying down specific criteria of purity for emulsifiers, stabilisers, thickeners and gelling agents for use in foodstuffs (OJ 1978 L 223/7)

Directive 78/664 laying down specific criteria of purity for antioxidants which may be used in foodstuffs intended for human consumption (OJ 1978 L 223/30)

Directive 79/693 on fruit jams, jellies and marmalades and chestnut purée (OJ 1979 L 205/5)
   M by Directive 88/593 (OJ 1988 L 318/44)

Directive 79/796 laying down Community methods of analysis for testing certain sugars intended for human consumption (OJ 1979 L 239/24)

Directive 79/1066 laying down Community methods of analysis for testing coffee and chicory extracts (OJ 1979 L 327/17)

Directive 79/1067 laying down Community methods of analysis for testing certain partly or wholly dehydrated preserved milks for human consumption (OJ 1979 L 327/29)

Directive 80/590 determining the symbol that may accompany materials and articles intended to come into contact with foodstuffs (OJ 1980 L 151/21)

Directive 80/766 laying down the Community method of analysis for official control of the vinyl chloride monomer level in materials and articles which are intended to come into contact with foodstuffs (OJ 1980 L 213/42)

Directive 80/777 on the exploitation and marketing of natural mineral waters (OJ 1980 L 229/1)
   M by Directive 85/7 (OJ 1985 L 2/22)

Directive 80/891 on the Community method of analysis for determining the erucic acid content in oils and fats intended to be used as such for human consumption and foodstuffs containing added oils or fats (OJ 1980 L 254/35)

Decision 80/1073 establishing a new Statute for the Advisory Committee on Foodstuffs (OJ 1980 L 318/28)

Recommendation 80/1089 on tests relating to the safety evaluation of food additives (OJ 1980 L 320/36)

Directive 81/432 laying down the Community method of analysis for the official control of vinyl chloride released by materials and articles into foodstuffs (OJ 1981 L 167/6)

Directive 81/712 laying down Community methods of analysis for verifying that certain additives used in foodstuffs satisfy criteria of purity (OJ 1981 L 257/1)

Directive 82/711 laying down the basic rules necessary for testing migration of the constituents of plastic materials and articles intended to come into contact with foodstuffs (OJ 1981 L 297/26)

Directive 83/229 on materials and articles made of regenerated cellulose film intended to come into contact with foodstuffs (OJ 1983 L 123/31)
   M by Directive 86/388 (OJ 1986 L 228/32)

Directive 83/417 on certain lactoproteins (caseins and caseinates) intended for human consumption (OJ 1983 L 237/25)

Directive 83/463 introducing temporary measures for the designation of certain ingredients in the labelling of foodstuffs for sale to the ultimate consumer (OJ 1983 L 255/1)

Directive 84/500 on ceramic articles intended to come into contact with foodstuffs (OJ 1984 L 277/12)

Directive 85/7 amending a series of Directives on the involvement of the Standing Committee for Foodstuffs (OJ 1985 L 2/22)

Directive 85/503 on methods of analysis for edible caseins and caseinates (OJ 1985 L 308/12)

Directive 85/572 laying down the list of simulants to be used for the testing of migration of constituents of plastic materials and articles intended to come into contact with foodstuffs (OJ 1985 372/14)

Directive 85/573 amending 77/436/EEC on coffee and chicory extracts (OJ 1985 L 372/22)

Directive 85/585 amending 64/54/EEC on preservatives authorised for use in foodstuffs intended for human consumption (OJ 1985 L 372/43)

Directive 85/591 on the introduction of Community methods of sampling and analysis for monitoring foodstuffs intended for human consumption (OJ 1985 L 372/50)

Directive 86/424 laying down methods of sampling for chemical analysis of edible caseins and caseinates (OJ 1986 L 243/29)

Directive 87/524 laying down Community methods of sampling for chemical analysis for monitoring preserved milk products (OJ 1987 L 306/24)

Directive 88/344 on extraction solvents used in the production of foodstuffs and food ingredients (OJ 1988 L 157/28)

Directive 88/388 on flavourings for use in foodstuffs and on source materials for their production (OJ 1988 L 184/61)

Directive 89/107 on food additives authorised for use in foodstuffs intended for human consumption (OJ 1989 L 40/27)

Directive 89/109 on materials and articles intended to come into contact with foodstuffs (OJ 1989 L 40/38)

PROPRIETARY MEDICINAL PRODUCTS

Directive 65/65 on provisions relating to proprietary medicinal products (OJ 1965 22/369)

Directive 75/318 on analytical, pharmaco-toxicological and clinical standards and protocols in respect of the testing of proprietary medicinal products (OJ 1975 L 147/1)

Directive 75/319 on provisions laid down by law, regulation or administrative action relating to proprietary medicinal products (OJ 1975 L 147/13)

Directive 78/25 on colouring matters which may be added to medicinal products (OJ 1978 L 11/18)

Directive 81/851 on veterinary medicinal products (OJ 1981 L 317/1)

Directive 81/852 on analytical, pharmaco-toxological and clinical standards and protocols in respect of testing veterinary medicinal products (OJ 1981 L 317/16)
   M by Directive 87/20 (OJ 1987 15/34)

Directive 87/22 on the marketing of high-technology medicinal products, particularly those derived from biotechnology (OJ 1987 L 15/38)

Recommendation 87/176 on tests relating to the placing on the market of proprietary medicinal products (OJ 1987 L 73/1)

COSMETICS

Directive 76/768 on cosmetic products (OJ 1976 L 262/169)
   M by Directive 87/137 (OJ 1987 L 56/20)
   M by Directive 88/233 (OJ 1988 L 105/11)
   M by Directive 88/667 (OJ 1988 L 382/46)
   M by Directive 89/174 (OJ 1989 L 64/10)

Directive 80/1335 on methods of analysis necessary for checking the composition of cosmetic products (OJ 1980 L 383/27)
  M by Directive 87/143 (OJ 1987 L 57/56)

Directive 82/434 on methods of analysis necessary for checking the composition of cosmetic products (OJ 1982 L 185/1)

Directive 83/514 on methods of analysis necessary for checking the composition of cosmetic products (OJ 1983 L 291/9)

Directive 85/490 on methods of analysis necessary for checking the composition of cosmetic products (OJ 1985 L 295/30)

Directive 87/137 adapting to technical progress Annexes II, III, IV, V and VI to Directive 76/768/EEC on cosmetic products (OJ 1987 L 56/20)

TEXTILES

Directive 71/307 on textile names (OJ 1971 L 185/16)
  C by Directive 75/36 (OJ 1975 L 14/15)
  M by Directive 83/623 (OJ 1983 L 353/8)
  M by Directive 87/140 (OJ 1987 L 56/24)

Directive 72/276 on certain methods of quantitative analysis of binary textile fibre mixtures (OJ 1972 L 173/1)
  M by Directive 81/75 (OJ 1975 L 57/23)
  M by Directive 87/184 (OJ 1987 L 75/21)

Directive 73/44 on quantitative analysis of ternary fibre mixtures (OJ 1973 L 83/1)

Recommendation 87/142 on certain methods for the removal of non-fibrous matter prior to quantitiative analysis of fibre mixtures (OJ 1987 L 57/52)

Recommendation 87/185 on quantitative methods of analysis for the identification of acrylic and modacrylic fibres, chlorofibres and trivilyl fibres (OJ 1987 L 75/28)

DANGEROUS SUBSTANCES

Directive 67/548 on the classification, packaging and labelling of dangerous substances (OJ 1967 196/1)
  M by Directive 87/302 (OJ 1987 L 133/1)
  M by Directive 87/432 (OJ 1987 L 239/1)
  M by Directive 88/490 (OJ 1988 L 259/1)

Directive 73/173 on the classification, packaging and labelling of dangerous preparations (solvents) (OJ 1973 L 189/7)
  M by Directive 80/1271 (OJ 1980 L 375/70)
  M by Directive 82/473 (OJ 1982 L 213/17)
  M by Directive 88/379 (OJ 1988 L 187/14)

Directive 76/769 on restrictions on the marketing and use of certain dangerous substances and preparations (OJ 1976 L 262/201)
  M by Directive 85/467 (OJ 1985 L 269/56)
  M by Directive 85/610 (OJ 1985 L 375/1)

Directive 78/631 on the classification, packaging and labelling of dangerous preparations (pesticides) (OJ 1978 L 206/13)
  M by Directive 81/187 (OJ 1981 L 88/29)
  M by Directive 84/291 (OJ 1984 L 144/1)

FERTILISERS

Directive 76/116 on fertilisers (OJ 1976 L 24/21)
  M by Directive 88/183 (OJ 1988 L 83/33)
  M by Directive 89/284 (OJ 1989 L 111/34)

Directive 77/535 on methods of sampling and analysis for fertilisers (OJ 1977 L 213/1)
  M by Directive 79/138 (OJ 1977 L 39/3)
  C by Directive 87/566 (OJ 1987 L 342/32)

Directive 80/876 on straight ammonium nitrate fertilisers of high nitrogen content (OJ 1980 L 250/7)

Directive 87/94 on procedures for the control of characteristics of, limits for and resistance to detonation of straight ammonium nitrate fertilisers of high nitrogen content (OJ 1987 L 38/1)
  M by Directive 88/126 (OJ 1988 L 63/12)

OTHER SECTORS

Directive 68/89 on the classification of wood in the rough (OJ 1968 L 32/12)

Directive 69/493 on crystal glass (OJ 1969 L 326/36)

Directive 73/404 on detergents (OJ 1973 L 347/51)
  M by Directive 86/94 (OJ 1986 L 80/51)

Directive 75/324 on aerosol dispensers (OJ 1975 L 147/40)

Directive 76/767 on common provisions for pressure vessels and methods for inspecting them (OJ 1976 L 262/153)
  M by Directive 87/354 (OJ 1987 L 192/43)
  M by Directive 88/665 (OJ 1988 L 382/42)

Directive 77/728 on the classification, packaging and labelling of paints, varnishes, printing inks, adhesives and similar products (OJ 1977 L 303/23)
  M by Directive 83/265 (OJ 1983 L 147/11)
  M by Directive 86/508 (OJ 1986 L 295/31)
  M by Directive 88/379 (OJ 1988 L 187/14)

Directive 84/525 on seamless steel gas cylinders (OJ 1984 L 300/1)

Directive 84/526 on seamless unalloyed-aluminium and aluminium-alloy gas cylinders (OJ 1984 L 300/20)

Directive 84/528 on welded unalloyed steel gas cylinders (OJ 1984 L 300/48)

Directive 84/527 on common provisions for lifting and mechanical handling appliances (OJ 1984 L 300/72)
  M by Directive 88/665 (OJ 1988 L 382/42)

Directive 84/529 on electrically operated lifts (OJ 1984 L 300/86)
  M by Directive 86/312 (OJ 1986 L 196/56)

Directive 84/530 on common provisions for appliances using gaseous fuels, safety and control devices for these appliances and methods of surveillance of them (OJ 1984 L 300/95)
  M by Directive 87/354 (OJ 1984 L 192/43)
  M by Directive 88/665 (OJ 1988 L 382/42)

Directive 84/531 on appliances using gaseous fuels for instantaneous production of hot water for sanitary purposes (OJ 1984 L 300/106)

Directive 84/532 on common provisions for construction plant and equipment (OJ 1984 L 300/111)
  M by Directives 84/533–538 (OJ 1984 L 300/123–171)
  M by Directive 88/665 (OJ 1988 L 382/42)

Recommendation 84/549 on the implementation of harmonisation in the field of telecommunications (OJ 1984 L 298/49)

Directive 86/361 on the initial stage of mutual recognition of type-approval for telecommunications terminal equipment (OJ 1986 L 217/21)

Directive 86/529 on the adoption of common technical specifications for the MAC/packet family of standards for direct satellite television broadcasting (OJ 1986 L 311/28)

Directive 86/663 on self-propelled industrial trucks (OJ 1986 L 384/12)

Directive 87/54 on the legal protection of topographies of semiconductor products (OJ 1987 L 24/36)

Directive 87/354 amending certain directives on industrial products with respect to the distinctive numbers and letters indicating the member states (OJ 1987 L 192/43)

Directive 87/372 on frequency bands to be reserved for the co-ordinated introduction of public pan-European cellular digital land-based mobile communications in the Community (OJ 1987 L 196/85)

Directive 87/404 on simple pressure vessels (OJ 1987 L 220/48)

Directive 88/301 on competition in the markets for telecommunications terminal equipment (OJ 1988 L 131/73)

Directive 89/104 on trade marks (OJ 1989 L 40/1)

Directive 89/106 on construction products (OJ 1989 L 40/12)

Directive 89/336 on electromagnetic compatibility (OJ 1989 L 139/19)

CONSUMER INFORMATION, EDUCATION AND REPRESENTATION

Directive 71/307 on textile names (OJ 1971 L 185/16)
  M by Directive 83/623 (OJ 1983 L 353/8)
  M by Directive 87/140 (OJ 1987 L 56/24)

PROTECTION OF HEALTH AND SAFETY

Directive 81/602 on the prohibition of certain substances having a hormonal action and of any substances having a thyrostatic action (OJ 1981 L 222/32)

Directive 85/358 supplementing Directive 81/602/EEC on the prohibition of certain substances having a hormonal action and of any substances having a thyrostatic action (OJ 1985 L 191/46)
   M by Directive 3768/85 (OJ 1985 L 362/8)
   M by Directive 88/146 (OJ 1988 L 70/16)

Directive 85/649 prohibiting the use in livestock farming of certain substances having a hormonal action (OJ 1985 L 382/228)

Directive 86/138 concerning a demonstration project with a view to introducing a Community system of information on accidents involving consumer products (OJ 1986 L 109/23)

Directive 87/357 on products which, appearing to be other than they are, endanger the health or safety of consumers (OJ 1987 L 192/49)

Directive 88/146 prohibiting the use in livestock farming of certain substances having a hormonal action (OJ 1988 L 70/16)

Directive 88/299 on trade in animals treated with certain substances having a hormonal action and their meat (as referred to in Art. 7 of Directive 88/146/EEC) (OJ 1988 L 128/36)

Regulation 88/983 laying down special provisions on the marketing of olive oil containing undesirable substances (OJ 1988 L 98/36)

Directive 88/378 concerning the safety of toys (OJ 1988 L 187/1)

Directive 88/379 on provisions relating to the classification, packaging and labelling of dangerous preparations (OJ 1988 L 187/14)

Directive 89/437 on hygiene and health problems affecting production and the placing on the market of egg products (OJ 1989 L 212/87)

PROTECTION OF ECONOMIC INTERESTS

Directive 75/106 on the making up by volume of certain prepackaged liquids (OJ 1975 L 42/1)
   M by Directive 79/1005 (OJ 1979 L 308/25)
   M by Directive 85/10 (OJ 1985 L 4/20)
   M by Directive 88/316 (OJ 1988 L 143/26)

Directive 75/107 on bottles used as measuring containers (OJ 1975 L 42/14)

Directive 76/211 on the making up by weight or volume of certain prepackaged products (OJ 1976 L 46/1)

Directive 79/112 on the labelling, presentation and advertising of foodstuffs for sale to the ultimate consumer (OJ 1979 L 33/1)
   M by Directive 85/7 (OJ 1985 L 2/22)
   M by Directive 86/197 (OJ 1986 L 144/38)

Directive 79/530 on the indication by labelling of the energy consumption of household appliances (OJ 1979 L 145/1)

Directive 79/531 applying to electric ovens Directive 79/530/EEC on the indication by labelling of the energy consumption of domestic appliances (OJ 1979 L 145/7)

Directive 79/581 on consumer protection in the indication of the prices of foodstuffs (OJ 1979 L 158/19)
   M by Directive 88/315 (OJ 1988 L 142/23)

Directive 80/232 on the ranges of nominal quantities and nominal capacities permitted for certain prepackaged products (OJ 1980 L 51/1)
   M by Directive 86/96 (OJ 1986 L 80/55)
   M by Directive 87/356 (OJ 1987 L 192/48)

Directive 83/463 introducing temporary measures for the designation of certain ingredients in the labelling of foodstuffs for sale to the ultimate consumer (OJ 1983 L 255/1)

Directive 87/250 on the indication of alcoholic strength by volume in the labelling of alcoholic beverages for sale to the ultimate consumer (OJ 1987 L 113/57)

Regulation 1898/87 on the protection of designations used in marketing milk and milk products (OJ 1987 L 182/36)
   M by Regulation 222/88 (OJ 1988 L 28/1)

Directive 88/314 on consumer protection by indication of prices on non-food products (OJ 1988 L 142/19)

Directives 89/393–398 on foodstuffs labelling and advertising (OJ 1989 L 186/13–17)

Directive 89/451 on the labelling of sparkling wine (OJ 1989 L 202/12)

HEALTH PROTECTION

Directive 77/312 on biological screening of the population for lead (OJ 1977 L 105/10)

Directive 84/466 laying down basic measures for the radiation protection of persons undergoing medical examination or treatment (OJ 1984 L 265/1)

Directive 89/105 on measures regulating the prices of medicinal products for human use and their inclusion in the scope of national health insurance systems (OJ 1989 L 40/8)

PROTECTION OF ANIMALS

Directive 86/609 on the protection of animals used for experimental and other scientific purposes (OJ 1986 L 358/1)

Index